The Public Life of Privacy
in Nineteenth-Century
American Literature

NEW AMERICANISTS   A Series Edited by Donald E. Pease

STACEY MARGOLIS

The Public Life of Privacy in Nineteenth-Century American Literature

Duke University Press   DURHAM AND LONDON   2005

© 2005 Duke University Press
All rights reserved
Designed by Erin Kirk New
Typeset in Minion by Keystone Typesetting, Inc.
Library of Congress Cataloging-in-Publication Data appear
on the last printed page of this book.

Portions of chapters 3, 5, and 6 appeared, respectively, in *PMLA* (March 2001): 329–43; *High Anxieties: Cultural Studies in Addiction*, edited by Marc Redfield and Janet Farrell Brodie (2002); and *Novel: A Forum on Fiction* (summer 2001); 391–410. I thank the MLA, the University of California Press, and *Novel* for permission to reprint.

FOR ANDREW AND CHARLES

Contents

Acknowledgments ix

Introduction: The Limits of Privacy 1

PART ONE Discipline and Punish

1. *The Blithedale Romance* and Other Tales of Association 17
2. The Rules of the Game: Punishment in *The Wide Wide World* 51

PART TWO Race and the Law

3. *Huckleberry Finn;* or, Consequences 81
4. The Veil of Cedars: Charles Chesnutt and Conversion 107

PART THREE The Public Life

5. Addiction and the Ends of Desire 141
6. Homo-Formalism: Analogy in *The Sacred Fount* 169

Notes 197

Index 231

Acknowledgments

This book began as my dissertation at the University of Chicago, was reconceived and substantially revised during a postdoctoral fellowship at the California Institute of Technology, and was completed at the University of Utah. I am grateful to the faculties of each of these institutions, especially my colleagues at Utah, who welcomed me warmly into the English department long before I became a full-fledged member. Teachers, friends, and colleagues have made valuable contributions to this project; I am pleased to be able to thank them here: Lauren Berlant, Bill Brown, Gillian Brown, Eleanor Courtemanche, Stuart Culver, Kevin Gilmartin, Howard Horwitz, Cathy Jurca, Walter Benn Michaels, Donald Pease, Matt Potolsky, Cindy Weinstein, and Barry Weller. I would also like to thank my parents, Sheila and Steve Margolis, my sister, Robin Winer, and my in-laws, Harry and Margo Franta. My greatest debt, both personal and intellectual, is to Andrew Franta. Because every page bears some trace of his remarkable intelligence, I dedicate this book to him, and to our son, Charles Magnus.

INTRODUCTION   The Limits of Privacy

Edward Bellamy's collection *"The Blindman's World" and Other Stories* (1898) is framed by two stories of vexed privacy. In the first, "The Blindman's World," S. Erastus Larrabee, a professor of astronomy, passes out while studying Mars through his telescope and wakes up with the sense that something has happened to him in the interim, something "strange and startling," that he cannot remember.[1] Soon, the "desire to know" his own inaccessible "impressions" and "experiences" becomes an obsession: "It seemed intolerable that I should have secrets from myself, that my soul should withhold its experiences from my intellect" (7). In the second story, the final one in the volume, "To Whom This May Come," the hero is shipwrecked on his way from Calcutta to New York. During the wreck he passes out, only to wake up and find himself stranded on an island of mind readers. His first reaction is "panic" at finding himself "among people who, while inscrutable to me, knew my every thought" (397). And although he quickly discovers that he can exercise the same restraint over thoughts that he exercises with relative ease over speech, he goes on to suggest that such restraint has its limits: "Indeed, among the mind-readers, politeness never can extend to the point of insincerity, as among talking nations, seeing that it is always one another's real and inmost thought that they read" (398).

What is striking about these stories is that they represent individuals who have interiority—"real and inmost thought"—without having privacy. In "The Blindman's World" the individual's own thoughts cannot be considered private because he has no direct access to them; in "To Whom This May Come" the individual's thoughts cannot be considered private because everyone has access to them. In each story, Bellamy imagines a world in which individuals do not simple experience their own inmost thoughts but rather come into relation with them indirectly, through the production of formal or public traces. Professor Larrabee finally learns about his adventures on Mars when he discovers a strange text that turns out to be his own diary: "I was astounded, on looking more closely, to observe that the handwriting was my own.... These written sheets apparently contained the longed-for but despaired-of record of those hours when I was absent from my body" (8). Written when he was asleep and read with suspense (as though it were a story about someone else), the text becomes the "trace" of his own experience; it is "the record of what I had seen and known during those hours of which my waking memory showed no trace" (7). In "To Whom This May Come," the narrator discovers that mind reading gives one access not only to the interiority of other people but also to one's own "character": "I learned that mind-reading is chiefly held desirable, not for the knowledge of others which it gives its possessors, but for the self-knowledge which is its reflex effect. Of all they see in the minds of others, that which concerns them most is the reflection of themselves, the photographs of their own characters" (410). In these stories, Bellamy transforms commonsense accounts of privacy, creating individuals who no longer have the ability either to gain or to police access to their own thoughts. In both cases, being inserted into unfamiliar systems of social organization leads to strange scenarios in which self-knowledge either depends on the mediation of the formal trace or becomes a "reflex effect" of publicity.

However fantastical Bellamy's scenarios may appear, they cannot easily be classed as science fiction, if only because the world they represent—in which the individual begins to be defined in terms of his formal or social effects—was already coming into existence in the second half of the nineteenth century. Indeed, Bellamy's stories might best be understood as thought experiments designed to explore the changing conditions of subjectivity brought about by new technologies of social organization that privileged public effects over private intentions and feelings.[2] These stories are illuminating, moreover, because the technologies they represent cannot be adequately understood in the Foucauldian terms of surveillance and discipline that have become so familiar in literary and cultural studies. From Bellamy's perspective, individual subjectivity depends on such mediation without necessarily being disciplined by it. By living in a world of surveillance that extends to the contents of their minds, their "real and inmost thought," the mind readers in "To Whom This May Come" do not conform their thoughts to some acceptable "norm." Instead, they seek out this surveillance because it makes their own thoughts newly or uniquely legible: a mind reader's "mental and moral self" is "made objective to him" by his fellows and thus "can be contemplated by him as impartially as if it were another's" (411). Surveillance, from this perspective, is not a tool of social discipline but, surprisingly, a kind of heuristic device, a way of placing oneself in relation to the world. Bellamy's stories, while imagining utopian alternatives to everyday life, emblematize the importance of public effects in nineteenth-century America as well as suggest that technologies designed to account for such effects have no predictable political content.

My central claim in this volume is that such counterintuitive accounts of privacy inform an important strain of the American novel, one that has been both misrecognized and misread. In the chapters that follow I argue that one tradition of the American novel that runs from Nathaniel Hawthorne to Henry James, hitherto viewed as deeply committed to the exploration of interiority, in fact repeatedly articulates subjects that can only be understood—can only understand themselves—through the production of public effects. Like Bellamy's foreign travelers, characters in novels by Hawthorne, James, Susan Warner, Mark Twain, Charles Chesnutt, and Pauline Hopkins are confronted by the surprising evidence of their own effects on other people, evidence that has the power to transform their self-conceptions. More specifically, what unites the texts under examination here is their sense of the ways in which social categories like race and sexuality along with politico-legal forms like partisanship and negligence made it possible to imagine that an individual's public effects could eclipse the authority exercised by her private feelings and intentions. My claim is that these and other nineteenth-century texts work to disarticulate privacy and individuality by emphasizing what seems external, even peripheral, to the self—not only the accidents and mistakes that define individuals in Hawthorne, Warner, and Twain, but the public codification of bodies that transforms identity in Chesnutt, Hopkins, and James.

In this book I thus treat a central tradition of the American novel as a series of thought experiments that attempt to define, analyze, and critique a modern world beginning to be characterized as much by its interest in effects as by its interest in intentions. To argue that a central tradition of the American novel subordinates individual feeling and experience to the world of social effects is to challenge familiar and convincing ways of characterizing nineteenth-century American culture. Some of the most influential critics of the past twenty years have insisted that post–Civil War America is dominated by an ideology of privacy that defines subjects in terms of interiority, intimacy, and desire. These scholars have generally understood the nineteenth-century American novel in terms either of the market (which defines individuals in relation to their desires and social life in relation to contract)[3] or of the domestic (which defines individuals in relation to their feelings and social life in relation to the home).[4] The basic premise of both schools of thought is that the United States was (and continues to be) ruled by an ideology that privileges the individual; that imagines the private life as a protected zone of intimacy that is immune from politics; that assumes freedom of movement, contract, and belief; and that grants a shield of abstraction in the public sphere.[5]

One could argue that it is this commitment to the power of liberal individualism that links recent literary scholarship to earlier accounts of the period by such scholars as F. O. Matthiessen, Lionel Trilling, and Richard Chase. But where Trilling, to take one example, reads *Adventures of Huckleberry Finn* as the tale of a "heroic character" who "discards the moral code" of a corrupt society when he "resolves to help Jim in his escape from slavery,"[6] recent scholars have been more interested in the inherent contradictions of liberal individualism and the role of literature in perpetuating or demystifying it. Thus, Sacvan Bercovitch, like Trilling, recognizes a commitment to the autonomous individual in the works of "classic writers" like Emerson, Thoreau, Hawthorne, and Whitman, but understands this commitment as a form of liberal bad faith. No matter how critical these writers were of particular social problems, he argues, they must be seen as complacently protecting more general "cultural norms": "Their works are characterized by an unmediated relation between the facts of American life and the ideals of liberal free enterprise." And thus, he concludes, "The works of our classic writers show more clearly than any others I know how American radicalism could be turned into a force against any form of change that would decisively alter the norms, ideals, and structures of American culture."[7]

Recent work in American history, however, has begun to challenge this picture of a nineteenth century ruled by liberal individualism, arguing that American culture was, in fact, dominated by extensive systems of social regulation and committed to the primacy of public rather than private interest.[8] According to William Novak, the notion of a nineteenth-century America defined by limited government, the free market, and the sanctity of individual autonomy is belied by the unprecedented expansion of what was known as "state police power"—the right of the state to promote public welfare by "regulating or even destroying private right, interest, liberty, or property."[9] Intrusive regulation was, he claims, absolutely central to an American culture of "positive governance" (9) that was expected to protect "public safety and security, public economy, public property, public mortality, and public health" (16). As he explains: "Nineteenth-century America was a *public* society in ways hard to imagine after the invention of twentieth-century privacy. Its governance was predicated on the elemental assumption that public interest was superior to private interest. Government and society were not created to protect preexisting rights, but to further the welfare of the whole people and community" (9). Nowhere is this desire to regulate in the public interest more dramatic than in the response to the "railroad revolution." As Barbara Young Welke points out, the dramatic rise in accidental injuries to railroad passengers led to myriad local ordinances to protect public safety: "Open platforms gave way to platforms with gates, gates to fully enclosed platforms. Unguarded crossings at grade were replaced by flagmen, and in turn manually operated gates were replaced by automatic gates and electric signals." These responses to the demand to reduce injury, Welke observes, "were part of a broader pattern of state assumption of responsibility to safeguard individual life and health even where that meant limiting individual freedom of action."[10]

What these histories of regulation make plain is the extent to which an industrializing America confronted a number of problems (like the increase of injuries from railroad accidents) that could not be solved by the market and, indeed, made no sense to think about in terms of contract. Even statistical approaches to chance and accident (increasingly central to the regulatory state) were understood to limit individual freedom. Ian Hacking, for example, argues that the rising importance of statistics in the nineteenth century demonstrates the belief that "technologies for classifying" seemingly random information could work as a form of "social control."[11] In other words, the "avalanche of printed numbers" that gave rise to the modern conception of probability also gave birth to the idea of "normalcy," an idea that came to have not only a descriptive but a coercive force. Because "most of the law-like regularities were first perceived in connection with deviancy: suicide, crime, vagrancy, madness, prostitution, disease," Hacking explains, statistical thinking has always been based on "the notion that one can improve—control—a deviant subpopulation by enumeration and classification" (3). Historians like Novak and Welke, as we have seen, place less importance on the attempt to classify the accidental than on the regulations designed to prevent accidents from happening in the first place. Yet both statistical thinking and governmental regulation have been understood as a limit to or, more forcefully, an assault on the individual's autonomy.

In this book I argue that the coercion of the individual ascribed to the well-regulated society is only part of the story. I contend that technologies of social organization created to control for the contingencies of individual action in a world increasingly perceived to be chaotic did not necessarily impede action and thus limit the individual's freedom. Instead, these technologies often worked to explain or ameliorate the effects of such action after the fact. The rise of tort law in the second half of the nineteenth century as a response to the ever-increasing number of accidental injuries is predicated on this retrospective (rather than coercive) account of action. As opposed to safety ordinances, which responded to accidents by attempting to prevent them, tort law responded to accidents by attempting to assign responsibility for what had already happened and to determine compensation for those already injured. The central problem confronted by tort law was how to define obligations between strangers—individuals who had no preexisting contractual or personal relationship—so that it could make determinations of culpability in the absence of any intention to harm (these were, after all, accidental injuries). By insisting that certain persons (or corporations) bear responsibility for the unintended consequences of their own actions, tort law began to define individuals almost strictly in terms of their effects.[12] In its focus on actions that are, by definition, beyond the individual's control, tort law exemplifies the way in which social technologies might organize or even redefine disparate individual actions without working as a form of "discipline."

While tort law is perhaps the most dramatic example of the kinds of social technologies addressed here, it is not the only one. The noncorporeal form of discipline so central to midcentury philosophies of child rearing, for example, can be understood less as a set of rules designed to conscript action than as a kind of feedback loop designed to let children know exactly what they have done. The discourse of addiction that emerged in the late nineteenth century insisted that the compulsion to use drugs was not an exaggerated form of desire but rather an evacuation of desire. The concept of addiction emptied out subjectivity and imagined that it could be replaced by a host of external forces. It thus became a system of medical classification that not only served as a tool of "normalization" but opened up new and unexpected forms of knowledge and identity.

Like Bellamy's stories, the tradition of the novel that forms the subject of this book responds to such emergent systems of social organization; systems that belie the ubiquity of liberal individualism without working as forms of coercion, that is, as modes of social discipline or social engineering. These novels explore the ways in which such technologies both force and enable individuals to come into relation with what have typically been considered private, and thus obvious and unmediated, forms of knowledge: experience, opinion, intention, and desire. In almost every one of these texts, individuals misrecognize their own effects in the world and depend on other people (or impersonal structures like the law) to make this connection for them. Interiority thus exists in these novels chiefly as a function of these seemingly endless attempts to connect actions with their unexpected consequences. Public effects become primary identity-making structures precisely because they are beyond the individual's control. But rather than depicting an engineered society from which subjectivity and agency are squeezed out, these novels see in the world of social effects new conditions of subjectivity and agency.

Although I have organized this book chronologically, beginning with Hawthorne and Warner and ending with Hopkins and James, my primary goal is not to trace the progress of this interest in the centrality of social effects from the 1850s through the turn of the century. Instead, I explore three different historical "moments" by examining the ways in which a particular problem is represented and imaginatively resolved by a contemporaneous pair of texts.

Part 1 of this work, which looks at Hawthorne, Warner, and the 1850s, focuses on the problem of self-regulation in relation to the disciplinary structures of the political party and the family. Both Hawthorne's *The Blithedale Romance* (1852) and Warner's *The Wide Wide World* (1850) ask what happens to the individual who inserts himself (or finds himself inserted) into such identity-making structures. Does the group rewrite the individual, replacing "authentic" interiority with collective intentions and desires? Or does the group nurture the individual, making the expression of true opinion or sentiment possible? In chapter 1 I argue that *The Blithedale Romance* tests the limits of both models in relation to the system of partisanship that dominated American politics in the 1840s and 1850s. In *Blithedale*, Hawthorne imagines that life in a commune sometimes works as a form of indoctrination (so that, for example, opinions become contagious) and sometimes works to liberate individual desires (so that the socialists find that the commune "seemed to authorize any individual, of either sex, to fall in love with any other, regardless of what would elsewhere be judged suitable and prudent").[13] In moving back and forth between the first model of group life and the second, Hawthorne begins to suggest that the voluntary group might work in a completely different way. Rather than as an agent of indoctrination or liberation, the group can be understood as a kind of mirror that puts the individual into a new and unexpected relation with his own opinions. Like Bellamy's mind readers, Hawthorne's Miles Coverdale begins to experience his fellow socialists as living reflections of his own interior states.

In chapter 2 I argue that Warner's *The Wide Wide World* works along similar lines to suggest that for the child the family is less a source of discipline than a mechanism that allows her to understand her own actions. While popular child-rearing guides like Lydia Maria Child's *The Mother's Book* (1831) and L. H. Sigourney's *Letters to Mothers* (1838) argued that effective punishment would ultimately produce well-behaved, self-regulating citizens, Warner creates a world in which the child loves punishment rather than learning to act so as to avoid it. Warner's Ellen Montgomery loves punishment, I argue, because it is only through punishment that she can get people to tell her what her actions mean and thus who she is. As John Humphreys, her "brother" and mentor, tells her after another in an endless series of mistakes: "You are no worse than before;—it has only made you see what you are."[14] To be self-regulating in *The Wide Wide World* is, Ellen realizes, to be unsure of exactly how one registers in the world.

Part 2 of this volume, on Twain, Chesnutt, and the post-Reconstruction era, focuses on racial identity and racism in relation to the legal structures of negligence and segregation. Both *Adventures of Huckleberry Finn* (1855) and *The House behind the Cedars* (1900), I argue, tease out from the logic of existing legal structures phantasmatic solutions to America's racial crisis. And in both cases this novelistic solution involves privileging what seems peripheral rather than intrinsic to the self—accidents over intentions in Twain, surface over depth in Chesnutt. Chapter 3 assesses the nature of sentiment in *Huckleberry Finn*, arguing that the novel works both to highlight Huck's change of heart toward Jim and to replace this sentimental model of responsibility with a model drawn from the emergent law of negligence (one powerful element of tort law). Twain, I argue, uses the basic logic of negligence to suggest that Huck's feelings are ultimately irrelevant to understanding how he has harmed Jim and that, by extension, the nation could be held accountable for the harms done to the freedmen. From the standpoint of negligence, the forty-dollar payment that ends the novel becomes a form of compensation, an evocation of the national promise to provide the freedmen with "forty acres and a mule." This chapter reads *Huckleberry Finn* as an implicit indictment of post-Reconstruction racism—not because it offers friendship as a model of reform, but because it imagines accountability for systematic harm even in the absence of malice.

In chapter 4 I argue that Chesnutt imagines the power of segregation law to assign identity based on "color" turned against itself. What would it mean, *The House behind the Cedars* asks, to take on the racial identity announced by one's appearance? The novel insists from beginning to end not on the power of heritage or blood, but on the power of the public image to enforce identity. Drawing on British conversion narratives in which Jews have the power to transform themselves into Christians (some of which, by Walter Scott, Edward Bulwer-Lytton, and Grace Aguilar, are cited in the novel), Chesnutt creates characters who deny that they are passing as white by insisting that they actually are as white as they appear to be. In *The House behind the Cedars*, Chesnutt proposes that interior and exterior are not in competition (as does the model of passing) but exist in a kind of symbiosis: the external does not hide but rather dictates interiority.

Part 3, on Hopkins, James, and the turn of the century, focuses on the limits of desire in relation to the construction of relatively new forms of public identity. Here I argue that both Hopkins and James see the medicalization of "perversions" like addiction and homosexuality less as modes of repression than as deeply productive social forms. In Hopkins's *Of One Blood* (1902–1903) and James's *The Sacred Fount* (1901), the discourses of addiction and homosexuality, which appear to understand individuals in terms of their uncontrollable desires, are transformed into ways of understanding individuals in almost purely formal terms. In both the hollow racial subject in

Hopkins and the subject of analogy in James, identity depends on form. I begin chapter 5 by analyzing the rhetoric of addiction at the turn of the century. In contrast to cultural critics who have read addiction on the model of the market (in which consumers feel compelled to buy), I argue that a powerful competing model of addiction was also at work during this period, one that understood the addict less as having uncontrollable desires than as having been evacuated and effectively "replaced" by the drug itself. In Henry Coles's *Confessions of an American Opium Eater* (1895), for example, the addict takes on the phantasmatic body of the drug: "Though human blood runs in his veins, it is little better than poppy juice; he is no longer really a man, but a malignant essence in forming a cadaverous human shape."[15] Drawing on this second model of addiction, Hopkins (as well as Frank Norris and Jack London) devises both new social formations and new ways of understanding individual identity. In *Of One Blood*, the "blood" of race is like opium in its ability to replace the subject, producing a peculiar kind of collective memory—for example, Reuel Briggs's ability to speak an African language he's never learned and recognize people he's never met—that unites the racial group. Indeed, Hopkins's version of modern racial identity takes up and redeploys the logic of addiction.

In chapter 6 I argue that James's *The Sacred Fount* represents homosexuality as a formal system for producing identity, a system that might be used to think about the construction of identity in general. James's narrator's attempt to make sense of desire by arranging the novel's lovers according to the logic of analogy (*A* is secretly victimizing *B* just as *C* is secretly victimizing *D*) suggests not only that sexual love is a form of vampirism but that hidden desires can be tracked through an algebraic formula. Rather than repressing a specifically homosexual desire, James makes such desires emblematic. *The Sacred Fount* uses the formal symmetry of same-sex desire— unlike the other lovers, the narrator and his companion are represented as mirror images of one another—to literalize or embody the analogies through which characters come to know themselves. Embodying analogy in the form of two male lovers helps James to represent even more dramatically than vampirism the fear of a self made legible by unknown desires.

Each of these chapters reads literary texts in conjunction with important contemporaneous discourses not simply to elucidate historical context, but to suggest that these discourses are themselves the starting point for novelistic analysis. Unlike the New Historicism, however, which refuses to make distinctions between fictional and nonfictional texts, this study suggests that the novel is self-consciously interested in the formal features of these extra-literary discourses and, in fact, creates formal correlatives in order to analyze their logic and explore their impact. In *Huckleberry Finn*, for instance, the emergence of the law of negligence does not function merely as the novel's relevant legal and historical context but is reflected in its form. The logic of retrospection (enforced by Tom's withholding of information) requires Huck to reconsider, after the fact, what he had been doing at the Phelps farm: not freeing Jim but playing a game. Through enforced retrospection, in other words, Twain dramatizes the disorienting effects of a world in which individual action is continually being redefined by other people.

In addition to reading the novel as it engages contemporaneous discourses, each of the three parts of this volume pairs canonical and noncanonical texts as a way of suggesting connections and correspondences that bridge traditional generic categories (because, for example, over the last thirty years, African American and women's fiction have become distinct genres in the critical canon). In so doing, I follow in the footsteps of important revisionist critics who have seen African American and women's writing not in isolation but in an ongoing dialogue with "classic" American fiction.[16] The implicit argument of each part is that novels depicting very different social issues and addressed to very different audiences can, at the same time, be understood as central to a broader cultural dynamic, the interest of which is not limited by the gender, race, or class of the author or implied audience. If Susan Warner, for example, writes most obviously within the tradition of the domestic novel, her concern with the consequences of group life in *The Wide Wide World* links her project very clearly to Hawthorne's investigation of partisanship in *The Blithedale Romance*. Read together, these novels suggest a concern with the unpredictable effects of identity-making groups that reconceives the family in the same terms as the party and that pertains to women as much as men. Rather than simply "transcending" gender, however, this concern with group life helps to supplement and contextualize the unique situation of women at midcentury. Along the same lines, under the rubric of privacy I bring together in this book a series of social issues (race, sexuality, the market, domesticity, and the law) that Americanists tend to treat singly or in pairs and I argue that they must be treated as integral parts of a larger cultural transformation that the novel helps illuminate. Simply put, this transformation encompasses a range of issues because it marks the emergence of a new form of sociality in which individuals are understood as social beings not because of their feelings, desires, or intentions but because of the various and inevitable traces they leave on the world.

Privacy has become a vexed issue in some of the most interesting recent criticism of American culture, especially for those critics who see it as a particularly harmful form of liberal ideology. According to Lauren Berlant, an investment in privacy is one manifestation of a broadly sentimental American culture, which privileges individual stories of pain over questions about structural inequality and injustice. When pain masquerades as politics, she claims, politics itself is evacuated of content and robbed of its power to mobilize individuals:

> Can we say something general then, about the contradictions deliberately or inevitably animated by politically motivated deployments of sentimental rhetoric? Here is a hypothesis: when sentimentality meets politics, it uses personal stories to tell of structural effects, but in so doing it risks thwarting its very attempt to perform rhetorically a scene of pain that must be soothed politically. Because the ideology of true feeling cannot admit the nonuniversality of pain, its cases become all jumbled together and the ethical imperative toward social transformation is replaced by a civic-minded but passive ideal of empathy. The political as a place of acts oriented toward publicness becomes replaced by a world of private thoughts, leanings, and gestures.[17]

From this perspective, liberal individualism, in its sentimental mode, deflates the "imperative toward social transformation" and discourages "acts oriented toward publicness" by convincing people that "empathy" alone counts as viable political action. The commitment to privacy fuels political paralysis.

In its focus on empathy as distraction, Berlant's work serves as a powerful corrective to much recent scholarship on the politics of sentiment and feeling and on the "right to privacy."[18] For Berlant, popular culture, even when it attempts political critique, only enforces a kind of impotent sentimental politics (which has its roots in mid-nineteenth-century women's fiction) by promoting the "universalism" of pain and the "redemptiveness of personal suffering."[19] More generally, popular culture (as well as "official" discourses like the law) must be read ideologically because they represent the world of private life not only as a world of pain but as a realm of freedom, a space protected from the instabilities and contradictions of politics. Thus, while "the critique of patriarchal familialism constantly put forth by sentimental forms can be used to argue against the normativity of the family . . . the sacred discourse of family values within this very domain works to preserve the fantasy of the family as the smallest space of sociability in which flow, intimacy, and identification across difference can bridge life across generations."[20] This "sacred discourse," which sanctifies privacy and intimacy, serves ultimately to disguise or make more palatable the power that is always at work in these supposedly "protected" spaces.

Michael Warner's recent work on privacy makes absolutely clear the Foucauldian roots of such an analysis. Like Berlant, Warner argues against the politically paralyzing consequences of the liberal commitment to privacy. In elaborating his theory of alternative public spheres (which he calls "counterpublics"), forms of public life that "are teaching us to recognize in newer and deeper ways how privacy is constructed" and "how private life can be made publicly relevant," Warner draws on and reinterprets Foucault's account of shifting and decentralized forms of power.[21] In a theory developed through a series of studies—in particular, *Madness and Civilization*, *Discipline and Punish*, and *The History of Sexuality*—Foucault tracks the workings of power in precisely those private places imagined to be protected or immune from social discipline. According to Warner, "In the domains of reason, justice, and personal life, Foucault's three major treatises show that the modern order requires relations of power that saturate civil society and the most intimate dimensions of personhood. The very private life thought to be the locus of freedom and rights was instead the laboratory of a regulatory order, one that could by no means be equated with the state or even with a class that ruled indirectly through the state" (157). In other words, the belief in the freedom of private life is simply a testament to the effectiveness of modern forms of social discipline, in which subjects need not be punished because they have been trained to control themselves.

In this book I both draw on these insights—especially the understanding of privacy as a form or structure that has potentially counterintuitive implications—and propose that the "publicness" of privacy was imagined in very different terms in nineteenth-century American literature. This version of privacy is best understood in relation to Foucault's account of the "problematic," a form of analysis that takes as its object not disciplinary structures but modes of understanding and judgment. Indeed, Warner's own thinking about privacy relies on this less familiar Foucauldian paradigm, which he describes as "not just an intellectual tangle," but "the practical horizon of intelligibility within which problems come to matter for people" (154). It is a form, in other words, of what Foucault calls "archeology," the description of an "archive" or "the set of rules which at a given period and for a given society define . . . the limits and forms of the sayable."[22] The novelistic tradition I examine here transforms publicness into this kind of problematic. It is treated, in other words, less as a space of exposure, surveillance, or discipline than as a condition of intelligibility for individual action. To return to the example of *Huckleberry Finn*'s account of negligence, the law from this standpoint represents a way of defining behavior in terms of its consequences, so that Huck comes to understand what he is responsible for—what he has actually done to Jim—only in relation to a series of other people's revelations. In this dependence on outsiders to explain the meaning of his own actions, Huck resembles the mind readers in Bellamy's tale, who discover their own characters in the minds of other people. In much the same way, individuals in the novels treated here find themselves inserted into systems of social organization—the party, the family, the law, the "science" of race or sexuality—that cannot simply be understood as normalizing. This is not to suggest that such systems did not perform a disciplinary function; rather, it is to argue that this function does not exhaust their social utility. In the pages that follow, I examine the way in which the American novel treats publicness as a condition of intelligibility and privacy as a limit case for thinking about how individuals confront themselves in and through social systems.

PART ONE Discipline and Punish

CHAPTER ONE   *The Blithedale Romance* and Other Tales of Association

The opening chapter of *The Blithedale Romance* (1852) begins with a description of a veiled woman and ends with a description of a masked one. Reflecting on "the wonderful exhibition of the Veiled Lady," Miles Coverdale imagines that the "misty drapery" that shields the star of the performance from the "material world" has provided her with "many of the privileges of a disembodied spirit."[1] When, at the end of this scene, he discusses with Old Moodie the well-known writer Zenobia, he claims that her "public name" works as "a sort of mask in which she comes before the world, retaining all the privileges of privacy" (8). For Coverdale, these two celebrities seem virtually interchangeable; he suggests at one point that Zenobia's mask is "a contrivance . . . like the white drapery of the Veiled Lady, only a little more transparent" (8). And yet it will quickly become evident that the novel depends on the difference between these kinds of veils. If the Veiled Lady's drapery turns out to be a prison, which does not so much shield her from her audience as discipline her by ensuring that she act on command, then Zenobia's pen name seems to be a form of liberation, a way of asserting control over something as ephemeral as her public image. What these two very different senses of the public "mask" suggest is that, from the very beginning of this novel about the vexed nature of group life, the group is imagined to have two competing effects on the individual. On the one hand, the group appears to indoctrinate, so that the individual must bend to its will; on the other, it appears to be quite malleable, subject to the individual's will. It is as though Hawthorne could not quite make up his mind about the individual's ability to maintain her integrity in the midst of a crowd; where

Zenobia is powerful, the Veiled Lady is powerless. This concern with the mysterious effects of group life persists even when *Blithedale* shifts from the public world to the semiprivate one, from the stage in Boston to the commune at Blithedale. The various affiliations and disaffiliations that constitute the plot can thus be read as instances of a more fundamental question: What happens when one becomes a member of a group?

This desire to think in rather abstract terms about the conflicting effects of group affiliation registers *The Blithedale Romance*'s engagement with the politically and economically modernizing world of midcentury America. After all, the political context of the novel and the scene of its writing were saturated by questions of group identification and affiliation: the 1840s saw not only the consolidation of the Whigs and Democrats as rival national parties but also the intensification of sectionalism with respect to the question of slavery, the expansion of religious and social reform movements, and the rise of various experimental utopian communities. When we remember that the immediate popularity of *The Scarlet Letter* was predicated on the partisan controversy recounted in "The Custom House" and that the contemporary interest in *Blithedale* was typically an interest in the satiric portraits of Brook Farm's earliest members, Hawthorne's personal connection to these issues of political affiliation seems indisputable.

But what is more interesting about such a political scene, especially in relation to *Blithedale*, is the general implication (often quite vehemently contested) that individual interests are best expressed and individual influence felt most forcefully through acts of affiliation. In America, Alexis de Tocqueville remarks, "there is no end which the human will despairs of attaining through the combined power of individuals united into a society." He explains: "As soon as several of the inhabitants of the United States have taken up an opinion or a feeling which they wish to promote in the world, they look out for mutual assistance; and as soon as they have found each other out, they combine. From that moment they are no longer isolated men, but a power seen from afar, whose actions serve for an example, and whose language is listened to."[2] It was, according to one historian, "the Era of Association."[3] Societies proliferated not only for the advancement of political causes—abolition, temperance, penal reform—but also for self-improvement (literary clubs), entertainment (sports clubs), and moral uplift (tract societies).

Despite this antebellum passion for "joining," questions of voluntary association have rarely been mentioned in recent criticism of Hawthorne's fiction. Indeed, beginning with Sacvan Bercovitch's influential reading of *The Scarlet Letter*, scholarship has focused almost exclusively on the problem of the nation. Bercovitch argues that the hidden logic of not only Hawthorne's novels but "all our mid-nineteenth-century classics" is a commitment to what he calls American "liberal ideology."[4] For Bercovitch, in other words, a novel like *The Scarlet Letter* sustains the idea of American individualism by endorsing a number of its fundamental beliefs: "The belief that social change follows from self-realization, not vice-versa; that true revolution is therefore an issue of individual growth rather than group action; and that the conflict it entails between self and society centers not on schemes for institutional change, whether by reform or transformation, but on the freedom of the individual 'to begin anew'—which is to say, on one's resistance to all institutional controls" (125). From this perspective, novelistic dissent makes sense only within the compromising terms of "liberalism" and thus serves to mask and maintain a more stable national consensus. Conversely, Lauren Berlant argues that Hawthorne's fiction must be read as a relentless critique of American political culture. In the broadest terms, she argues that his fiction "critiques and counters the hegemonizing strategies and privileges of 'official' national identity" by corralling "popular memory" into a critical form of "counter-memory."[5] Because national ideology works through the "symbolic and practical orchestration of public mentality," literature becomes central not only to the task of producing citizens but also to that of producing critical citizenship. If Bercovitch's account suggests that ideology is the logic that organizes American culture in all of its manifestations, encompassing both justification and dissent, Berlant's account suggests that "popular memory" might represent the "destabilizing" (194) fractures in this "official" story.[6]

From the perspective of ideology, these accounts make competing claims. From the perspective of American literary culture, however, they share certain key assumptions about the primacy of the national ideological frame to political and literary thought. Dividing American culture into official and unofficial knowledge or into the stabilizing force of consensus and the destabilizing force of radical dissent assumes that the nation is the primary form through which all political action and theory is processed. The basic logic of this position is that if Hawthorne is thinking politically, he must be thinking about the nation, so that if (according to Berlant) Hawthorne's fiction "threatens the nation's status as the ultimate political referent" (194), it does so by making the nation the ultimate literary referent, or if (according to Bercovitch) his fiction works as "thick propaganda" (89) for American liberalism, it does so by dissolving all partisan conflict into an assertion of an America that "transcended politics" (107). The implication of such accounts is that a text like "The Custom House" (or even *Blithedale*) must not be read in relation to the partisanship it explicitly describes but rather in relation to the "National Symbolic" under which specific disputes disappear into ideology.

Thinking solely in terms of the nation, however, inevitably means subordinating the question of partisanship; the two-party system is typically imagined as a lesser model of either the kind of discipline that happens on the national level or the kind of general consensus represented by national ideology. "The Custom House," Hawthorne's rather personal attack on the Salem Whigs who forced him out of his position as surveyor of U.S. Customs, goes a long way toward supporting such a view, dismissing the party system as one that exists merely to divvy up appointed offices and thus suggesting the poverty of actually existing democracy in America. Hawthorne's impatience with patronage is evident almost immediately in the fantasy that authorship might allow a kind of sympathetic relation with an audience defined as a "mass," a thing not divided up in advance by party or any other group loyalty but rather sorted out through the reader's relation to the author himself: "The truth seems to be . . . that when he casts his leaves forth upon the wind, the author addresses, not the many who will fling aside his volume, or never take it up, but the few who will understand him."[7] The fantasized decapitation that marks his transformation into a "politically dead man" (33) is certainly antithetical to the intimacy he imagines that a mass readership makes possible. Moreover, this scene of "revolutionary" political violence has also been read ironically, as a testament to the conservative nature of the two-party system. According to Jonathan Arac, for example, "the particular wit of the joke is that patronage changes are not 'revolution' but carry out the etymologically related action of 'rotation' in office: Revolutionary principle has become rotary patronage." Because, as Arac suggests (echoing a familiar contemporary critique of the two-party system), "consensus reigned between the two established parties" in 1850, he sees the party system itself as irrelevant to American politics, especially in relation to the larger question of national unity.[8]

The Blithedale Romance, I will argue in this chapter, turns this familiar hierarchy on its head by subordinating questions of national politics and national identity to the questions posed by the system of partisanship. Hawthorne's interest in the dynamics of partisanship does not mean that he simply disregards the problems of nation or of citizenship. Rather, what Hawthorne's work makes clear is that the nation in the mid-nineteenth century was not only experienced in terms of affiliative structures like party (so that one's relation to the political nation took shape within partisan practices) but conceptualized in these terms as well. Beginning in the 1790s and culminating in the years following the Jackson administration there was, as Ronald Formisano puts it, a "transformation of political culture" that was characterized by the establishment of well-defined, tightly organized, and widely supported national parties.[9] Even those historians who dispute the claim that the high visibility of parties on the political scene in the early nineteenth century meant high levels of grassroots participation do not dispute the fact that participation in politics at this moment was virtually synonymous with partisanship.[10] Thus the claim that the parties were basically in agreement (in that neither one sought to overthrow the government it was seeking to run) is at once a broadly true and a rather empty characterization of midcentury politics.

For Hawthorne, what is most significant about the party system is the fluidity of the affiliations it creates. That one is not born into a party (the pressures of family tradition aside) but can affiliate or disaffiliate at will suggests that party, far from being subordinate to nation, is the form through which notions of political compacts can be tested and through which tacit "consent" can be made explicit. Critics have been quick to note the ways in which Hawthorne's single sustained effort in political propaganda—his campaign biography of Franklin Pierce—argues for the preservation of the union "as it is" over any attempt to risk that union through sectional loyalties. Slavery, he suggests in one of the biography's most infamous passages, must be seen "as one of those evils which divine Providence does not leave to be remedied by human contrivances, but which, in its own good time, by some means impossible to be anticipated, but of the simplest and easiest operation, when all its uses shall have been fulfilled, it causes to vanish like a dream."[11] What often gets left out of the analysis of *The Life of Franklin Pierce*, however, is the way in which Hawthorne, rather than simply refusing to countenance sectional divisions over slavery, transfers these divisions from the nation to the national Democratic Party.

In the sections of the biography that concern the antislavery threat to the unity of the Democrats, Pierce no longer represents the power of compromise in the service of national unity; instead, he represents the power of principle. Hawthorne dramatizes Pierce's commitment to dividing the party along ideological lines, even to the point of risking a rupture between his pro-Compromise Democrats and the antislavery Democrats, a rupture that could cost him the election: "General Pierce could not consent that his party should gain a nominal triumph, at the expense of what he looked upon as its real integrity and life" (421). Pierce proves himself a "statesman of practical sagacity" (416), by proving both that he "loves his country as it is," "that great and sacred reality—his whole, united, native country—better than the mistiness of a philanthropic theory" (371), and that, in his willingness to sacrifice party cohesion to his sense of "right," he does not love his *party* "as it is." What Hawthorne's tract finally suggests is that party bears the burden of both national consensus (uniting members across sectional lines) and national reform (allowing "principle" to trump compromise). Indeed, party might be understood as the mechanism through which the collective consciousness that is the idealized form of the nation takes shape.

Hawthorne, I am arguing, is not invoking some type of utopian collective form against the pitfalls of national citizenship but is instead examining the unpredictable effects of political affiliations on the individuals who affiliate and on the political systems ruled by such affiliations. In so doing, he links voluntary group ties like the party and the commune to largely involuntary ones like the family and the nation. In attempting to represent the immediate and personal experience of affiliation through Coverdale's first-person narration, *Blithedale* imagines what it would mean either to speak through the group or to be completely dissolved into the group. In the process, Hawthorne produces (and ultimately rejects) two counternarratives that might be labeled the romance of choice and the romance of discipline. In the former, the group is imagined to act only to promote the individual's desires; in the latter, the group infiltrates the individual and transforms him in its own image. In fact, *Blithedale* might best be read as a thought experiment on the nature of affiliation, in which both the flatness of the "paint and pasteboard" (2) characters and the limitations of the narrator's point of view are specifically designed to explore the mysterious effects of group life on those who join. Hawthorne's project in *Blithedale*, then, is to think in abstract terms about affiliative groups, not in order to create "thick propaganda" for such organizations or to "critique and counter" them, but to analyze how they work and how they affect the mechanisms of choice and desire. Indeed, Hawthorne suggests that it is only through acts of affiliation that individuals come to understand their own positions and opinions.

Discipline and Pleasure

In "The Custom House," the unforeseen consequences of party affiliation provoke a retreat from public life into the intimate world of domesticity; Hawthorne imagines the mundane living room rather than the mundane office as the proper frame for "Romance." While "public office" undermines the artistic "character" by destroying "an entire class of susceptibilities, and a gift connected with them" (28–29), the isolation of the domestic sphere cultivates such susceptibilities, becoming (in Hawthorne's familiar line) "a neutral territory, somewhere between the real world and fairy-land, where the Actual and the Imaginary may meet and each imbue itself with the nature of the other" (28). In such a scheme, the violence and betrayal of political life can be replaced by the "sympathy" emblematized by the home, which allows the writer to indulge "an autobiographical impulse" (4) and to suppose a personal relation with the public "without violating either the reader's rights or his own" (5).[12]

Two years after "The Custom House," Hawthorne begins *Blithedale* with a depiction of an artist who makes a similar retreat from public to private space. As the novel opens, Coverdale is leaving the "wonderful exhibition" (5) of the Veiled Lady for his "cosey pair of bachelor rooms" (10), a retreat that, due to its location in "one of the midmost houses of a brick-block" of Boston (10), he in turn abandons for rural Blithedale, a community that represents to him "a world-wide distance from the system of society that shackled us at breakfast time" (13). That Coverdale imagines himself escaping from a "system of society" rather than a mere location in space both connects this scene to "The Custom House"—each text moves from the artificiality of system to the authenticity of intimate relations—and marks its difference. For Coverdale's escape to Blithedale is represented not as a move from public commitments to private life but as a move away from "the languor and vague wretchedness of an indolent or half-occupied man" (124) and toward "a purpose of life, worthy of the extremest self-devotion" (123). It is a move, in other words, away from privacy and toward politics.

What makes the communal experiment at Blithedale "political" is the fact that it attempts to organize a heterogeneous community of individuals on the model of the family and thus to replace competition with intimacy. "We had left the rusty iron frame-work of society behind us," according to Coverdale, "for the sake of showing mankind the example of a life governed by other than the false and cruel principles, on which human society has all along been based" (18–19). In *Blithedale*, then, intimacy represents not an escape from politics but a new form of political life: "We sought to profit by mutual aid, instead of wresting it by the strong hand from an enemy, or filching it craftily from those less shrewd than ourselves . . . or winning it by selfish competition with a neighbor" (19). The communal experiment at Blithedale might thus be read as a move away from both the market-dominated life of Boston (which threatens communal ties by fostering competition for scarce resources) and its party-dominated politics (which threaten the sanctity of individual opinion by fostering blind obedience to its dictates).

It is in this attempt to build politics on relations of intimacy, rather than replacing politics with intimacy, that *Blithedale* draws on Charles Fourier's theories of "Association" and his vision of the commune or "phalanx" in which political system is subordinated to individual desire.[13] The novel raises the issue of his influence explicitly when a convalescent Miles Coverdale claims that "Fourier's works, in a series of horribly tedious volumes, attracted a good deal of my attention, from the analogy which I could not but recognize between his system and our own" (49).[14] Fourier's vision of communal life depends on a commitment to the inviolable individuality and radical freedom of choice that Coverdale himself advocates throughout the novel. Indeed, Fourier's particular brand of socialism works both as a critique of market-dominated society and as an elaborate attempt to redeem and perfect a kind of market-based individualism. (This aspect of Fourierism might account for the fact that Albert Brisbane's 1840 translation of Fourier begins by defending private property as "the greatest guarantee of individual liberty.")[15] While never openly explored by the novel, the Fourierist account of what happens to individual desire within the confines of the utopian community is, I will argue, nevertheless central to its account of affiliation. Even after Coverdale denies the analogy he has just proposed— "There was far less resemblance, it is true, than the world chose to imagine; inasmuch as the two theories differed, as widely as the zenith from the nadir, in their main principles" (49)—Fourier haunts *Blithedale*.

According to Fourier, the problem with "Civilization," by which he means the market-dominated moment in which he writes, is (strangely enough) its asceticism, its denial of pleasure in the name of "morality." By contrast, Fourier's utopian community, Harmony, recognizes that pleasure, far from posing a threat to social order (this is the fundamental mistake made by the "philosophers" and "moralists" he derides), is itself the only conceivable end of social existence.[16] Thus, Fourier's commitment to pleasure is both a commitment to recognizing the significance of what seem to be the individual's most trivial desires and to seeing in desire a kind of divine inspiration: "Questions regarding gallantry and the love of eating are treated facetiously by the Civilised, who do not comprehend the importance that God attaches to our pleasures. Voluptuousness is the sole arm which God can employ to master us and lead us to carry out his designs; he rules the universe *by Attraction and not by Force*; therefore the enjoyments of his creatures are the most important object of the calculations of God."[17] The theory of "passionate attraction,"[18] the basis of much of Fourier's socialism, is precisely this belief that God has designed the passions for the individual's own good. And it is, arguably, this notion of order by attraction that set Fourier and his American followers apart from contemporary utopian communities like the Shakers and the Rappites (which Brisbane dismisses as "monotonous and monastic" [29]). The brilliance of Fourier's Harmony is both that it takes desire as its foundation and that it considers no desire too strange or too insignificant to be cultivated by the community. Harmony uses rather than denies the passions, allowing the individual to fulfill even (or especially) the most perverse desires by making the satisfaction of desire the ultimate social good. Indeed, in Harmony the community is necessarily subordinate to desire; in Fourier's eyes, Harmony exists only for the satisfaction of the individual.

"The merchants are free today, but the social body is not so in its relations with them; for we are compelled to make purchases."[19] By arguing that market-based freedom masks an alarming unfreedom, Fourier makes a case against the liberal defense of the free market that sees random individual choices miraculously adding up to social harmony. As Fourier sees it, the market is premised on promises of abundance that it cannot, by its very nature, deliver. The problem is not only that individuals experience constraint rather than freedom (or, in Fourier's words, "Force" rather than "Attraction"), but that they are necessarily subject to limitation rather than abundance. For the logic of the free market, which organizes demand for a scarcity of resources, makes the world into a zero-sum game in which a gain for one causes a loss for another; pleasure for one requires another's pain. And thus freedom of contract, far from working to advance the best interests of all parties, produces "two kinds of interest, collective and individual," which necessarily conflict, so that "every person engaged in an industry is at war with the mass, and malevolent toward it from personal interest."[20] The ultimate problem with civilization's dependence on the market—the reason such a system inevitably produces more misery than pleasure—is not desire itself (which is, after all, God-given) but incoherence and disorder, the "invisible hand" that does less to help satisfy desire than to frustrate and repress it.

The question that Fourier asks relentlessly in his writings is how one might create a viable social order that poses no threat to the individual, denies the individual nothing, and indeed takes individual satisfaction as the aim of its existence. The answer, he suggests, to this desire for unrestrained desire is, paradoxically, more organization. In Harmony, the key to happiness is a kind of hyperorganization. Even the briefest glance at Fourier's writings makes clear the depth of his commitment to arranging and anatomizing (for the purpose of both diagnosis and recommendation), his endless production of outlines, graphs, charts, and series: "The nine known passions are *the five sensual appetites* which exercise a greater or lesser degree of control over each individual, and *the four simple appetites of the soul.*"[21] Fourier's recommendations are offered up in the same spirit. He proposes that the effects of individual desire on the community as a whole depend entirely on how such desires are arranged: "The passions can only be harmonized if they are allowed to develop in an orderly fashion within the progressive series or series of groups. Outside of this mechanism the passions are only unchained tigers, incomprehensible enigmas."[22] The perfectly organized group (rather than the amorphous mass of civilized society) promises to transform desire from a threat into something more like a social bond. In Harmony, everything depends on the group; in Fourier's writings, everything depends on the *theory* of groups: "A Theory of Groups!!! What is its object? It is to ascertain by what methods the associative bond is established, so impracticable within the customs of civilization."[23] Within the "mechanism" of the group, the individual's most bizarre desires (the craving for "old hens," the love of "amorous heel scratching")[24] are not imagined to pressure the community—

to pit the interests of one against those of the mass—but to liberate the individuals who comprise the community.

The cultivation of "bizarre" desires in Harmony, something that Fourier describes in great detail, performs a kind of social service; allowing some people to do the strange things no one else wants to do ends up freeing everyone from "repugnant, disgusting, and degrading" labor. For example, because "no passion is more marked in children from ten to twelve years of age than that of filth and dirt," Harmony forms children into cleaning crews—"The Little Hordes"—that serve the community by indulging in the dirty work the adult population hates but its younger members love.[25] Moreover, because groups are constructed and maintained solely around the individual's own passions—the basis of Fourier's theory of "attractive industry"—the cultivation of desire helps cement social bonds: "In the theory of the passions the term group refers to a number of individuals who are united by a shared taste for the exercise of a particular function."[26] Groups are thus formed through "spontaneous association without compulsory ties"; they are united by "ardent and blind passion for a brand of industry or kind of pleasure common to all the members."[27] Under the theory of attractive industry, one works at the industry one loves, so that in Harmony even labor is transformed into pleasure.

The form of social organization most amenable to individual fulfillment, it turns out, not only cultivates clearly defined and spontaneously constructed groups but also the thematic arrangement of these groups (the vegetable-growing groups, for example) into a proper series: "In large associations, it is necessary to class the workmen in groups homogenous in tastes, and connect those groups together in an ascending and descending serie [sic], in order to develop the inclinations of each individual and excite the emulation, which arises from a methodical opposition of contrasts or differences of tastes."[28] Each individual is expected to cultivate a variety of passions and thus plays a part in a number of different groups. Each group is part of a tightly organized series; the artful arrangement of series makes up the "Phalanx," Harmony's equivalent of the state. If, for example, "three individuals—A, B, C" who "like their bread salted in different ways"—formed the center of three different groups, they would constitute "a passionate series of *breadists* or bread-lovers." They would become, "that is, an affiliation of groups with graduated and contrasted tastes. Their joint activity and their cabalistic discords would create the intrigues necessary to bake excellent bread and grow fine wheat."²⁹ Competition, rather than a matter of each against all, is harnessed by the series, becoming less the function of the individual against the mass and more a product of group solidarity. Fourier's theory of "attractive industry" creates a system in which supply and demand can never be at odds so that there is no need to marshal resources or adjudicate competing claims. Harmony replaces economy with organization.

By generating harmony rather than discord out of the radical proliferation of desires, Fourier creates a world that Roland Barthes has likened to an "ideal orgy": "a fantasmatic site, contra-civilized, where no one refuses himself to anyone, the purpose not being to multiply partners . . . but to abolish the wound of denial."³⁰ In such a structure, intimacy is no longer the domain of the couple or the family (civilized forms that Fourier hated) but instead describes the relation among a wide variety of unrelated people. If his desiring individual thus depends on the organization for fulfillment, he is also imagined to be radically self-sufficient and impervious to influence. It is as if, as one of Fourier's American disciples put it, each individual were his own system: "The Soul, the Me, the Mover, manifesting itself thus only by its passions, may be regarded as their sum, or one grand Immortal Passion."³¹ Harmony makes no claim to produce the passions; rather, it makes the free expression of passion possible. The trick, according to Fourier, is not to change desires themselves—to make them amenable to communal life—but to construct a system that would enable them to flourish. Designed as a kind of federation of individual passions, the group is never experienced as a limit to what one can do; it does not impinge on the individual or his self-conceptions in any way. Indeed it is only within the organization of the group and the series that the individual can truly experience and fulfill his desires.

Fourier imagined that the new social forms produced by Harmony would depend on architecture, and he pictured an elaborate "phalanstery" or "Palace" that would eliminate the monopoly of the isolated nuclear family and contribute to what Barthes calls "an over-all science of human space."³² Brisbane explains that "all varieties and kinds of edifices, which are necessary to man, and which are now scattered and isolated, will be combined and interwoven in one vast construction, which will form the Palace of a Phalanx."³³ The phalanstery arranges bodies in space just as the system of "attractive labor" classes individuals in groups and series. To take the "new amorous institutions" as an example, not only are there particular groups (the virginal "Vestalate" and the more promiscuous "Damselate"; not to mention the "Striplings," who are too old to be classed as children and too young for sexual classification) and particular times (the Damsels "participate in the court of love each evening from nine to ten") but particular spaces are arranged to accommodate each hourly activity and each chosen identity.[34] While the Vestals have chosen chastity, the architecture of the phalanstery ensures that they are true to their word: "The lodgings of the Vestals are arranged in such a way as to leave no room for doubt about their private life."[35] In Fourier's plan, architecture overcomes epistemological skepticism. The emphasis in the phalanstery is on the creation of public space and the arrangement of private space such that the individual inhabitants never completely disappear, or cease to register in the overall community. But if this looks like the attempt to eradicate private space, it also might be read as the attempt to rethink the concept of privacy. After all, in Fourier's view it is only within such spatial arrangements that the individual becomes free to experience, without repression, a true interiority.

Thus architecture produces Harmony. Fourier's sense of how the publicness of communal life would work runs directly contrary to more familiar Foucauldian accounts, in which the structure of the panopticon—where prisoners are controlled by the very fact of being continuously watched—represents the disciplinary structure of modernity.[36] Being watched, in other words, not only ensures conformity to a certain model of behavior through the threat of punishment but also convinces the individual to cooperate, to become her own disciplinarian. What we produce in such a world, according to Foucault, is the regime of the normal. In Harmony, however, such manipulation of public and private space is intended to undo civilization's need for repression by ensuring the vast proliferation of desire. If the arrangements of space in the phalanstery might be seen as "individuating," they must not be understood as "normalizing" precisely because the point of the baroque social structure is to encourage the widest possible expression of perverse individual desire and, indeed, to make the expression of this desire possible.

If, as I suggested earlier, Fourier haunts *Blithedale*, it is as an ever-present fantasy of how group life might work. This fantasy—enacted, as I will explore below, in Coverdale's obsession with free choice—is, in essence, the idea that the individual could be freed *by* rather than *from* the group. The interest of the testing of Fourier in *Blithedale*, however, becomes much clearer in relation to popular celebrations of Fourierism (including political tracts by Brisbane and Parke Godwin). One such celebration—"Meadow-Farm: A Tale of Association," which appeared anonymously in the *Knickerbocker* in 1843—is important in this context not only because it depicts a Harmony-like commune, but because it explicitly links socialist theory to questions of political partisanship by pitting the freedom of socialists against the slavery of partisans. Given the connections between tale and novel, I want to consider briefly the ways in which "Meadow-Farm," in making different kinds of claims about the power of space, the power of influence, and the difference between "what man can do alone, and what he can accomplish collectively," throws into relief the political issues at the center of *Blithedale*.[37]

A Tale of Association

"Meadow-Farm" is about the success of a Vermont commune and was clearly designed as propaganda for a particular version of Christian socialism. Serialized in the years just after Hawthorne's departure from Brook Farm, the story shares with *Blithedale* the bare bones of its plot: in the serial a hard-headed philanthropist, his dreamier associate, and two sisters help found a commune wherein they pledge, like the Blithedalers, "to avoid the rivalry and competition which causes one man to raise himself at the expense of another's ruin; which makes one man's loss another's gain, and separates instead of uniting men in the social state" (June, 544). And, despite the fact that the commune in "Meadow-Farm" looks more like a village (full of private homes and monogamous couples) than a phalanstery, like *Blithedale* the tale makes a point of drawing attention to its Fourierist roots. Rufus Gilbert, the farm's founder and spiritual leader, having steered clear of all theory ("Instead of studying mental philosophy in Brown or Locke or Stewart, he studied it in living subjects" [May, 435]), seems to have spontaneously generated his own theory of "association": "It might seem incredible that a young man, in the seclusion of an inland village, should originate a scheme upon principles which have made the name of Fourier immortal; for at this time doctrines of association had hardly gained a hearing abroad, much less in this country. But it must be remembered that the same circumstances impressed the mind of Rufus which had impressed the minds of others; the same evils existed in his village as in other places, and the pervading spirit of the age touched him and guided his thoughts, though he knew it not" (May, 441). In the end, we might hold "the pervading spirit of the age" responsible for the fact that both "Meadow-Farm" and *Blithedale* are concerned with tracking the effects of affiliative life in relation to both socialist theory (Fourier) and political practice (party).

As it promises, "Meadow-Farm" pursues the connection with Fourier's theory. An interest in reforming native architecture, for instance, drives the initial plans for the commune: "If I were as sanguine as you are," Rufus tells his more "visionary" friend Philip Welton, "I should long ago have set out on a crusade against mean houses; have preached the one idea of a better architecture for the farms and villages from Maine to Georgia" (May, 441). The point in Fourier's Harmony is to so effectively arrange bodies in relation to one another that one could imagine each individual as the center of a perfectly ordered association—and, in turn, imagine the association as a kind of human mechanism for fulfilling each individual's desires. The point in "Meadow-Farm," however, is to beautify the domestic arrangements that are already in existence, to make private homes "more alluring" (May, 440) for their downtrodden inhabitants. It would not be stretching the point to say that whereas the purpose of architectural reform in Fourier is to make all space public space, the purpose of reform in "Meadow-Farm" is to eradicate public space altogether: "I have been led to believe, by the feelings I always have when I approach this place," Rufus claims while admiring a particularly charming cottage, "that if our people had more comfortable homes they would love to stay in them better, and would not seek the tavern and store so much" (May, 440).

At the same time, Meadow-Farm, like Harmony, is marked by the desire for epistemological certainty, which translates into the desire for perfect transparency in social and personal relations. As "Meadow-Farm" would have it, the effect of this desire in everyday life in America is the production of both democratic institutions and a republic of spies:

> This curious and, as it is called, meddlesome spirit, which Americans show in the affairs of their neighbors, is in fact the instinct of self-preservation in our people. It is a better habit than an idle curiosity, however it may be denominated. It matters little who comes or goes, or what the habits and opinions, of people who live in countries where a military power is ever ready to support the established authority of the land. Not so with us. We require no passports in passing from village to village, from state to state; every man is free to move as he pleases; but there is constantly over every man a jealous scrutiny, and not so much over his personal movements, as over the most important part of him, his

opinions and habits.... As we live and move and have our being as a nation by the action of this public sentiment, is it not a necessary consequence that we are curious and meddlesome, and often annoying, toward those who come among us to see the strange anomaly, a self-governing people? (September, 231)

In other words, openness of space and freedom of movement, far from liberating individuals from the surveillance of their neighbors, ends up enforcing the "jealous scrutiny" of "every man." At Meadow-Farm, by contrast, certainty about "the most important part" of one's fellow socialists is produced neither by spying nor by the arrangement of public space (indeed in Rufus's case, "the domestic arrangements of the house were such that he could retire and be as solitary as a hermit" [September, 239]), but by individual consent alone. Because no "habit" or "opinion" is irrelevant to the "public sentiment," the Meadow-Farmers attempt to reform politics by agreeing to disclose personal information. Thus, "having separated from the others in their walk" in order to talk privately, Rufus's sister Clara and her suitor John Stewart must remind themselves (even in the midst of personal confessions) of their "solemn agreement" with the community "to divulge all secrets." When Rufus overhears their decision to immediately inform the group of their engagement, he tells John that his "honesty alone" makes him "worthy of any woman" (September, 230).

In "Meadow-Farm," the commitment to the public expression of private opinion sets this particular community apart not only from everyday life in America (which requires constant surveillance), but from other affiliative groups, especially party. Despite the fact that political parties define themselves, like the commune at Meadow-Farm, as associations united by "one common interest" (June, 544), they are, in the view of the commune, insufficiently committed to individual opinion. Party arises at a number of key moments in the tale, each time in order to highlight both the intolerance of partisans for differences of opinion and the indifference of partisans to their own opinions. According to the tale's narrator (an outside observer who often plays the part of the chorus), partisans of any stripe can be characterized in the following terms: "Having few facts, and those often distorted by the newspaper, which is the party organ, reading only one side of the question, whatever it may be, and not entitled to have any opinion in truth, they rush into the wildest extravagances and utter the foulest anathemas against their opponents" (June, 549). Defined by their vehemence in fighting with their opponents, partisans in this tale are imagined to have no opinions of their own. This lack, it seems worth noting, is not understood as an empty-headed commitment to the party line. Indeed, "party men" in "Meadow-Farm" are represented as being devoted to their party without having any idea what their party line might be. "Grounds, Sir!" explains the Whig committee man when Rufus asks him to describe his candidate's positions: "Sir, he is a Whig; he was born a Whig; he has lived a Whig, and will die a Whig. What more can you ask? He never opposes his party; he is a man we can rely upon; we know where to find him; he is a man to stick to the party, if the party go to the d——l; and that's what I call being a patriot" (September, 232). The problem with party, it seems, is that like some kind of parasite it replaces the individual's devotion to his own opinions with a deep and abiding devotion to itself.

Throughout "Meadow-Farm" much is made of the fact that the socialists (often suspected of being as "bigoted and sectarian" [September, 237] as the partisans who surround them) are in fact committed to the sanctity of personal opinion. Written into the Farm's bylaws is "a clause which stated that no one should be censured for opinion's sake upon any subject, political or religious, 'as men have not the control of their opinions, but must follow the course of evidence or argument wherever they may lead'" (June, 546). That this freedom of opinion leads to no disputes among the socialists, no conflicts of any kind, is as the story hints entirely due to Rufus's "influence." For the openness of Meadow-Farm depends on the subtle control of Rufus, who is imagined to have "a very different power . . . over the minds of men" than "the bustling importance of the village politician." As the narrator puts it, Rufus has "acquired" this power to influence "from Heaven": it was "the power of superior virtue, the majesty of an elevated mind, a dictatorship derived from God" (May, 434). In the logic of "Meadow-Farm," the fact that Rufus influences his followers by his virtuous example rather than by bribery or force makes all the difference; the commune he creates—committed to both individual opinion and the influence of Rufus's opinion—becomes something like a democratic dictatorship. Thus those of Meadow-Farm seem to have escaped from the tyranny of party into the tyranny of the charismatic leader.

It was the fear of this kind of inescapable influence (emanating from an individual or a group) that generated the various forms of opposition to the period's general passion for association. Ralph Waldo Emerson, when approached by the Ripleys about joining Brook Farm in 1840, made it clear that suspicions about the threat to the sanctity of individual opinion extended to any kind of affiliative group:

> Shall I raise the siege of this hencoop & march baffled away to a pretended siege of Babylon? It seems to me that to do so were to dodge the problem I am set to solve, & to hide my impotency in the thick of the crowd. I can see too afar, that I should not find myself more than now—no, not so much, in that select, but not by me selected fraternity. Moreover, to join this body would be to traverse all my long trumpeted theory, and the instinct which spoke from it, that one man is a counterpoise to a city,—that a man is stronger than a city, that his solitude is more prevalent & beneficent than the concert of crowds.[38]

From one perspective, the problem Emerson identifies here is that no group, not even an affiliative group, can adequately reflect the individual's desires; Brook Farm, the "select, but not by me selected fraternity," is believed to be not quite amorphous enough to count as a "crowd" and not quite "select" enough to count as family. But Emerson's distaste, in the end, has less to do with his inability to select his own fraternity than with his sense that fraternities are inherently corrupting. In "The American Scholar," he makes more explicit the general problem with affiliative groups that are imagined to reconstruct the individual in their own image: "Is it not the chief disgrace in the world not to be a unit;—not to be reckoned one character;—not to yield that peculiar fruit which each man was created to bear, but to be reckoned in the gross, in the hundred, or the thousand, of the party, the section, to which we belong; and our opinion predicted geographically, as the north, or the south?"[39] Emerson transforms affiliation into a series of equations, whereby joining a group is equivalent to conforming to prepackaged opinion, and conformity to such opinion is equivalent to giving up individuality altogether. The dynamics of the "party," for Emerson, are so powerful a mechanism of conformity that the group becomes a kind of map that can not only predict and make legible individual opinion, but can simply replace it.

Emerson's commitment to solitude, both literal and figurative, recalls familiar republican doubts about the power of faction. In his 1796 Farewell Address, George Washington delivered a version of this position that remained influential for antebellum opponents of the party system. Focusing on "the baneful effects of the Spirit of Party," which "agitates the Community with ill founded jealousies and false alarms," Washington argued that such "combinations or Associations... are likely, in the course of time and things, to become potent engines, by which cunning, ambitious, and unprincipled men will be enabled to subvert the power of the People and to usurp for themselves the reins of government."[40] Thomas Jefferson comes even closer to Emerson's sense that the real danger of party is its ability to corrupt not the nation but the individual: "I never submitted the whole system of my opinions to the creed of any party of men whatever in religion, in philosophy, in politics, or in anything else where I was capable of thinking for myself. Such an addiction is the last degradation of a free and moral agent. If I could not go to heaven but with a party, I would not go there at all."[41]

Such suspicions only intensified during the rise of the second party system when political activity became virtually unimaginable outside the confines of party; while proponents of the party system saw it as the most democratic way to create, out of scattered individual interests, a unified public voice, critics saw it as a dangerous form of indoctrination. What newly minted partisans imagined as loyalty, opponents imagined as a much more sinister form of coercion, "by which a man is bound to surrender his principles upon the altar of party."[42] Where partisans saw a "band of brothers"[43] engaged in political battle, opponents saw "branded sheep ... who, when argued with, merely bid you look at their brand."[44]

It is true that, as the second party system took shape, the structure of the party itself came to overshadow both the principles it initially stood for and the commitment to democratic procedure. According to Richard Hofstadter, Martin Van Buren and other Albany Regency spokesmen who pushed so hard to establish strong national parties at the earliest stages of their formation "were moved by a new passion that would have seemed strange, possibly even sinister, to their predecessors—the passion for organization."[45] Certainly, one of the most dramatic differences between the second party system and the first is the establishment of elaborate national organizations by both Whigs and Democrats; party committees organized members (with widely divergent results) from the school district to the congressional district to the national convention. The function of such machinery, according to activists, was to consolidate a vast network of partisans into a unified public voice, a process often compared to military training: "Parties in our republic," claimed the editor of the *New York Globe*, "in their contests, may be compared to contending armies; there must be system, discipline, order, regularity, union, and concert of action."[46] On the grassroots level, this discipline involved the production of member loyalty through the parades, campaign barbecues, and rallies that were designed to heighten enthusiasm for the party organization if not the party's candidate. It also involved vigilance on the part of individual partisans; party newspapers made incessant calls for self-sacrifice: "We hold it a principle . . . that every man should sacrifice his own private opinions and feelings to the good of his party—and the man who will not do it is unworthy to be supported by a party, for any post of honor or profit."[47]

As the parody of partisanship in "Meadow-Farm" makes clear, this commitment to structure and to organization rather than conscience and conviction was the central point of contention for those who were suspicious of the two-party system. Francis Lieber, in his 1839 *Manual of Political Ethics*, claimed that while party has always been a legitimate and necessary part of "free countries," it nevertheless poses a danger to the individual, whose "own judgment and even moral feeling may become warped and distorted" by mere party zeal. He suggests that the danger of party lies in its propensity to indoctrinate, and thus to shift the very terms of individual judgment: "[As partisans] we shall judge of those things *by* which alone parties can be truly measured, such as justice, the prosperity of the whole country, truth, right, which are indeed the first principles upon which all politics shall move, by the standard derived *from* the party, thus making that which ought to be the standard the thing to be measured, and that which ought to be measured the standard, as inflamed sects will sometimes measure the truth by their tenets, not their tenets by the truth."[48] In the strongest terms, bending to this kind of partisan influence was represented as a form of slavery, in which one sacrificed on the "altar" of party the dignity of living by conscience. The Whig committee man in "Meadow-Farm," dazzled by the superior reasoning of Rufus (who refuses all party affiliation), claims, "Would to God I were free to act myself! Oh! this slavery of party; this slavery of the soul! How much meaner and baser is it than any bonds of the body!" (September, 233).

What is surprising, then, about the vehement defense of partisanship in the 1840s is that it was couched in nearly the same terms as the opposition to party. Rather than a tool of indoctrination, defenders imagined party to be a tool with which individuals could more forcefully express their own interests and opinions. To antebellum partisans, political organizations not only conducted a massive public service—creating an institutionalized opposition that would ensure a check on those in power, disseminating political information to far-flung populations, and assuaging sectional conflict by cementing ideological bonds across different regions—but worked to give voice to scattered individual opinions. There was, in fact, a sense among advocates that the party, rather than corrupting the individual's opinions, might act as a public extension and amplification of the individual's voice. The party, according to proponents, was literally built on individual opinion: "Those who stay away from the caucuses and primary meetings of the party," claimed one local paper, "have no right, afterwards, to complain if the proceedings are not to their wish; it is their business to attend, take an active part, express their opinions and wishes, and endeavor to make the action of the party what they think it ought to be."[49] From this perspective, parties were thought to be aggregations of individuals rather than engines of indoctrination; they were, at bottom, tools with which individuals with similar opinions could act more effectively in public. One might even claim that, in the eyes of proponents, parties are built on the model of Fourier's Harmony, in which the individual is inserted into a social structure without being, in any essential way, transformed by it. Thus, the machinery of the system enhances and makes possible the individuality it only seems to threaten. In a world in which one's inclusion in a group was more often than not involuntary, party politics represented itself as a romance of affiliation, a belief in the freedom to enforce one's opinions, pick one's associates, and choose— Democrat or Whig—one's own identity.

The "theory of groups" articulated by Fourier and his followers as well as by partisans and their critics marks the emergence of two competing models of group life at midcentury, two competing accounts of what happens to the individual who inserts herself into the party or the commune. In the first model, the group is imagined to replace the individual's opinions and interests with its own program, thus transforming the individual into a true "member" by a rather shady process of indoctrination. In the second model, the group is imagined to be an extension of the individual, a tool that can be used to fulfill desires or make interests register in the public sphere. If these are the predominant ways of characterizing the antebellum world of affiliation, however, they are not the only ways. What, for example, are we to make of Fourier's insistence that there be obstacles to desire, his claim that "cabalistic discords" are necessary not only for producing "excellent bread" but for sustaining "individual and collective happiness"?[50] From the perspective of the obstacle, the hierarchical structure of Harmony might be better understood as a complicated way of putting individuals into relation with their desires. Barthes is helpful here, drawing attention to the ways in which a myriad of devices work to elicit or to heighten desire. In Harmony, Barthes argues, an institution like the "Angelicate" (which serves the community as prostitutes) does not merely fulfill but actually "*conducts* desire: as though, left on his own, every man were incapable of knowing whom to desire, as though he were blind, powerless to invent his desire, as though it were always up to others to show us *where the desirable is*."[51]

According to political theorist Frederick Grimke, partisanship might perform a similar function. In *The Nature and Tendency of Free Institutions* (1848), he claimed that because "in a democratic republic, the people themselves compose all existing parties," "opinions are not only submitted to examination, but they are submitted to the examination of those who are immediately affected by them."[52] This kind of political education, in which those "affected" by politics are encouraged to make critical judgments, looks a bit like Berlant's account of "critical citizenship," although Grimke describes the effects of such an education in very different terms. Individuals, he claims, often enter parties not from political conviction, but "from motives which are of a purely personal or private character" (180). And yet, the mere fact of partisanship produces a kind of political enlightenment: "The connection which has taken place between politics and private manners brings the former more completely within the reach of everyone," so that "in spite of the eternal wrangling of parties, or rather in consequence of it, a greater amount of knowledge, a keener sagacity, and juster views are created than would otherwise exist" (185). Party, from this perspective, does not produce opinion but makes judgments about opinion possible. Implicit in Grimke's analysis of party is the Fourier-like suggestion that individuals are often in a kind of "lag" with respect to their own opinions. What emerges from such theories is the idea that the group might work neither as a form of indoctrination nor as a tool for the expression of individual opinion, but rather as a structure through which one comes to know one's own opinions. Association, in other words, might be a form of education, but it is an education in the individual's own interests.

Hawthorne's novel of communal life takes shape within this debate about the power of the affiliative group. At the center of *Blithedale* are the two competing versions of affiliation that emerge through competing fantasies of group life, one represented by Coverdale's commitment to "choice" and the other by Hollingsworth's commitment to "discipline." Indeed, in Hollingsworth's and Coverdale's competing fantasies—Hollingsworth's dream of a prison that molds the individual and Coverdale's dream of a community that reflects his own desires—we have competing versions of utopia that are analogous to the competing visions of party. It is the conflict between these two ways of imagining the individual's relation to the group that organizes Hawthorne's narrative from its first scene. And yet, *Blithedale*'s complicated account of personal, social, and textual "influence" develops the possibility, implicit in Fourier and Grimke, that the group might function as a different kind of "mechanism" altogether, one that neither liberates nor eradicates the individual's interests and opinions but that works as a kind of mirror that puts him into relation with himself. It is only through public acts of affiliation, the novel suggests, that the individual comes to have a sense of his own interests.

The Romance of Affiliation

"Real life," as Coverdale claims, while straining to hear Zenobia and Westervelt discuss their private life, "never arranges itself exactly like a romance" (97). If "real life" involves contingency—Zenobia and Westervelt, much to Coverdale's dismay, wander out of earshot—romance involves the ability to transform contingencies into certainties, to make the world submit to individual will. According to Hawthorne's preface to the novel, this is precisely what it means to turn "real life" into romance; *Blithedale* as a textual project (like Blithedale as a socialist experiment) gives the individual "a license with regard to every-day Probability, in view of the improved effects which he is bound to produce thereby" (2). From one perspective, then, Coverdale is wrong about the way in which "real life arranges itself" at Blithedale. For what makes this particular socialist experiment "utopian" for Coverdale is neither that it prioritizes the spiritual over the material nor that it fosters equality and "brotherhood" among those of different classes, but that it provides the individual with a radical—indeed seemingly magical—freedom of choice.

What Coverdale suggests about social equality among the Zenobias and Silas Fosters of the world, for example, is that it is prized (or, more accurately, accepted without complaint) primarily because it feels uncoerced. Sitting down to his first communal meal at Blithedale, Coverdale wonders "whether some of us—and Zenobia among the rest—would so quietly have taken our places among these good people, save for the cherished consciousness that it was not by necessity, but choice" (23). Rather than the escape from the commercialism of Boston, it is this sanctity of choice that, in Coverdale's eyes, truly separates Blithedale from the outside world. Because trade is central to this particular utopian experiment—"one of the first questions raised" there is how they will manage to "compete with the market-gardeners round Boston" (20)—what makes life in Boston appear so distasteful, it turns out, is not trade itself, but coercion, the limits that the market inevitably places on consumers. Thus, when Coverdale claims that in the city "every son of woman both perpetuates and suffers his share of the common evil, whether he chooses it or no" (19), the implication is that the true "evil" is precisely this lack of choice. In Coverdale's utopian community there are, it appears, no such restrictions on what one can choose to do. And thus it comes as no surprise that he describes every crisis in the novel in terms of a choice. Coverdale's own dramatic break with Hollingsworth turns on an ultimatum: "Be with me . . . or be against me! There is no third choice for you" (125). A few scenes later, when Coverdale tracks down Priscilla in Boston, his only concern is to find out whether she has left of her "own free will": "Is it your choice to go?" he asks her (158–59). Both of the interpolated "legends" that prove to be crucial turning points in the plot—Zenobia's "Silvery Veil," which marks Priscilla's recapture, and Coverdale's "Fauntleroy," which reveals her history—depend on this fantasized freedom to exercise one's will. While in the first legend, Theodore seals his own fate by rejecting the Veiled Lady's offer ("Thou hast made thy choice" [105]), in the second Old Moodie reveals his power over Zenobia by refusing to claim his inheritance (he lives in poverty "of [his] own choice" [177]).

For Coverdale, this investment in free choice is so powerful that it promises to do away with the constraints of individuality itself. At its most radical, his refusal to acknowledge limits to choice requires him to imagine that individuals can choose their own origins, can construct for themselves not only a new family but a new family history. Coverdale begins his stay at the farm with an illness that, by wasting his body, allows him to rebuild it, and thus serves to literalize the fantasy of rebirth; his convalescence seems to him "an avenue between two existences; the low-arched and darksome doorway, through which I crept out of a life of old conventionalism, on my hands and knees, as it were" (56). Reborn into a body he designs himself—he pictures himself memorialized as a founder of the commune, "painted in my shirt-sleeves, and with the sleeves rolled up, to show my muscular development" (120)—Coverdale becomes, "in literal and physical truth ... quite another man" (57). Given Coverdale's desire to cast his venture at Blithedale as a rebirth, his sense of Hollingsworth's concern, his "more than brotherly attendance" (38) on him through his sickness, might best be read not as a homoerotic attachment (as many critics have suggested)[53] but as a filial one. Hollingsworth's domestic role in this scene—there seems to be "something of the woman moulded into [his] great stalwart frame" (39)—and the intimation that it is he who brings Coverdale back to life, suggests that in this rebirth fantasy, Coverdale's friend has become his mother. Indeed, the absolute authority of desire here, the need to imagine that everything, even biology, is subordinate to it, might be seen as the driving force behind a system that, as Coverdale sees it, requires one to be reborn into a new body and seems "to authorize any individual, of either sex, to fall in love with any other, regardless of what would elsewhere be judged suitable and prudent" (67). By this logic, it would make no difference whether Coverdale is in love with Hollingsworth or wants to be his son, so long as his desire determines their relationship.

This kind of magical noncontingency goes well beyond the idealization of free choice, which for Coverdale means "the cherished consciousness" that he sacrifices comfort and authority, "not by necessity, but choice." The amazing prevalence of what at first seem like coincidences in *Blithedale* suggests that in such a world one's wildest dreams really do come true. If Zenobia hopes aloud, for example, that the firelight from the windows of the farm-house "may serve to guide some wayfarer to shelter," she has no sooner finished speaking than "there came a knock at the house-door" (24) from the snow-covered wayfarers Hollingsworth and Priscilla. If Coverdale fantasizes about seeing Zenobia's naked form immortalized in the "cold decorum" of "marble" (41), by the end of the novel she is literally frozen into "the marble image of a death-agony" (216). And if Coverdale early on quips that Zenobia is "a sister of the Veiled Lady" (42), he soon discovers that they are, in fact, sisters.

Given Hawthorne's desire to picture a community built on the sanctity of individual desire—a utopia akin to Fourier's in which other people present no obstacle to the fulfillment of one's desires—the novel's obsession with individuals who can make the world submit to their will begins to make sense. The creation of an intimate community at Blithedale, a community built on "brotherhood" and that "seemed to authorize any individual, of either sex, to fall in love with any other," in no way overrides the commitment to the primacy of the individual. If the burden of Fourier's Harmony is to replace expensive and dirty private homes with magnificent public spaces designed to accommodate the entire range of possible activities (he recommended that Harmonists change occupations every two hours), the burden of Blithedale is to combine the "advantages of an associated life" (75) with the comforts of privacy.[54] The Blithedalers "had the privilege of building cottages for their own residence . . . thus laying a hearthstone and fencing in a home, private and peculiar, to all desirable extent" (75). One might argue that Hawthorne simply makes explicit what goes unspoken in Fourier's writings—the sense in which the group, understood as enabling rather than limiting the individual, allows the individual to maintain at all times and under all circumstances a kind of perfect privacy. Accordingly, each character is not only caught up in a love story (indeed, the emergence of the couple is the only thing that seems to threaten the "brotherhood" of Blithedale) but represented as in some way masked, veiled, or shielded from the watchful eye of the group. Zenobia is called, even by the Blithedalers, by her pen name, which works as "a sort of mask," Priscilla has her veil, Old Moodie his eye patch, and Coverdale his "hermitage." That each is imagined to exist within some form of prophylaxis suggests that individuals might believe themselves capable of remaining essentially private, unchanged and unchangeable, even in the midst of "association."

And yet, for every moment in the text that celebrates the individual's inviolability there is an equal and opposite sense of the individual's vulnerability to the group's influence. Hollingsworth's particular vision of reform gives us a glimpse of this very different version of group life. Like Fourier, Hollingsworth has an obsession with architecture, the creation of physical structures that, by organizing bodies in relation to one another, produce spiritual harmony. Hollingsworth is not only a prison reformer, it turns out, but a prison designer, who finds in the pastoral world of Blithedale the perfect "foundation" for "the construction of an edifice" (52) that will house his pet project. Unlike Fourier, however (whom he dismisses as a "nauseous villain" [50]), Hollingsworth designs this perfected social space not in order to liberate desire but to foster moral influence: "the reform and mental culture of our criminal brethren" (52). Thus, if Coverdale dreams of a world in which everyone has free choice, Hollingsworth dreams of a world in which everyone is subject to indoctrination. Indeed, his desire to reform criminals seems almost secondary to his desire to influence his fellow Blithedalers: "What I desire to know of you," he tells Coverdale, "is . . . whether I am to look for your co-operation in this great scheme of good. Take it up with me! Be my brother in it!" (123). That Hollingsworth might actually possess the power of influence he desires becomes clear during this conversation with Coverdale, who fears that Hollingsworth's very touch might transform him into a proselyte: "Had I but touched his extended hand, Hollingsworth's magnetism would perhaps have penetrated me with his own conception of all these matters" (124).

What is truly remarkable about this kind of influence, however, is that it is imagined to reside not in one charismatic individual like Hollingsworth but rather in the entire group. Undermining Coverdale's belief in his own "repellent and self-defensive energy" (43) is the fact that he represents his experience of Blithedale as a series of influences. Taking the desire for intimacy and brotherhood to its logical end, these influences cannot be explained as "love" and yet seem to erase the line between self and other: "Zenobia's sphere, I imagine, impressed itself powerfully on mine, and transformed me" (43); "I beheld all these things as through old Moodie's eyes" (79); "It was not till I had quitted my three friends that they first began to encroach upon my dreams" (142). There is a kind of contagiousness to life at Blithedale that seems to be a product of communal life itself—the mere proximity of other socialists—rather than the power of any one individual's influence. So contagious is life in the commune that, as Coverdale suggests, not only are they affected by one another, so that "if one of us happened to give his neighbor a box on the ear, the tingle was immediately felt, on the same side of everybody's head" (129), but by the inanimate objects that surround them as well: "The clods of earth, which we so constantly belabored and turned over, were never etherealized into thought. Our thoughts, on the contrary, were fast becoming cloddish" (61). In much the same way, Priscilla, holding a "sealed letter," magically begins to look like its author, Margaret Fuller. And in the process of denying the possibility—"How could I possibly make myself resemble this lady, merely by holding her letter in my hand?" (48)—she suggests that the letter itself, like the clods of earth, might in fact be contagious. On one reading of the novel, the perfect emblem of this kind of magical influence is the Veiled Lady, the mesmerized subject of Professor Westervelt, who serves as evidence of "the miraculous power of one human being over the will and passions of another" (183). Her veil, rather than a form of protection from the public eye, represents both her complete passivity and her vulnerability to such influence. As Westervelt's popular stage production and Zenobia's legend make clear, the "powerful enchantment" (107) of the veil transforms her into a kind of puppet.

As I have already suggested, *Blithedale* alternates between these two accounts of communal life: the account that imagines collectivity as a federation in which communal ties do not impinge on the individual, represented by the masks and veils that shield the Blithedalers from one another, and the account that imagines collectivity producing an indoctrination that magically transforms individuals into carbon copies of one another. In the broadest terms, it is the commitment to both accounts that defines the utopian community: "Altogether, by projecting our minds outward, we had imparted a show of novelty to existence, and contemplated it as hopefully as if the soil, beneath our feet, had not been fathom deep with the dust of deluded generations, on every one of which, as on ourselves, the world had imposed itself as a hitherto unwedded bride" (119). Coverdale describes a community in which it is possible to imagine both "projecting the mind outward" and thus remaking the world in the image of its inhabitants, and having the world "impose itself," so that one is remade from the outside in. From paragraph to paragraph, sentence to sentence, the narrative moves between the first model and the second.

Coverdale's hermitage is a case in point. The hermitage itself, "a kind of leafy cave, high upward into the air, among the midmost branches of a white-pine tree" (91), has most often been read by critics as Coverdale's desperate attempt to maintain the purity of the self amid threats of dissolution into the intimate community. This is, in fact, how Coverdale himself reads his desire for his "leafy cave," which serves as a retreat from the community that itself serves as a retreat from Boston: "I was so constituted as to need these occasional retirements, even in a life like that of Blithedale, which was itself characterized by a remoteness from the world. Unless renewed by a yet farther withdrawal towards the inner circle of self-communion, I lost the better part of my individuality" (91). In *Walden*, Thoreau famously asks, "What sort of space is that which separates a man from his fellows and makes him solitary?"[55] He goes on to suggest that privacy might not be a matter of space, isolation, or seclusion at all. In *Blithedale*, on the other hand, Coverdale, who is provided with no mask against the community, seems to accord real power to physical seclusion; the "inner circle of self-communion" he seeks is, in other words, not merely metaphorical. Ensconced in his "hollow chamber of rare seclusion" (91), Coverdale claims: "This hermitage was my one exclusive possession, while I counted myself a brother of the socialists. It symbolized my individuality and aided me in keeping it inviolate" (92). From this perspective, one could recast Thoreau's question in Coverdale's terms: "What sort of space is that which separates a man from his fellows and makes his individuality inviolate?"

Many critics have made this question, and this scene of hiding, central to the novel. As Gordon Hutner has argued, the problem Coverdale has with close proximity to others is best read as the threat of intimacy: "For Coverdale, close personal relations intrude upon the best parts of one's individuality. The poet fears that once his vigorously reserved privacy is surrendered, his individuality will be lost, and he will be seen under the unsettlingly democratic light of being certainly no better and perhaps a good deal worse than others."[56] And while Gillian Brown provides a very different reading of the novel, in which individuality is read in relation to femininity and desire, she shares this sense of Coverdale's resistance to intimacy. For Brown, "the experiences in Coverdale's sick-chamber disclose and amplify the danger in his usual consumerist pleasure: the risk of subjection to desire."[57] In response to this threat, his "voyeurism" performs "self-protective psychic work"—"the maintenance of a particular masculine identity" (117, 115)—by distancing him from any real engagement with the objects of his desire. On this reading, Coverdale perfectly diagnoses his own problem as a need to protect his individuality by avoiding intimacy with others, by watching instead of participating.[58] Berlant's reading of *Blithedale* suggests that Coverdale's commitment to the personal (not only his desire to protect himself but his desire to see the utopian project as a love story) is the political center of the novel and the focus of Hawthorne's critique: "In Hawthorne's work love usually, but not always, provides the comfort of personal origins, personalities, and characters, and ultimately denies the potential strength in thinking through collective history (in America, a utopian concept), collective experience, collective consciousness." In her reading Hollingsworth emerges as the hero precisely because, unlike Coverdale, he "refuses to honor the differences between the individual and the collective, public and private, spirit and politics."[59]

And yet Coverdale's sense of the hermitage as a place of solitude, a retreat from the pressures of intimacy or political engagement, is an idea that the novel consistently undermines. In fact, the name of the retreat itself serves as the novel's only (albeit oblique) reference to the world of party politics: Hermitage is also the name of the Nashville plantation owned by Andrew Jackson, who remained the most recognizable symbol of American partisanship well into the 1840s. It seems fitting then that this space of retreat registers the world of politics not only in its name but in its ability to bring Coverdale into relation with his fellow socialists. Far from removing Coverdale from the pressures of the community, the hermitage serves as a window onto other people's lives. And the opinions that this space of self-communion enables him to express—his sense, for example, that "our especial scheme of reform, which, from my observatory, I could take in with the bodily eye, looked so ridiculous that it was impossible not to laugh aloud" (94)—appear, on closer inspection, to derive from other people. Indeed, this belief in the ridiculousness of the communal experiment is attributed throughout the novel not only to Hollingsworth, who believes Blithedale to be a "wretched, unsubstantial scheme" (121), but also to Westervelt, whom Coverdale has just encountered in the woods near the hermitage.

The way in which the hermitage fails to enable the honest expression of a hidden opinion but instead stages the collapse of different points of view quickly becomes apparent to Coverdale himself. Having retreated to the tree house to assert his inviolability, Coverdale finds himself inadvertently looking at the world "through [Westervelt's] eyes, more than [his] own" (94). It is Westervelt's "sceptical and sneering view," Coverdale claims, that "filled my mental vision in regard to all life's better purposes" (94). This very escape to the hermitage is, in fact, initiated by what looks like a scene of imitation: Coverdale, confronting the sardonic Westervelt, claims that "the fantasy of his spectral character so wrought upon me, together with the contagion of his strange mirth on my sympathies, that I soon began to laugh as loudly as himself" (89). So strongly does Westervelt's presence register in the hermitage that when Coverdale finds himself wanting to "laugh out loud" at his fellow reformers, the "peculiar laugh" he then hears turns out to be *not* his own laugh but his rival's: "While thus musing, I heard, with perfect distinctness, somewhere in the woods beneath, the peculiar laugh, which I have described as one of the disagreeable characteristics of Professor Westervelt" (94).

There is a similar moment a bit later in the novel, after Coverdale has retreated from Blithedale yet again, this time for a boardinghouse in the city. "No sagacious man," he claims, "will long retain his sagacity, if he live exclusively among reformers and progressive people, without periodically returning into the settled system of things, to correct himself by a new observation from that old stand-point" (130). What Coverdale discovers, however, is that there is no returning to an "old stand-point." Once affiliated with the Blithedalers, Coverdale is no longer in a position to refuse the effects of affiliation. At the very moment that Coverdale believes himself rid of them, they have already made their claims on him: "It was not till I had quitted my three friends that they first began to encroach upon my dreams. In those of last night, Hollingsworth and Zenobia, standing on either side of my bed, had bent across it to exchange a kiss of passion. Priscilla, beholding this—for she seemed to be peering in at the chamber window—had melted gradually away, and left only the sadness of her expression in my heart" (142). Here Coverdale not only internalizes Hollingsworth and Zenobia's desire for one another but also experiences Priscilla's desire and thus her sadness as his own. At this point in the novel, no amount of space will truly separate Coverdale from his fellows; there is no refuge that will make his individuality inviolate.

One way of negotiating these competing claims would be to say that Hawthorne was, in the end, unable or unwilling to resolve these contradictory accounts of group life and thus let them both stand in the text. And yet, in light of Fourier's and Grimke's contemporary accounts of affiliation, the contradictions that fuel *Blithedale* might instead be understood as working toward an altogether different model of group life. The endless confusions between inside and outside, individual and group, public and private (so that it is never clear whether it is Priscilla's sadness or Coverdale's; Westervelt's laugh or Coverdale's; Hollingsworth's opinion or Coverdale's) suggest that in *Blithedale*, privacy is best understood as a formal device, a way of thinking about the relevance of the external to our attempts to define or understand interiority. In this novel, questions about privacy—about the relation between insides and outsides—work neither to police nor to collapse the boundary that divides the individual from the social, but to produce strange scenarios in which these relations are transformed and reversed, so that what should be internal is often confronted as if from outside the self, and what should be external is experienced as an interior state. Priscilla's sadness is experienced as if it were Coverdale's; Coverdale's own laugh appears to have come from someone else. *Blithedale*'s insistence on the power of surfaces (including the expressions of the body) suggests that Hawthorne sees visuality as the mechanism through which the effects of group life can best be represented. Within such a model of the group, Coverdale's confusions in the tree house and the boardinghouse do not work as evidence that he has been taken over by desires that are somehow alien to him. Rather, these scenes suggest that he confronts internal states as though they were embodied in other people. One's fellows, in this model, do not so much change one as make it known that a change has taken place; they become, in effect, representations of that change.

This emphasis on the power of visuality also explains the interest that Coverdale takes in waifish Priscilla rather than the more voluptuous Zenobia. For Priscilla, the novel takes great pains to suggest, has the ability to arrange "sights." Paired with Coverdale's voyeurism is Priscilla's mastery of the spectacle. It is of course true that her career as the Veiled Lady is represented as her imprisonment by Westervelt rather than the product of her own conniving. And yet, countering all of Coverdale's assertions about her essential passivity are his accounts of her creation of spectacles at Blithedale through which she manipulates the commune's central players. Here I have in mind, for one, the hints that she displays her helplessness—"she ran faulteringly, and often tumbled on the grass" (68)—for the benefit of her protectors, who "were all conscious of a pleasant weakness in the girl, and considered her not quite able to look after her own interests" (69), and for another, the suggestion that the turning point in the plot—Zenobia's disinheritance—is, in fact, the product of Priscilla's manipulation. Having arrived at Blithedale to check on his daughter, Old Moodie, from "behind the trunk of a tree," sees Priscilla through the farmhouse window "playfully drawing along Zenobia." Watching Old Moodie watching his daughters, Coverdale not only claims that he "was convinced that this pretty sight must have been purposely arranged by Priscilla, for the old man to see," but also intimates that she arranges the more troubling part of this scene by goading Zenobia into giving her "a haughty look, as from a mistress to a dependent" (82). It is, we are to assume, this final look in a complicated circuit of sight lines—from Coverdale to Old Moodie, from Old Moodie to Zenobia, from Zenobia to Priscilla—that prompts Old Moodie to disinherit Zenobia and will his fortune to Priscilla.

But what is truly extraordinary about Priscilla is that she functions for

Coverdale as a kind of living mirror, so that her passivity actually functions (like her ability to arrange sights) to provoke her fellow socialists. Her life is represented as a series of mysterious transformations in which, chameleonlike, she takes on the shape of her surroundings. Having been "bred up, no doubt, in some close nook," some "small, close room" (33, 31), Priscilla appears stunted, a "slim and unsubstantial girl" who, on her arrival, takes up only a "little space" (25) in Hollingsworth's arms. In her career as the Veiled Lady she becomes veillike: "There was a lack of human substance in her; it seemed as if, were she to stand up in a sunbeam, it would pass right through her figure, and trace out the cracked and dusty window-panes upon the naked floor" (171). Blithedale stimulates "these sudden transformations" (56). Not only does she appear to be "the true offspring of both parents and the reflection of their state" (171), she serves as both "the soft reflection" of Hollingsworth's "more powerful existence" (114) and the mirror image of Zenobia's beauty: "It was as if, in her spiritual visits to her brilliant sister, a portion of the latter's brightness had permeated our dim Priscilla, and still lingered, shedding a faint illumination through the cheerless chamber" (172). No wonder, then, that all of Zenobia's attempts to thwart her are attempts to have her hidden, once again, under the veil. From this perspective, the scene in which Coverdale is possessed by Priscilla's sadness might just as easily be read as a scene in which Coverdale's sadness is represented for him by Priscilla's mirrorlike face.

The significant thing about the centrality of sight in *Blithedale* is that it cannot be understood as a form of "discipline." Like the organization of sight in the phalanstery, visuality at Blithedale does not advance the project of normalization; it does not, in other words, function as surveillance designed to prompt individuals to conform to a certain model of behavior. What Coverdale sees when he watches his fellows (whom Hawthorne has already suggested are two-dimensional) are living reflections of himself. When he confronts Westervelt, for example, he imagines his rival's face not only as a "mask" but as "polished steel" (159), a mirror in which Coverdale sees the reflection of his own contempt for the commune for the first time. (Westervelt's ability to enter the community and serve this function for Coverdale underscores the sense in which the affiliative community, like marriage, can introduce strangers into the family.) Confronting Zenobia after her break with Hollingsworth, Coverdale does not simply witness her grief. Instead, he sees in it a version of his own: "It suits me not to explain what was the analogy that I saw, or imagined, between Zenobia's situation and mine" (205). This is the first glimpse of what will become Coverdale's final "confession"—that he had been, from the beginning, in love with Priscilla. The power of "analogy" in this text—such that Coverdale's grief can be represented for him by other people (by Priscilla in his dream and by Zenobia at Eliot's Pulpit)—lies in the suggestion that Coverdale is not hiding a secret love so much as discovering one. Here, analogy does not transform the relation between self and other but instead puts the individual into an unexpected relation with himself. That you could be dependent on others to make known to you your own desires, could always be catching up to yourself, begins to explain the burden this novel places on love—and on Coverdale's confession. For love is imagined as a way of exploring the individual's indirect relation to what is considered most personal, most private. Thus, the rather anticlimactic confession of Coverdale's love actually represents in stark terms the imagined effects of associative life; it is a way of suggesting that someone else's love story might, in fact, turn out to be one's own love story after all. And from this perspective, other people begin to function neither as hindrances to nor expressions of one's desires, but as evidence of heretofore unknown desires that are nevertheless one's own.

Blithedale ultimately intervenes in debates about the promises and dangers of the affiliative group in the antebellum period by imagining the effects of such institutions on the individuals who inhabit them. Hawthorne demonstrates the way in which the affiliative group might be understood not only as a mode of education or a form of discipline but also as a mechanism for putting one in relation to oneself. Such a mechanism works, like the hermitage, to provide the individual with a new point of view. In other words, affiliation is both the assertion of an interest and the process of discovering interests one never knew one had, interests that are nonetheless personal. This sense of the individual's dependence on such social mechanisms provides us with a new perspective on the Veiled Lady. For if her image, with its suggestion that the self can be separate and isolate even in the midst of a crowd, can be read as the novel's most telling image of privacy, it is also, and most profoundly, an image of absence: "A blindfold prisoner" or "disembodied spirit" behind the veil, "she was wholly unconscious of being the central object to all those straining eyes" (185). The Veiled Lady thus exemplifies the power of affiliative structures by her exile from them. Cut off by the veil from the representations offered by the existence of other people, what should count as interiority simply ceases to exist.

CHAPTER TWO

The Rules of the Game: Punishment in *The Wide Wide World*

> "If ye love me, keep my commandments."
> "I wonder," thought Daisy, "what they are."
> SUSAN WARNER, *Melbourne House* (1864)

Susan Warner's *The Wide Wide World* (1850), one of the earliest American best-sellers, is famous for its heroine's tears. Barely a chapter of this six-hundred-page novel goes by in which the orphaned Ellen Montgomery finds no reason to cry. Indeed, so excessive are her tears—one critic has described her as "a weeper of artesian resources"[1]—that by the end of the novel, even fellow characters remark on it: "It doesn't take anything at all to make the tears come in her eyes," says her Aunt Keith. "The other day I didn't know whether to laugh or be vexed at the way she went on with a kitten. . . . I wish you had seen her! I am not sure she didn't cry over that."[2] Feminist critics of the 1970s and 1980s, who rediscovered Warner (along with a host of other midcentury domestic novelists), attempted to redeem the novel's long-suffering heroine by reading her tears as a representation of and a serious response to the social and political constraints on middle-class women. Jane Tompkins famously claimed that Warner's endorsement of female submission and self-denial was itself an assertion of spiritual power, a guide to success and survival in a world that denied women power over anything but themselves. As Tompkins put it, "Instead of initiating her into society, the heroine's experience teaches her how to withdraw into the citadel of herself. The Christian precepts she internalizes teach her not how to succeed in the marketplace, or implement her purposes in the world, but how to become a saint who makes herself malleable to the will of others."[3]

What makes *The Wide Wide World* so remarkable, however, is the way in which it continually imagines tears brought about less by sadness or sentimentality than by an outraged sense of justice. Countless episodes of crying are instigated by Ellen's belief that her rights have been violated—she has had her property taken away, she has been misrepresented, she has been unfairly punished: " 'Stop! stop!' said Ellen wildly [to her Aunt Fortune],—'you must not speak to me so! Mamma never did, and you have no *right* to!' " (159). It is this version of Ellen—the enraged and indignant woman rather than the self-effacing and submissive child—that has attracted so much recent critical attention. Against the contention that *The Wide Wide World* both documents and endorses submissiveness (and saintliness) in its white middle-class heroine, an array of more recent scholars have seen in Ellen's rebellious passion a more critical, more "subversive" account of female rage and desire.[4] Critics like Susan Williams, G. M. Goshgarian, Veronica Stewart, Marianne Noble, and Jana Argersinger argue that the novel's Christian didacticism (which counsels, through the voice of Ellen's long-suffering mother, "though we *must* sorrow, we must not rebel" [12]) barely masks the sexual perversity and naked desire for power that is at the heart of Ellen's story.[5] According to Noble, *The Wide Wide World* reveals such desires even when it is at its most didactic, articulating "fantasies" of violence and domination that "can function as expressions of a taboo desire for erotic pleasure." Such fantasies are, for Noble, a form of "sentimental masochism" that provides "a volatile and transgressive idiom of desire" and thus "turns one of the greatest weapons of the patriarchy—the eroticization of domination—into a form of pleasure and agency."[6] Rather than acquiring a diminished form of power by evacuating the self of desire, Ellen submits to her various disciplinarians because, as Noble suggests, a perverse and exaggerated experience of surrender is exactly what she desires.

Whether critics find that Ellen learns to control her desires (and thus becomes a model of true womanhood) or that she learns to express these desires covertly (and thus rebels against this stereotype), they inevitably read *The Wide Wide World* as a type of bildungsroman. Critics of all stripes see the novel in terms of Ellen's gradual progression from helpless orphan to self-sufficient evangelical Christian. Another way to express this point would be to say that while critics have been arguing for years about what Ellen learns, they all seem to agree that she learns something.[7] According to Richard Brodhead, through Ellen's education Warner tracks a broad cultural shift in child-rearing practices—from a disciplinary system based on command and corporal punishment that attempts to control the body to one based on love and reason that convinces the child to control herself. Following Foucault, Brodhead claims that such an education (a new regime he calls "postcorporal discipline"), while presenting itself as more humane and less coercive than corporal punishment, produces instead a more absolute control over the child. As Brodhead puts it, "In its heightened emphasis on introjection, the discipline of love reveals itself as a mechanism . . . not for the mitigation of authority but really for the extension of its regulating hold. When loved parents are properly enshrined in the sanctuary of mind, no space is out of their sight."[8] Love, in *The Wide Wide World*, is not a refuge from power but proves instead to be the most efficient way of enforcing obedience to a set code of conduct: "Ellen's achievement as the novel plots it is to move toward ever more perfect internalizations of parental authority" (34).

But if Brodhead sets out to prove that *The Wide Wide World* depends on a peculiarly modern form of discipline, his analysis also serves to underscore the fact that education is necessarily a process of internalization. And thus to write about Ellen's education, no matter what form this education takes, is to focus on the way that Ellen internalizes a code of behavior or a set of new skills or a series of facts. From this perspective, Brodhead does not so much change the terms of analysis as make these terms explicit: Ellen is the subject of an effective program of education—she both stands in for and instructs the young readers of Warner's novel. By the end, Ellen is imagined to have become a perfectly self-regulating body: according to Noble, she "achieves the non-corporeal ideal"; according to Isabelle White, she "has internalized authority by making it her own"; according to Shirley Foster and Judy Simons, she succeeds in reaching an "ideal Christian state via obedience to a heavenly authority."[9] In turn, critics have claimed, Ellen's achievement of this perfected self then serves as a model for her readers. Tompkins is not alone in arguing that *The Wide Wide World* must be read as a kind of moral training manual: "Sanctified by the sacrifice of her own will, [Ellen] becomes a mentor by example, teaching lessons in submissiveness through her humble bearing, downcast eyes, unruffled brow, and 'peculiar grave look.'"[10] In such readings, Warner's novel is thought to enact the kind of training it envisions for its heroine.

The problem with this way of seeing *The Wide Wide World*, however, is that it depends on a form of self-transparency and self-regulation (so that the individual always knows what she is doing and what her actions mean) that the novel simply denies. If education is absolutely central to this novel, then it works in a curious way. Rather than a teleological process whereby students acquire knowledge and learn to master different subjects, education proves to be a complete failure, a process of repetition that requires students continually to make the same mistakes and submit to endless punishment. In fact, mistakes rather than achievements take on an enormous significance in Ellen's career, not merely because she needs people to tell her what to do and how to live, but because it is only by making mistakes that she can get people to tell her what she *has* done and thus who she already is. What makes John Humphreys (her adopted brother, teacher, and future husband) so indispensable for Ellen is that he not only knows everything about her and seems to see everything she does, but that he never tires of analyzing her mistakes and her failures. In response to Ellen's confession of religious doubt after the death of Alice Humphreys, John insists, "There is something wrong then with you, Ellie." What is wrong, he explains, is that she has not devoted "sufficient time" to her "Bible and prayer" (471). Indeed, John's very indispensability to Ellen's training means that she can never prevent bad actions or avoid making mistakes. Because she is never given a set of rules by which to govern her behavior, Ellen can never know with any amount of certainty whether what she does is right or wrong before she actually does it. And if, from this perspective, *The Wide Wide World* is, as Tompkins has suggested, "a kind of bildungsroman in reverse," it is not because Ellen ultimately learns to "forget self" but because she cannot learn anything at all.[11]

It is in this denial of the fantasy of self-regulation that one can locate Warner's crucial difference from midcentury sentimental writers like Maria Cummins, Fanny Fern, Harriet Beecher Stowe, and Martha Finely, with whom she is so often lumped together. Certainly, by the time the typical sentimental heroine has come of age, she knows exactly what is expected of her. To take one example, Cummins's *The Lamplighter* (an 1854 best-seller) follows the career of an orphan named Gerty Amory who, like Ellen, is trained by a series of adopted families to control her passionate temper. Unlike Ellen, however, Gerty soon needs no external supervision at all: "Gertrude had often found in time and the soothing influences of religious faith some alleviation to her trials; but never until this night, did she feel a spirit not of earth, coming forth from the very chaos of sorrow into which she was plunged, and enkindling within her the flame of a higher and nobler sensation than she ever yet had cherished."[12] It is this "nobler sensation," which seems to emerge from within herself, that throughout the rest of the novel efficiently regulates her behavior. By drawing this contrast I do not mean to suggest that Warner has no place in the domestic tradition (more than thirty years of criticism has proven otherwise). Rather, I am suggesting that the repeated failure of Ellen's education—her need for endless punishment—represents a significant departure from this tradition, and one that needs to be addressed on its own terms.

Indeed, Warner's novel might be more profitably read within the tradition of the novel this book describes—a tradition that begins to define the individual against rather than in relation to her own intentions. Just as in *The Blithedale Romance*, where party works as a kind of feedback loop through which one can learn one's own opinions, in *The Wide Wide World* the domestic sphere works as a kind of feedback loop through which one discovers one's effects on the world. For Warner, the home becomes a testing ground, a more circumscribed realm in which one might finally discover how one's actions register once they are performed. Far from shunning the "wide wide world" in favor of the safety of the domestic (Charles Kingsley retitled the novel "The Narrow Narrow World"),[13] Warner registers in Ellen's endless disorientation the same cultural dynamic that drives Hawthorne in *Blithedale*—the way in which the affiliative group might serve as a kind of living mirror for its members. And in Ellen's commitment to making mistakes (so that she can get people to tell her what she's done) Warner describes what looks like the prehistory of negligence—the rise of a system designed to control for accidents by holding individuals accountable for the unforeseen consequences of their actions. That is, in the domestic sphere Warner conceives, Ellen exists only insofar as she makes mistakes.

What Warner explores in *The Wide Wide World* is a fantasy of domestic life in which the domestic realm is made perfect not through its warmth and intimacy or its ability to discipline and control its members, but through its commitment to judgment and interpretation. Ellen's caretakers (John, more than anyone else) seem to concern themselves almost entirely with observing, correcting, and reporting on Ellen's every move. As Tompkins has proposed, "To read *The Wide Wide World* is to experience life as if everything that happened to you, every thought that passed through your mind, every feeling you ever had, deserved the most minute consideration."[14] But the point of the novel is not, as Tompkins suggests, to validate Ellen's behavior; it is instead to evaluate it and explain where it went wrong. The punishment John continually metes out thus rewards Ellen not by enabling her to change but by providing her with moments of perfect legibility. Like Coverdale, Ellen can never escape the system she has entered; she can never complete her education because this process of punishment for mistakes is imagined to support the only viable form of self-relation.

Being "Weak," Keeping "Right"

Because Warner has been, of late, so central to critical accounts of the American domestic tradition, her rejection of one of its central conventions—the heroine's achievement of perfect self-regulation—bears closer examination. The novel's departure from convention is, fittingly, most conspicuous when Warner is at her most generic, during those moments in *The Wide Wide World* when she manipulates certain stock domestic scenes. The confession scene, for example, in which the young heroine is forced to admit her faults to a parent or mentor, is a staple of the midcentury "girls' novel" (a subset of the domestic novel in which Warner's work is often placed).[15] The point of this confessional moment in virtually all of the texts that use it is not only to humiliate and chasten the willful heroine—serving as a rite of passage or an initiation into adulthood—but to structure larger questions about the formal basis of subjectivity. In the confession and punishment scenes, the domestic novel fantasizes a culture powerful enough to transform its heroines into ideal subjects. One way, then, of understanding the peculiar subject produced by Warner's version of the domestic sphere is to look at the way the confession scene functions in what appear to be similar midcentury domestic novels.

In Cummins's *The Lamplighter*, eight-year-old Gerty begins her career in much the same way as Ellen, prey to a "violent temper, which, when roused, knew no restraint" (34). When she confesses to impulsively breaking the window of her tormentor Nan Grant, her reprimand—a silent look from her guardian Truman Flint and her mentor Willie Sullivan—seems to be magically transferred from their hearts to her own: "True now inquired what window; and Gerty unhesitatingly acknowledged what she had done, and avowed that she did it on purpose. True and Willie were shocked and silent. Gerty was silent, too, for the rest of the walk; there were clouds on her face, and she felt unhappy in her little heart" (50). Silence suffices as a reprimand in Cummins's world because of the strength of Gerty's conscience—the feeling of unhappiness "in her little heart." This scene is the beginning of Gerty's education, a process by which "the lessons that are divine, were implanted in her so naturally, and yet so forcibly, that she realized not the work that was going on" (67).

In this sense, Gerty represents the perfect product of what Brodhead describes as disciplinary intimacy. Chastened by the very existence of caring guardians in her youth, Gerty ultimately proves to be her own best disciplinarian. As if to assure the reader that Gerty's model behavior is the effect of self-government rather than immunity to passion, Cummins's novel creates periodic tests of her ability to control herself: "Gertrude's old temper rose at this insulting language, beat and throbbed in her chafed spirit, and even betrayed itself in the tips of her fingers, which trembled as they rested on the table near which she stood (having risen as Mr. Bruce spoke); but though this was an unlooked-for and unwonted rebellion of an old enemy, her feelings had too long been under strict regulation to yield to the blast, however sudden, and she replied in a tone which, though slightly agitated, was far from being angry" (234). That Gerty's struggle against herself is represented here as a struggle against her body (which registers and thus gives away her temper) makes this scene an enactment of the transformation that Brodhead describes: from corporal to postcorporal discipline; from an external force that controls the body to an internal force that controls the feelings. In the end, Truman Flint can die in Gerty's childhood not because his death proves to be a needed trial but because his work is already done.

In Martha Finely's *Elsie Dinsmore* (1868), the figure of authority, Elsie's father Horace Dinsmore, is overthrown rather than internalized only because Elsie has already internalized a "higher" authority. Elsie's confession scenes thus work in much the same way as Gerty's silent punishment: each enforces the dictates of the heroine's own conscience. Refusing her father's demand that she sing for his guests on the Sabbath (a situation that Finely, a fan of Warner's, lifted from Warner's 1864 novel *Melbourne House*), Elsie must, as the genre requires, confess her disobedience. But in this case the confession looks more like an admission of perfect obedience: "Thank you for your sympathy, Mr. Travilla, you are very kind; but I could not do it, because Jesus says, 'He that loveth father or mother more than me, is not worthy of me;' and I cannot disobey Him, even to please my own dear papa."[16] The punishment that follows—Elsie is condemned to sit on a stool until she passes out and injures her head—and which is meant to humiliate and humble her, ultimately works to convince Horace that "a parent has no right to coerce a child into doing violence to its conscience" (226). In other words, the punishment that Horace inflicts, a punishment that is presented as a literal act of violence against Elsie's conscience, transforms her into a martyr (complete with stigmata) rather than a penitent.

In *Elsie Dinsmore*, the trial of subduing the will need never be shown because it has already been effortlessly achieved. Thus, the struggle that Elsie must undergo is not so much a struggle with herself as a struggle of ostensibly competing masters or codes of conduct. Indeed, the climactic moment in the tale—the moment when Horace is changed from the "cold" disciplinarian she fears into the affectionate disciplinarian she loves—is presented as the reconciliation of these competing codes. In this scene, Elsie rejects the commands of her Aunt Enna and her grandparents in favor of her religious scruples. "It is," according to her grandmother, "a great piece of impertinence for a child of her years to set up her opinion against yours and mine; and I know very well it is nothing but an excuse, because she doesn't choose to be obliging" (202). But as usual, Elsie claims that her refusal to tell a fairy tale on Sunday is not a matter of opinion but of ethics: "'I offered to tell her a Bible story, or anything suitable for the Sabbath day,' replied Elsie, meekly, 'but I cannot tell the fairy tale, because it would be wrong'" (202). And it is, in this scene, Elsie's religious scuples that get the final word. Ultimately, Horace recognizes that her defiance represents not only a more perfect form of obedience to him—it is after all her refusal to "be made a slave to Enna's whims" (205)—but a model for him to follow: "Ah! if I were but half as good and pure as she is, I should be a better man than I am" (211).

In the end, what links *The Lamplighter* and *Elsie Dinsmore* to each other and to an array of domestic novels from the period is precisely this depiction of the sentimental heroine as the self-sufficient object of imitation. Each novel works to establish both the heroine's perfection and her unconsciousness of that perfection: "She's the most perfect lady I ever saw," says a young protégée of Gerty's, "and mother says she has beautiful manners, and I must take pattern by her" (194). Elsie's Aunt Adelaide claims, "readily as [she] gives up her own wishes to others on ordinary occasions, I have never known her to sacrifice principle. . . . Elsie is certainly very different from the rest of us, and if it is piety that makes her what she is, I think piety is a very lovely thing" (38). Serving as models for both the girls inside the story and the women who read the story, Gerty and Elsie help do for the reader what the disciplinarian in the text has done for them: internalize a moral code that prescripts action.

The confession scene in *The Wide Wide World* begins in the typical fashion: Ellen, having picked the prized piece of blue morocco out of a closed bag, offers her prize to her rival Margaret and then admits to the party of her playmates that she had gotten it by cheating: "'I am not modest! I am not generous! you mustn't say so' cried Ellen ... 'I don't deserve to be praised,—it was more Margaret's than mine. I oughtn't to have kept it at all—for I saw a little bit when I put my hand in. I didn't mean to, but I did!'" (294). While Margaret's sarcastic response both raises and denies the ostensible moral of this scene ("Here's a beautiful example of honour and honesty for you!"), John's initial response to Margaret's remark ("'I think it is,' said John, quietly") suggests that we read Ellen's confession generically (294). When John confronts Ellen directly about her cheating, however, he makes clear that the terms of the heroine's education have shifted quite significantly: "'You will wonder at me perhaps, Ellie,' said John, 'but I am not very sorry this has happened. You are no worse than before;—it has only made you see what you are—very, very weak,—quite unable to keep yourself right without constant help'" (296). While John claims that this "constant help" is to come from "our dear Savior" (297), his unwillingness to stop monitoring Ellen's behavior suggests that both he and she have more earthly help in mind. Accordingly, this scene does not form part of Ellen's education in self-sufficiency, but heralds instead her willing bondage to the system of endless punishment and correction that John orchestrates. It is only by way of John's assessment of her actions that Ellen can come to "see" what she is.

From John's point of view, this help comes in the form of commandments that provide Ellen with rules to obey and precepts to live by. Certainly, this element of their relationship has been most disturbing to critics, who have seen John primarily as a threat to Ellen's autonomy. Noble encapsulates the ethos of this criticism when she writes of John that he is "a representative of paternal law," and she links him implicitly to "a popular figure of female desire in the nineteenth century": "the authoritarian doctor who provided scripts by which women were to live."[17] There are any number of moments in the text that seem to bear out this reading, moments in which Ellen wants nothing more than to follow John's "scripts." If, for example, Alice's kindness fails to distract Ellen from her grief after her mother's death, John's demand that she follow a rigorous program of self-improvement succeeds: "What

[Alice] asked of her Ellen indeed *tried* to do; what John told her *was done*" (351). Indeed, more than one critic has pointed out that John is not merely the mouthpiece for "our dear Savior" but, for Ellen, actually comes to replace God as savior and disciplinarian:

> "I know all, Ellie," said he, still very kindly,—"I have seen all;—why do you shun me?" (296)

> "I do believe, Mr. John," she said, stammering, "that you know every thing I am thinking about." (317)

> It was well there was always somebody by, who, whatever he might himself be doing, never lost sight of her. If ever Ellen was in danger of bending too long over her studies or indulging herself too much in the sofa-corner, she was sure to be broken off to take an hour or two of smart exercise, riding or walking, or to recite some lesson. (464)

It comes as no surprise that Ellen can barely function when she is separated from her "brother": "But oh! I want my brother!—I don't know how to be happy or good either without him. I want him all the while" (544).

Yet, what the drama of John's authoritarianism seems to mask is that he fails both as an educator and as a disciplinarian not because Ellen rebels against his authority (she never does), but because the novel grants him a very different kind of authority. John fails as an educator because Ellen never becomes self-sufficient (it is virtually the end of the novel when she claims "I don't know how to be happy or good either without him" [544]), and he fails as a disciplinarian because she continues, despite his commands, to mistake her "duty." Not long after a family friend calls Ellen "a *perfectly* well-behaved child" (418), she is reprimanded by John for selfishly refusing to write a letter for a poor neighbor:

> "By the by, you are too busy, Ellie," said he. "Which of your studies shall we cut off?"
>
> "*Please*, Mr. John," said Ellen blushing,—"don't say any thing about that! I was not studying at all—I was just amusing myself with a book—I was only selfish and lazy."
>
> "*Only*—I would rather you were too busy, Ellie."
>
> Ellen's eyes filled.
>
> "I was wrong," she said,—"I knew it at the time,—at least as soon as you spoke I knew it; and a little before;—I was very wrong!" (463)

Where John never fails is in his role as interpreter. If he can neither teach Ellen nor prevent her from lapsing, he can offer up his endless assessments of her behavior: "Of one thing she was perfectly sure, whatever [John] might be doing,—that he saw and heard her; and equally sure that if any thing were not right she should sooner or later hear of it. But this was a censorship Ellen rather loved than feared" (461). Given the nature of their relationship, however, censorship is hardly the thing that Ellen loves. John's incessant correction cannot work as censorship because it depends on her having already taken some kind of action. John punishes, lectures, and corrects Ellen; he never prescripts her actions or prevents her from acting.

The difference between censorship (which would prevent mistakes) and punishment (which responds to mistakes) is clear in the scene in which John, promising Ellen that she might finally "know" herself to be one of "God's children," gives with one hand and takes away with the other (352–53). John suggests that the Bible provides perfect and unmistakable guidance for good behavior: "Carry your heart and life to the Bible and see how they agree. The Bible gives a great many signs and descriptions by which Christians may know themselves,—know both what they are and what they ought to be" (352). In virtually the same breath, however, he suggests the unreliability of the "heart" and of precepts like "O how love I thy law!" which he has commanded Ellen to study: "The Bible is full of them, Ellie; but you have need to ask for great help when you go to try yourself by them; the heart is deceitful" (352). Both universal laws and personal feelings are, in Ellen's world, decidedly unreliable guides: laws are difficult to interpret; feelings cannot always be trusted. Accordingly, Ellen is never sure whether she has in fact been doing what is right until John approves or disapproves of her behavior. In living out this fantasy of perfect legibility, Ellen never has to wait long for John's diagnosis. As she proudly tells her less critical friend Van Brunt, "It was only this morning he was telling me of something I did that was wrong" (414).

Against the domestic novel's vision of "pattern" behavior that is fit to be imitated, *The Wide Wide World* thus poses a rather unsettled universe. In the place of a heroine who represents a code of positive action, it offers a heroine who cannot reliably serve as a model beause she cannot tell right from wrong in advance. Warner represents the domestic sphere less as a space that produces the ideal woman than as a kind of theater in which the woman endlessly performs mistakes in order to be corrected. Indeed, Ellen's audience includes not only John but Alice, Mr. Marshman, Uncle Lindsay, and Aunt Fortune (who is rejected early on as an unsympathetic viewer), and this extended audience is both hypercritical and extremely vocal. Nothing is too insignificant to merit attention and discussion:

> "But do you know, Ellen, I am going to have a quarrel with you?"
> "What about?" said Ellen. "I don't believe it's any thing very bad, for you look pretty good-humored, considering."
> "Nothing *very* bad," said Alice, "but still enough to quarrel about. You have twice said '*ain't*' since I have been here."
> "Oh," said Ellen, laughing, "is that all?"
> "Yes," said Alice, "and my English ears don't like it at all." (221)

Ellen is never free of this intense scrutiny; even acquaintances are forever remarking on her pallor, her sad expression, her "sweetness of temper" (418). Yet like the public scrutiny in *Blithedale*, the world of supervision that Warner fantasizes does not work on the now ubiquitous model of the panopticon. Here, there is no regime of the normal that could help Ellen control herself, no amount of observation that could train her to follow rules, precisely because the norm and the rule do not exist. Rather, there are constantly shifting standards that require an endless stream of commentary. Thus Ellen loves punishment not, as some critics have argued, because she loves pain.[18] Rather, she loves punishment—and the pain that often accompanies it—because she loves judgment: " 'Pain! you needn't be afraid of giving me pain,' said Ellen fondly, throwing her arms around her,—'tell me dear Alice; is it something I have done that is wrong?' " (426).

The Cult of Self-Regulation

Warner's conception of the child's education seems all the more bizarre when read against the burgeoning discourse of child rearing that subtends so much domestic fiction. Countless treatises written for mothers (among the most influential are Lydia Maria Child's 1831 *The Mother's Book*, L. H. Sigourney's 1838 *Letters to Mothers*, and Catharine Sedgwick's 1835 *Home*)[19] argue that the primary goal of parenting is not simply to produce children who obey orders (out of fear, for instance), but to produce independent, self-regulating citizens. Cultivating this kind of self-regulation, domestic educators argue, requires not explicit rules that one might memorize but rather general principles that one might internalize, principles that would provide guidance in any contingency. According to Lydia Maria Child, "It is vain to load the understanding with rules, if the affections are not pure. In the first place, it is not possible to make rules enough to apply to all manner of cases; and if it were possible, a child would soon forget them. But if you inspire him with right *feelings*, they will govern his *actions*."[20] What makes this system of child rearing seem so modern is that parents are advised to model good behavior rather than lecturing about it in order to inculcate the "right feelings" in their children. As "creatures of imitation," children intuit the principles of good behavior by observing them in action rather than learning them by rote: "If they see a mother fond of finery, they become fond of finery; if they see her selfish, it makes them selfish" (22). This notion that children learn through imitation not only principles but also feelings makes possible the version of "pattern" behavior so beloved by the domestic novel.

In such a system, punishment is not a matter of justice exacted for wrong doing, but of training for the future. Wanting autonomy, children in these tracts often beg for punishment because they understand, as Child puts it, "the real use of punishment": it is "a means of helping [them] overcome what [is] wrong":

> I knew of a girl of five years old, who had the habit of biting her nails so close that her fingers were perpetually inflamed. Her mother had tried arguments, and various privations, without producing much effect. One day, the child, as usual, put her fingers to her mouth, to bite her nails; but suddenly withdrawing them, she came up to her mother's writing table, and said, "Mother, slap my hand smartly with your ruler every time I bite my nails, and then I shall remember." Her mother did as she was desired. . . . After a while she forgot herself, and bit her nails again; her mother was not in the room; but she went, of her own accord, and avowed the fact, saying, "Mother, give me a few more slaps than you did before; and see if that will make me remember it any longer." (36)

Corporal punishment, in this instance, is less about controlling the body than about reminding the child to control herself. And, unlike Ellen, the children who ask to be punished in these advice tracts eventually learn to internalize the principles (or feelings) that enable them to "keep themselves right" without external supervision. After demanding that her mother punish her, Child's resilient five-year-old nail biter "never needed correction for the same fault" (36).

What is at stake in the child-rearing literature is nothing less than the fate of the nation. As Sigourney writes,

> It seems now to be conceded, that the vital interests of our country, may be aided by the zeal of mothers. Exposed as it is, to the influx of untutored foreigners, often unfit for its institutions, or adverse to their spirit, it seems to have been made a repository for the waste and refuse of other nations. To neutralize this mass, to rule its fermentations, to prevent it from becoming a lava-stream in the garden of liberty, and to purify it for those channels where the life-blood of a nation circulates, is a work of power and peril. . . . The degree of [the mother's] diligence in preparing her children to be good subjects of a just government, will be the true measure of her patriotism.[21]

Sigourney's assessment of "untutored foreigners" who might pollute the body politic makes clear both the high stakes of childhood education and the class and racial politics at the heart of such advice literature. Like so many other middle-class advice-givers, Sigourney endorses a liberal model of personhood—the basis, she suggests, of American democracy—in which dependence is imagined always to be temporary, a stage in the individual's progress toward autonomy. What these writers propose is that self-government on the large scale depends on (and indeed grows out of) self-government by the individual.

In *The Wide Wide World*, patriotism and education come together in the figure of George Washington. During their first Christmas together John gives Ellen a copy of Mason Weems's biography of Washington as a gift, and she is instantly smitten: "Weims' [sic] Life of Washington was read, and read, and read over again, till she almost knew it by heart" (335). Memorizing Washington's life as a way of understanding her own would have been unsurprising in an age that made Washington the preeminent (and seemingly the only) model of American virtue. Indeed, by midcentury Weems's book had become established as a popular guidebook for children. As Marcus Cunliffe's influential introduction to the book points out, Weems virtually inaugurates a tradition in which biographers of Washington "emphasize what was 'normal' about him, what practical lessons his actions held for other Americans, what his countrymen could do to be like him."[22] Weems himself insists that it is in Washington's "private virtues" that "every youth is interested, because in these every youth may become a Washington—a Washington in piety and patriotism,—in industry and honour—and consequently a Washington, in what alone deserves the name self-esteem and universal respect" (5). The nineteenth-century children's literature that followed in the wake of Weems's *Life* uses the figure of the "normal," "private" Washington to model perfect self-regulation.²³

Initially at least, Warner follows the conventions of this tradition. She even uses Weems's *Life* as a model for her novel, borrowing well-known incidents from the book. In fact, the scene in *The Wide Wide World* discussed above in which Ellen confesses to cheating virtually announces itself as a reenactment of the famous scene in Weems's biography of young George and the cherry tree. In this legend, which Weems made ubiquitous in American folklore, young George immediately confesses his misdeed to his father: "With the sweet face of youth brightened with the inexpressible charm of all-conquering truth, he bravely cried out, '*I can't tell a lie, Pa; you know I can't tell a lie. I did cut it with my hatchet*' "(12). Ellen's own confession is merely a more tearful version of young George's; "I oughtn't to have kept it at all—for I saw a little bit when I put my hand in. I didn't mean to, but I did!" (294). Going beyond the typical sentimental confession, Warner's scene follows Weems's even down to the focus on the disciplinarian rather than the child. As Garry Wills argues, the intended moral of the cherry tree story was not directed at children, but at parents. Weems presents Washington's father "as another Ulysses,"²⁴ who cultivates honesty and integrity in his son by rewarding rather than punishing him for his confession: "*Run to my arms, you dearest boy*, cried his father in transports, *run to my arms; glad am I, George, that you killed my tree; for you have paid me for it a thousand fold. Such an act of heroism in my son, is more worth than a thousand trees, though blossomed with silver, and their fruits of purest gold*" (12). Child-rearing texts pick up and develop this analysis of Washington's upbringing, emphasizing not his father's influence but his mother's. According to Sigourney, for example, Washington's "undeviating integrity and unshaken self-command" are the direct result of "the agency exercised by [his] mother . . . in forming that character which the world delighted to honour" (126). In this account, Washington can work as a model for children precisely because his virtues are the products of proper training and are thus, ostensibly, attainable by everyone.²⁵

And it is on this subject of proper childhood discipline that Warner departs from her model. In the confession scene, John does not simply praise Ellen for her honesty in order to cultivate this virtue, but interprets the cheating itself as a crucial index of her character: "I am not very sorry this has happened. You are no worse than before;—it has only made you see what you are—very, very weak,—quite unable to keep yourself right without constant help" (296). What young George learns from his father is a form of self-reliance that makes his parents virtually obsolete. What Ellen learns from John is total dependence. It is not the cheating but John's interpretation of the cheating that makes Ellen "see what she is." In representing Ellen's dependence on a living, speaking interpreter, Warner also departs from more conventional readings of the cherry tree episode, in which it can be reduced to a simple precept. In one manual for children—*The Mount Vernon Reader, A course of Reading Lessons, selected with reference to their moral influence on the hearts and lives of the young, designed for the Middle Classes* (1840)—the moral of the story is quite simple: "No boy who has one particle of that noble spirit which George Washington had, will tell a lie. It is one of the most degrading of sins. There is no one, who does not regard a liar with contempt."[26] So strong was this imperative, that in E. D. E. N. Southworth's *Ishmael* (1863), the title character, in order to avoid any kind of misrepresentation, confesses to feeling a slight fear when racing into a burning building to rescue his enemies: "And once—I am ashamed to own it, but I will, because I know George Washington always owned his faults when he was a boy—once, I say, I was tempted to run away and leave the boys to their fate."[27]

Against Ellen's absolute dependence on correction, the Washington literature stresses the importance of rules and principles that can be internalized. This association is emblematized in Washington's own book of etiquette, *Rules of Civility and Decent Behavior in Company and Conversation*, which until the 1890s Washington was credited with writing as a schoolboy.[28] In this manuscript discovered among his papers after his death, Washington lists 110 rules, copied from other sources, meant to be a guide for day-to-day behavior.[29] The regulations are often quite mundane (something for which his biographers usually apologize), including, for example, this admonition: "Be not angry at table, whatever happens, and if you have reason to be so, show it not; put on a cheerful countenance, especially if there be strangers, for good humor makes one dish of meat a feast."[30] Demanding not honesty but the assumption of a false face, this rule flatly contradicts the principle for which Washington was most famous. Yet it is not the content of these rules but rather the apparent fact that the young Washington himself composed the rules that were to govern his behavior into adulthood that so impressed his nineteenth-century admirers. In a biographical sketch for *Harper's* in 1856,

John S. C. Abbott (author of moral tracts for children)[31] makes much of Washington's *Rules*: "Thus we see Washington, even in childhood, impelled by some inward monitor, acquiring an acquaintance with the important forms of business, investing his own nature with sublimity by the cultivation of a religious spirit, and carefully watching over his own words and his own actions, that dignity, decorum, and unaffected politeness might mark all his intercourse with his fellow-men."[32]

The Wide Wide World thus speaks with two voices. Ellen consistently praises Washington as a model of moral behavior, as when she tells her Scottish uncle that she loves Washington best of all because he "always did right" (515). At the same time, however, Ellen discovers that no rules gleaned from his life can guide her own. She ultimately finds, through a series of arguments with her Aunt Fortune and Uncle Lindsay, that honesty is not always the best policy. Despite the fact that she has "said the truth" to her Uncle Lindsay—that he was "not right" to take away her favorite book—this act of truth-telling turns out to be "wrong": that she in fact "spoke improperly" makes her uncle "justly displeased" (553). Propriety sometimes, but not always, trumps honesty as the required virtue. In *The Wide Wide World*, Washington's failure to perform his sanctioned role as a model for proper behavior enables John to emerge as a new kind of authority figure. He represents a form of education that, far from making individuals independent and self-regulating, creates a relationship stronger than familial or emotional bonds.

The Allure of Judgment

Despite Ellen's exemplary patriotism (she not only idolizes George Washington, but passionately defends the American "rebels" to her skeptical Scottish relatives), she never achieves the kind of self-regulation imagined to be both the product and the sign of American democracy. Instead, as we have seen, Ellen's story is marked from beginning to end by a kind of spectacular disorientation and an equally spectacular need for judgment. Warner goes out of her way to multiply these moments of uncertainty, beginning with Ellen's first solo shopping trip ("She felt confused, and almost confounded, by the incessant hum of voices, and moving crowd of strange people all around her" [45]) and continuing even after her move to Scotland near the end of the novel ("Oh, what shall I do! What will become of me if I do not watch over myself—there is no one to help me or lead me right—not a single one—all to lead me wrong! What will become of me?" [532]). If Ellen demands punishment, it is not so that she will eventually outgrow the need for it. Ellen demands punishment as part of an ongoing process of self-analysis; she makes mistakes in order to get people to respond.

This overwhelming feeling of uncertainty and the need for correction and punishment is one of the hallmarks of Warner's fiction. In the dozens of novels she published between 1852 and 1884 (the year before her death), virtually every one of her heroines suffers from some version of this need for correction.[33] And in every instance there is a man of God, modeled on John, who promises to fulfill it. On first inspection, this pattern suggests that Warner's desire to relive this relationship between Ellen and John was so strong that it fueled thirty years of fiction. Over and over in her work, a young woman very much like Ellen seeks a John-like mentor to help her "keep herself right" and to give her some idea of her proper role in the world. "Tell me how to do, sir, please," says Daisy Randolph to Mr. Dinwiddie in *Melbourne House* (1864), "I don't know how to be a Christian"; "What is the work of life?" Desire Burgoyne asks Max Iredell in *My Desire* (1879), "I wish you would tell me. That is something I occasionally puzzle about"; "Sometimes I am in great confusion, and can *not* understand myself," Rotha Carpenter confesses to her guardian, Digby Southwode, in *The Letter of Credit* (1882).[34] The tireless repetition of these narratives, in which the ideal mentor creates, Pygmalion-like, the perfect Christian and the perfect wife, might explain the fact that Warner's later novels were never as popular with readers as was *The Wide Wide World* and are now neglected by her critics.

Yet what is most interesting about this pattern is that, taken as a whole, it makes these particular instances of childish confusion seem like examples of a more profound, existential crisis. Warner's incessant return to this crisis, this need for "help," makes clear that the confusion in these novels is not simply the result of circumstance (Ellen and Rotha are orphans; Daisy's parents attempt to keep her in ignorance; Desire is trapped in her small town), but is imagined on some level to be the product of thought itself. What Warner's introspective but baffled heroines so powerfully dramatize is that self-reflection—the attempt to make sense of one's own thoughts and actions—can produce nothing but bewilderment. In response, Warner tests a variety of possible solutions to her heroines' inevitable disorientation. Could the ability to judge and correct the heroine's behavior be provided by a more "worldly" man? What about a woman?[35] What about the Bible itself, without the intervention of a more knowledgeable interpreter? Warner, in other words, did not merely repeat the relationship between Ellen and John in the novels that followed *The Wide Wide World*, she dissected and evaluated it, incorporating subtle variations in the relation between heroine and mentor. It is as if each novel were one element of a larger project designed to produce not the perfect Christian life but a life that provides the individual with a perfect, and seemingly impossible, form of self-knowledge.

In *The Old Helmet* (1863), for example, Eleanor Powle is engaged to marry the wealthy Mr. Carlisle (Lord Rythdale), but finds that the "sweets of her new position" leave her largely unsatisfied. Her trouble is that she "wants" something, something she cannot name but that seems to be embodied in the minister, Mr. Rhys, who offers her "a glimpse of a life she had never dreamed of," a life "quite unearthly in its spirit and aims" (1: 83, 92). Like *The Wide Wide World*, *The Old Helmet* establishes the heroine's confusion early on, her desire for clarity, and her search for someone to help her: "There seemed a great wall built up between her and the knowledge she wanted. Must it be so always?" (1: 31). Indeed, *The Old Helmet* is basically a retelling of Ellen's story, with a slightly older heroine and an English setting. But unlike *The Wide Wide World*, which quietly kills off Ellen's first (and relatively ineffectual) mentors—her mother and Alice—and replaces them with John, *The Old Helmet* forces Eleanor to choose between two possible mentors in the form of two competing suitors. Even their names—Lord Rythdale and Mr. Rhys—are designed to enhance their resemblance and their linked roles in the novel. If, looking from one to the other, Eleanor claims that "there was little in common between them; between the marked features and grave keen expression of the one face, and the cool, bright, somewhat supercilious eye and smile of the other," she also notes that "there was power in both faces . . . of different kinds; and power is attractive" (1: 51).

With the "supercilious" Rythdale and the "grave" Rhys, Warner seems to have taken John Humphreys and divided him into his component parts: the dictator whose power of command is experienced as both sexual thrill and sexual threat ("She was almost breathless with terror" [400]); and the judge whose criticism is experienced as a more comforting form of affection ("'You are a foolish child, Ellie,' said he gently, and kissing her again" [403]). Accordingly, in the first half of *The Old Helmet* Eleanor falls reluctantly under the control of Lord Rythdale, whose greatest pleasure, it seems, is to dominate her, and whose domination is quite frankly sexual: "'You little witch—' said he as he took possession of the just permitted lips,—'I will punish you for your naughtiness, by taking you home very soon—into my own management'" (1: 81). And in the second half, she happily submits herself to the tireless judgment of the more fatherly Mr. Rhys: "I felt I must come," Eleanor admits; "'You did very wrong,' said her companion" (1: 166). Moreover, by linking these figures, making them mirror images of one another (at one point, Eleanor looks over to where Rythdale had just been standing and sees that Rhys has taken his place), Warner manages to cloak the proper Rhys with some of Rythdale's sexual allure.

In *The Old Helmet*'s version of an Austen-like marriage plot, Eleanor's choice is clear to the reader long before it is clear to her: she must reject the wrong, threatening, "worldly" suitor in favor of the right, comforting, "spiritual" guide. What is at stake in Eleanor's choice, however, is more significant than the rejection of material for spiritual wealth (or the rejection of threatening for tamer sexuality). In rejecting Rythdale, Eleanor implicitly rejects government by explicit rules, a system in which she is always told exactly what to do. As her younger sister Julia explains, "Why you always do what [Rythdale] tells you. . . . He says 'Eleanor'—and you go that way; and he says 'Eleanor'—and you go the other way" (1: 86). When Eleanor acts rashly or unsuitably, Rythdale does not criticize her; he supplies her with rules that would prevent future errors and miscalculations. Discovering Eleanor alone at an evening church service, Rythdale demands that she not venture out at night without him to "protect" her reputation and prevent her from "going too far": "The Lady of Rythdale must not do anything unworthy of herself, or of me. . . . Eleanor—will you promise not to be naughty any more?" (1: 241–42). Eleanor ultimately rejects Rythdale less because his life is committed only to worldly ends than because his endless commands limit her freedom to act: "It seemed to Eleanor that fine bands of cobwebs had been cast round her, binding her hands and feet, which loved their liberty" (1: 80).

One might well ask how it is that a heroine so attracted to "power" is at the same time so protective of her "liberty." And in fact, this is an issue raised by a number of Warner's novels. In *The Letter of Credit*, young Rotha explains to Mr. Southwode that she must reject Christianity precisely because it limits what she can do.

> "Why do you not want to be a Christian, Rotha?"
> "I do not know," she answered slowly. "I suppose, I want to be free."

"Go on a little bit, and tell me what you mean by being 'free.'"

"Why—I mean, I suppose,—I *know* I mean, that I want to do what I like."

"You thought a Christian was a sort of a slave."

"Yes. Or a Servant. A servant he is; and a servant is not free. He has laws to mind." (153)

For Southwode, the problem of the Christian's "slavery" to God's law is solved when the Christian learns to love the law, when duty is what one "likes" to do. But for heroines like Rotha, Eleanor, and Ellen, being free does not mean freely choosing to do one's duty so much as choosing to act without the restrictions (or benefits) of the law. "Servants" have "laws to mind"; proper middle-class women do "what they like." How else are they to provoke a response in their proper middle-class suitors? Indeed, for Warner's heroines it is this freedom rather than conventional restrictions that transforms the relatively tame world of the domestic into a world of danger and drama. For Eleanor, the freedom she desires has itself produced the "mistaken" engagement to the dictatorial Rythdale: "What had she done? She was this man's promised wife; she had made her own bonds; it was her own doing; he had a right to her, he had claims upon her" (1: 245). Freedom to act, always closely guarded in these novels, means freedom to make mistakes.

In the end, the problem with Rythdale is not simply that he monitors Eleanor's behavior—following her to church meetings, forbidding her to go out alone or to meet Rhys—but that he monitors her for the wrong reasons. Rythdale's goal is to dictate behavior, to prevent her from doing what she likes. Rhys, on the other hand, monitors her behavior so that he can, after the fact, point out where she's gone wrong. Rather than telling her what to do, he questions and analyzes what she's already done. Thus when Eleanor declares that she "cannot" become a Christian, Rhys evaluates the source of her mistaken refusal simply to "accept" God's "conditions": "My friend, Jesus invites to no empty board—to no cold reception. On his part all is ready; the unreadiness lies somewhere with you, or the invitation would be accepted. In your case it is not the bodily frame that is palsied; it is the heart.... If you are entirely willing, the thing is done. If it be not done, it is because, somewhere, you are not willing—or do not believe" (2: 8). For Eleanor, this critique of her "unreadiness" is a revelation: "Could it be possible that she was not *willing*— or that she wanted *faith*—or that there was some secret corner of rebellion in her heart? It humbled her wonderfully to think it.... And she had thought herself all this while a subject for pity, not for blame; nay, for blame indeed, but not in this regard. Her mouth was stopped now" (2: 9). Rhys indeed "stops" Eleanor's "mouth," but not in the way Warner's critics have led us to expect. If he effectively robs her of the authority to evaluate her own behavior, it is because she seems incapable of true self-reflection. As Warner would have it, Rhys comes to Eleanor's rescue, curing her debilitating confusion with his own impeccable judgment. Rhys does not control Eleanor's behavior; he *reads* it.

With Rythdale, Eleanor is not free; with Rhys, Eleanor is free to err. Indeed, Eleanor (like Ellen) must make mistakes in order to solicit judgment and thus be acknowledged by those she thinks superior. Mistakes in Warner's world demand a response, and Rhys's response to Eleanor not only enables her to see herself clearly but also counts as evidence that her actions matter. Thus she cannot (as can so many other domestic heroines) dispense with this "correction." And accordingly, his role as her judge does not end even when Eleanor has been successfully humbled and converted. Nor does it end when they are married. By the end of the novel, Eleanor has traveled to Fiji in order to marry Rhys and join him in his missionary work, while Rhys has commenced what promises to be an endless commentary on Eleanor's various imperfections: she selfishly proposes to keep a gift of fruit; she gossips about their fellow missionaries. For Eleanor, as usual, his disapproval both acknowledges and elucidates her most mundane actions:

> Eleanor felt almost stunned with surprise and discomfort. This was the second time, in the few days that she had been with him, that he had found her wrong in something. It troubled her strangely; and the sense of how much he was better than she—how much higher his sphere of living than the one she moved in—pressed her heart down almost to the ground. . . . The feeling, how far he stood above her in knowledge and in goodness, while it was a secret and deep joy, yet gave her acute pain such as she never had felt before. She would not weep; it was a dry aching pain, that took part of its strength from the thought of having done or shewn something that he did not like. (2: 354–55)

That *The Old Helmet* virtually ends with this passage makes an important point about the fantasy of "power" at the heart of the novel. By the end of the story, the text's implied hierarchy has become Eleanor's own: Rhys, she imagines, stands "above her in knowledge and goodness"; she has been "pressed . . . almost to the ground." The fantasy enacted here, however, is not simply that Eleanor will submit to (or even rebel against) masculine "power."

Rather, it is that she will finally be able to subject herself to adequate judgment, regardless of whether this judgment brings her "joy" or "pain." Only through Rhys's eyes can Eleanor see what she has done—something, for example, worthy of "blame" rather than "pity." It is Rhys's look that clarifies Eleanor's vision; it is a "single ray of light" that "shewed her the darkness" in herself (1: 15).

In contrast to the stark choice offered to Eleanor in *The Old Helmet*, in *The Wide Wide World* Ellen is supplied with a series of weak (if well-meaning) mentors who must ultimately be rejected in favor of John—not only her mother and Alice but also the "old gentleman" in the department store, the "gentleman" on the ferry, and her friend (and tour guide) Ellen Chauncey. What links these figures is their literal, physical weakness; all of them, despite the fact that they manage to "rescue" Ellen at various times of crisis, are marked by age (too young or too old) or by sickness. Mrs. Montgomery and Alice eventually die; both old gentlemen simply disappear. Ellen Chauncey, who is younger but more informed than Ellen, enters the text as Ellen's guide to the treacherous social world of the Marshmans and defends Ellen against her old enemy, Margaret Dunscombe. One way of reading Warner's strange decision to give Ellen and her new friend the same name—"How shall we know which is which?" (284), asks Ellen Chauncey—is as an attempt to provide Ellen with a kind of living mirror that gives her the ability to gain a different perspective on herself. If, for example, Ellen is clearly indignant at the way she is treated by the other children, she remains "grave" and quiet; it is Ellen Chauncey who bravely talks back: "'For shame, William!' cried little Ellen Chauncey;—'didn't I tell you she was one of grandpapa's guests?'" (285–86). The problem, however, is that Ellen Chauncey, rather than providing clarity, only reflects Ellen's own confusion. When it comes to playing a Bible game on a Sunday, Ellen refuses because, as she explains tentatively, "I have a kind of *feeling* that I ought not to do it" (310). Ellen Chauncey, on the other hand, is a willing participant until she hears of Ellen's reservations: "*Do you think it is wicked, Ellen?*" (310). Useless for Ellen as a source of judgment, Ellen Chauncey has, by the end of the Marshman episode, virtually disappeared from the novel.

More important, however, *The Wide Wide World* (like *The Old Helmet*) is interested not only in trading weakness for "power" but in testing different versions of authority and different kinds of power. Thus, over the course of the novel, Ellen encounters—and rejects—a number of more plausible substitutes for John: not only (as we have seen) George Washington, but also her Aunt Fortune and her Uncle Lindsay.

Aunt Fortune, a domestic tyrant and the first real figure of authority in the text, is almost immediately dismissed as a brute. Ostensibly, she is vilified because she is unfeeling (Ellen's various troubles are, in Miss Fortune's home, "unsoothed by one word of kindness or sympathy" [139]) and because her home is a place of work rather than of middle-class leisure and refinement: indeed, Ellen is called on not only to clean her own room ("It was a rather disagreeable surprise to find her bed still unmade" [113]), but also to wash dishes, iron, and churn butter. And yet, as most of the early scenes in Aunt Fortune's home suggest, her primary sin in the economy of the novel is that she withholds information. When, for example, Ellen asks for permission to go to school, Aunt Fortune simply agrees, leaving Ellen to discover for herself the impossibility of getting to a school four miles away: "But Aunt Fortune, do please tell me what I am to do. How can I know unless you tell me? What way is there that I can go to school?" (139). As she explains to Alice, who will win her heart by promising to teach her arithmetic, grammar, French, and history, "That's another of my troubles,—there's nobody that can tell me anything" (155). As we have seen, what Ellen wants is not simply information but information about herself. And Miss Fortune is remarkably tight-lipped, not letting on when she receives word of Mrs. Montgomery's death or when she gets engaged to Mr. Van Brunt (thereby changing Ellen's status in her home), or when she receives a packet of letters from Ellen's parents directing her to live with her relatives in Scotland. In Miss Fortune, Warner represents the world of corporal punishment—not because she is physically abusive (although she does force Ellen to work and, in one early scene, boxes Ellen's ears), but because her punishments are, in a sense, nonverbal. Miss Fortune must be rejected because while she registers Ellen's mistakes she makes no attempt to explain and correct them.

Ellen's uncle, and adoptive father, Mr. Lindsay, serves as a similar figure of illegitimate power. Like Rythdale, Lindsay is immediately recognizable as a false mentor less for his worldliness than for his propensity to command, his desire to shape Ellen's character by giving her rules to obey: "Forget that you were American, Ellen,—you belong to me; your name is not Montgomery any more,—it is Lindsay;—and I will not have you call me 'uncle'—I am your father;—you are my own little daughter, and must do precisely what I tell you" (510). In fact, there is very little difference between Eleanor Powle's relation to her fiancé and Ellen Montgomery's relation to her uncle: both men extort affection, demand obedience, and have an almost magical power of influence. As in so many of Warner's novels, this power is experienced as both sexual thrill and sexual threat. For Ellen, Lindsay not only attempts to replace John's authority but also his status as object of desire. After she is forced by her uncle to drink wine (something the Humphreys frown on), Ellen dreams of John as a wrathful king who refuses to take a glass of wine from her: "But raising the sword of state, silver scabbard and all, he with a tremendous swing of it dashed the glass out of her hands; and then as she stood abashed, he went forward with one of his old grave kind looks to kiss her" (520). The kiss that wakes her from the dream, however, is her uncle's: "As the kiss touched her lips Ellen opened her eyes to find her brother transformed into Mr. Lindsay" (520). Transforming lover into brother and brother into uncle, Ellen's dream shuffles and confuses familial relationships, registering both the allure of John's punishments and the threat of Lindsay's very different brand of power.

The thrill for Ellen is in the punishment precisely because it proves that her various decisions and actions matter in the world; in this way one might call the thrill autoerotic. Accordingly, her new life with her dictatorial uncle is decidedly unthrilling: "No one now knew always what she was thinking of, nor if they did would patiently draw out her thoughts, canvass them, set them right or show them wrong" (538). Lindsay (like Rythdale) represents the authority of the set rule that hijacks speech and the established law that conscripts behavior: "I lay my commands upon you," her uncle tells her when she hesitates to call him father in public, "whenever the like questions may be asked again, that you answer simply according to what I have told you, without any explanation or addition" (526). Just as Rhys "stops" Eleanor's "mouth," the Lindsays find numerous ways of keeping Ellen from speaking: "Mrs. Lindsay touched her lips; a way of silencing her that Ellen particularly disliked, and which both Mr. Lindsay and his mother was accustomed to use" (541). From this perspective, Lindsay's kiss, which awakens her into a nightmare world of regulations, might be read as yet another way of stopping Ellen's mouth. But unlike Rhys, Lindsay does not replace his charge's false assessments of her own behavior with his own opinions. Like Miss Fortune's regime, Mr. Lindsay's is marked by its silence, especially in the face of any conflict with Ellen. After an argument in which Ellen admits to her uncle that she loves the Humphreys "a thousand times more" than her blood relations, Lindsay refuses the John-like role of interpreter: "She was exceedingly sorry the next minute after she had said this.... No answer was made. Ellen dared not look at any body, and needed not; she wished the silence might be broken; but nothing was heard except a low 'whew!' from Mr. Lindsay, till he rose up and left the room" (530). Lindsay's displeasure is both so obvious that it needs no explanation, and so cryptic that it throws Ellen into confusion: "What shall I do? what shall I do? she said to herself" (530). For Ellen, John's punishments are forms of communication—the one thing she can depend on is that "if anything were not right she should sooner or later hear of it" (461). Mr. Lindsay's punishments, however, are imagined to speak for themselves and thus replace explanation and correction.

In relation to both the power of command and the cult of self-control, Warner's commitment to punishment as a form of self-relation rather than as a spur to self-discipline—her commitment to the necessary endlessness of punishment and correction—looks quite perverse. By the end of *The Wide Wide World* we discover that, despite the fantasy of living by God's word, there will be no moral to any story, no emergent set of rules that will govern behavior. Indeed, the very end of the novel, which has John finally tracking down Ellen in her new home in Scotland, does not (as domestic fiction tells us it should) mark the end of her career as his student and the beginning of her career as his wife. Instead, it announces the continuation of her education. Ellen, as always, pines only for correction: "John, what shall I do without you?—If I could see you once in a while—but there is no one here—not a single one—to help me to keep right" (561). Even the final chapter, unpublished in Warner's lifetime, which describes their marriage and return to America, ends with this hope: " 'Well,' said Ellen presently—'I am very glad of it! You will tell me if I do anything wrong, and it will be just like old times. How I have longed for those old times! Oh!' and she covered her face with her hands, 'sometimes I am almost afraid I am too happy' " (583). In the end, what is so curious about Ellen's story is that love is imagined to work not as a form of discipline but as an excuse for making punishment never-ending. The novel does not, it must be noted, imagine that Ellen loves John and thus lets him control her. Instead, it imagines that by loving him Ellen ensures that there will be no end to their relation as master and pupil.

In so much of the best scholarship on domestic fiction over the past twenty years, the power of women's literature is ideological—it creates subjects who know how to act.[36] Warner's insight is to imagine that literature inevitably fails in its mission to prescribe action. Instead, Warner posits not a utopia of lawlessness (this is the lesson that Rotha, who wants to have no "laws to mind," must learn by the end of *The Letter of Credit*), but a world of competing and conflicting actions that must be explained and evaluated. In *The Wide Wide World* this difference between determining behavior and understanding behavior is the difference between deciding to tell the truth because it is "right" and discovering after the fact that one's truth-telling has actually done harm. Warner thus grants a very different kind of authority to narrative. In her view, narrative has the authority both to represent behavior that requires judgment and to provide an occasion for exercising judgment. Far from the novelistic universe of conformity and compliance, Warner has constructed a world in which judgment matters.

Warner's departure from the cult of self-regulation—in her insistence that mistakes are inevitable and that education is never-ending—must be understood as just that: a departure rather than a critique. Warner is not (as some have suggested) posing a protofeminist communitarian fantasy as an alternative to the harsh masculine world of possessive individualism. Indeed, she does not critique the cult of self-regulation at all. Instead, she analyzes it. In *The Wide Wide World*, Warner investigates the practical and philosophical limits of self-regulation, asking how one can ever know, in a world of disorienting complexity, exactly what one has done or is responsible for. From this perspective, Ellen's perpetual confusion is not the product of her class, her youth, or her gender. It is a product of modernity itself. While Elizabeth Barnes has also seen Ellen as the representation of a much broader cultural dynamic, this dynamic is, in her eyes, republican rather than modern: "In surrendering herself to an irresistible paternal influence, the domestic heroine represents not only the ideal of women but the perfect liberal individual, self-mastered and ultimately reconciled to her domestic situation."[37] Yet, what I have argued in this chapter is that Ellen is imagined against rather than within the republican cult of self-regulation. Moreover, this nonliberal model of the self (in which one requires the judgment of other people and so can never become autonomous) is just as central to nineteenth-century American culture as is possessive individualism. As I show in the next chapter, by the late nineteenth century negligence law emerges as a way of dealing with and formalizing these issues of agency and responsibility. In 1851, however, Warner's fantasy is that you could encounter an idealized, personal authority—closer to home than God but more critical than a mother—who would tirelessly narrate for you the effects of your behavior.

PART TWO | Race and the Law

CHAPTER THREE   *Huckleberry Finn*; or, Consequences

> "You are very kind; but there must be some mistake. I have not killed anything."
> "Your house did, anyway," replied the little old woman, with a laugh; "and that is the same thing."
> L. FRANK BAUM, *The Wonderful Wizard of Oz* (1900)

When, in 1953, Leo Marx proclaimed the "slapstick" ending of *Adventures of Huckleberry Finn* (1885) a "failure," he set off a critical debate about the relative merits of the novel that shows no sign of slowing down. Marx's critique of Twain was also directed against Twain's defenders, Lionel Trilling and T.S. Eliot, both of whom had written influential celebrations of *Huckleberry Finn*. Trilling praises the novel not only for its innovative style and lack of sentimentality but also for its "moral passion," especially in relation to Huck's crisis of conscience in which he decides to "go to hell" rather than abandon Jim. According to Trilling, *Huckleberry Finn* is "one of the world's great books and one of the central documents of American culture."[1] For Marx, however, this kind of idolatry had served only to blind readers to the novel's serious flaws, its "glaring lapse of moral imagination."[2] Against Trilling and Eliot, Marx argues that the extended description of Huck's and Tom's efforts to free a slave who, it turns out, is already free undermines the moral seriousness of the first part of the novel. What was initially a noble quest for Jim's freedom becomes nothing more than a game played at his expense: "During the final extravaganza we are forced to put aside many of the mature emotions evoked earlier by the vivid rendering of Jim's fear of capture, the tenderness of Huck's and Jim's regard for each other, and Huck's excruciating moments of wavering between honesty and respectability. . . . The conclusion, in short, is farce, but the rest of the novel is not" (294).[3]

In recent years, which have seen repeated challenges to *Huckleberry Finn*'s place in the canon and the curriculum, the terms of the debate have not changed very much. Defenders of the novel still praise the moral power of Huck's commitment to freeing Jim, and detractors still wonder if such commitment overrides the novel's various flaws—its casual racism, its lampooning of Jim, and its transformation of a serious crisis into a game. Against what seems to be a stalemate, two critics writing in the late 1990s—Jane Smiley and Jonathan Arac—attempt to do something new, to shift the focus of critique away from the novel to the social consequences of its canonization. In forceful polemics against the continued investment in *Huckleberry Finn* as an American classic—Arac's *"Huckleberry Finn" as Idol and Target: The Functions of Criticism in Our Time* and Smiley's "Say It Ain't So, Huck: Second Thoughts on Mark Twain's 'Masterpiece' "—Arac and Smiley do not ask if *Huckleberry Finn* is a good or bad book but rather if it has good or bad effects.[4] To claim, then (as a number of Smiley's respondents in *Harper's* did about her essay), that these two works misread the novel or refuse to attend to its historical context is to miss the point.[5] Smiley and Arac have far less interest in interpreting the novel than in addressing the way it has been used and, as Arac puts it, the "cultural work" (21) it continues to perform. They are making claims not so much about what *Huckleberry Finn* means as about what it does.

Thus, despite the fact that Arac confesses early on that he believes "*Huckleberry Finn* is a wonderful book" (16), his goal is to assess the consequences of excessive admiration, to "explore how Twain's book came to be endowed with the values of Americanness and anti-racism, and with what effects" (vii). Predictably, these effects are shown to be devastating. In Arac's view, the novel's prominent and seemingly unshakable position as a "quintessentially American book" (vii) has led to "white" complacency about racism ("northern liberal smugness" [65]), the legitimation of racial epithets, and the delegitimation of African American experience. For Arac and Smiley, the novel's pernicious influence is demonstrated most clearly in the way that a series of well-known critics have made Huck's change of heart about Jim (Huck's decision in chapter 31 to "go to hell") serve as a model of social responsibility. What mid-twentieth-century critics admired as a form of redemption, Arac and Smiley see as a distasteful form of liberal bad faith: the problem, in Smiley's terms, is the sense that if "Huck *feels* positive toward Jim, and *loves* him, and *thinks* of him as a man, then that's enough. He doesn't actually have to act in accordance with his feelings" (63). It is this investment in good intentions (both in the novel and in celebrations of the novel) that, more than anything else, bothers Arac and Smiley. After all, what could be more politically suspect than to applaud moral courage that can never be translated into social change?

One could argue that the reading of chapter 31 to which Arac and Smiley object—the reading of Huck's decision to help Jim as moral triumph—has never been as influential, at least in literary circles, as they seem to believe. Critics have been claiming since the 1960s that the futility of Huck's decision to free Jim, as well as the entire "evasion" sequence at the Phelps farm, must be read as a satire of white complacency and of the perils of legal freedom for blacks in late-nineteenth-century America. This reading is developed brilliantly by Laurence Holland in what is by far the best, if least cited, essay on the novel. In "A 'Raft of Trouble': Word and Deed in *Huckleberry Finn*" Holland argues that the novel undercuts the importance of Huck's change of heart: the necessity and the futility of his decision to free an already-free Jim satirize the fact that in the post-Reconstruction era (and, Holland suggests, even "in more recent decades") black Americans were systematically denied civil and economic rights and thus, in a real sense, still needed to be freed.[6] In much the same way, Russell Reising has weighed in against those critics who relegate the racial violence of *Huckleberry Finn* to a past that is "diffused . . . with a nostalgic gloss" as a way of avoiding the "presentness" of Twain's nightmare America.[7]

The interest of Smiley's and Arac's polemics is that they effectively invalidate all such defenses of the novel. At issue in these arguments is not what Twain intended or even what the novel really means (if these things are different) but how it has been and continues to be experienced by readers. Arac, for example, argues that to defend *Huckleberry Finn*'s treatment of Jim or its use of racial epithets by pointing to the novel's irony is to dismiss the legitimate concerns of African Americans who experience the book not as a satire of racial injustice but as a form of racial insult. "If civil rights means anything," he asks, "shouldn't it mean that African Americans ought to have a real voice in public definitions of what counts as a model of enlightened race relations?" (9). While Arac's and Smiley's claims about *Huckleberry Finn* put the two critics in the paradoxical position of attempting to rescue black readers from the "racist" effects of arguments by black intellectuals like Ralph Ellison and Toni Morrison (who have eloquently defended the novel),[8] the more general problem that Arac and Smiley have with any appeal to the novel's real meaning is that its meaning has been overshadowed by its powerful cultural effects. Indeed, Arac's project is a kind of postdeconstructive attempt to treat *Huckleberry Finn* not as itself a chain of uncontrollable iterations but as an object that fosters a chain of prescribed responses (that the novel is quintessentially American, that it is antiracist, that black readers who hate it must be wrong), so that "what counts is not the attitudes that the book supposedly teaches, but rather the opportunity the book provides for the incessant reiteration, the ritual repetition, of practical behavior" (11).

To hold Twain accountable for the effects of his novel is, for Arac and Smiley, to demonstrate a commitment to effect over intention that they claim most Americans refuse to countenance.[9] The problem with liberal readers of Twain is that they insist on reducing everything—including racism—to sentiment. "White Americans," Smiley argues, "always think racism is a feeling, and they reject it or they embrace it. To most Americans it seems more honorable and nicer to reject it, so they do, but they almost invariably fail to understand that how they feel means very little to black Americans, who understand racism as a way of structuring American culture, American politics, and the American economy" (63). For Arac, it is defenders of the novel who make this mistake, acting "as if racism were only a matter of specific intention to harm, of attitude rather than habitual practice and social structure" (13).

To make this case against white Americans or the liberal reader is to advance certain claims about what it means to be responsible for racism and, more generally, about the connections among what we do, what we intend, and what happens to us or to the people around us. It is, in fact, to make the claim that we can be held responsible not only for what we mean (or what we mean to do) but also for the unintended effects of what we do. On this account, our actions can count as racist even, according to Arac, if we "don't know it" and even if we have no "specific intention to harm" (13). It is in making this claim, I think, that Arac and Smiley are most interesting, most convincing, and, ironically enough, most indebted to *Huckleberry Finn*. For in their belief in responsibility for effects rather than for intentions, they are clearly the inheritors of a nineteenth-century cultural shift in notions of accountability that involved not only the rise of a new legal paradigm (the law of negligence) but also the social satire of a novel like *Huckleberry Finn*.

Far from being irrelevant to questions of institutionalized racism, Twain's novel is centrally concerned with the production of effects and the assignment of responsibility for them. *Huckleberry Finn* participates in this cultural shift in the conception of responsibility by articulating a form of moral action on which individual intentions and feelings finally have no bearing. Indeed, because intention and feeling, for all their differences, are both ways of explaining action in terms of psychology, they are equally irrelevant to the model of action explored here. This model disarticulates interior and exterior, motivation and effect—it depends on a discrepancy between what the individual thinks he's done and what he discovers he has actually done. In this chapter, I argue that Twain's interest in exploring the ways in which a wide variety of unknowing people could be held responsible for Jim's fate and be made to compensate him for his injuries must be read as an attempt to imagine what it would mean to extend the logic of negligence to the national level. And in this commitment to examining unintentional harms, Twain not only makes his strongest case against postbellum racism but also proves himself the intellectual forerunner of social critics like Arac and Smiley. For, from this perspective, *Huckleberry Finn* is an attempt to imagine accountability even in the absence of malice.

"How a Body Can See and Don't See at the Same Time"

Whether they like it or hate it, critics of *Huckleberry Finn* have always seen the real drama of the novel in Huck's internal conflict, the contest (as Twain once put it) between his conscience and his heart, so that the suspense for the reader lies in the uncertainty of Huck's decision for or against helping Jim. In the drawn-out interior monologue at the center of chapter 31, Huck convinces himself that he must fight his bad impulse to steal Jim by giving in to the dictates of official "Sunday school" morality: "It hit me all of a sudden that here was the plain hand of Providence slapping me in the face and letting me know my wickedness was being watched all the time from up there in heaven, whilst I was stealing a poor old woman's nigger that hadn't ever done me no harm" (270). Huck decides to be "bad" when his sentimental attachment to Jim overrides his obligations to Miss Watson: "Somehow I couldn't seem to strike no places to harden me against him, but only the other kind" (271). The sense that at this moment of decision Huck risks something for Jim—his status back home (such as it is) or even his soul—has always grounded defenses of the novel. But even detractors have made this scene the moral center of the novel, debating whether or not Huck's willingness to prolong Jim's captivity at the Phelps farm or his unwillingness to stop using racial epithets undermines the heroism of his decision. In fact, the commitment to the soundness of Huck's "heart" is the one thing that most supporters and detractors of the novel have always had in common. Thus Marx, the novel's most famous detractor, claiming that Huck's "victory over his 'yaller dog' conscience" in chapter 31 ultimately "assumes heroic size" (301), sounds a great deal like Trilling, the novel's most famous supporter, who claims that Huck "becomes an heroic character when, on the urging of affection, [he] discards the moral code he has always taken for granted and resolves to help Jim in his escape from slavery" (107).

This sense that what counts in chapter 31 is Huck's "heart" hardly seems surprising because it is intention rather than action that gets the final word. Announcing his decision to destroy the letter he has written to Miss Watson disclosing Jim's whereabouts, Huck says, "It was awful thoughts, and awful words, but they was said. And I let them stay said; and never thought no more about reforming" (272). While it is clear what it would mean to let a letter stay written (by not ripping it up), it is not as easy to picture what it would mean to let words, once uttered, "stay said." But one might make the case for the priority of intention in this novel by asserting that the permanence of these words consists in the purity of the intention that produced them, in Huck's determined refusal to change his mind. The novel dramatizes this commitment to intention over action most explicitly in the way that it neatly undoes the action of this key scene: Huck demonstrates his loyalty to Jim by ripping up the letter he has just written. The fact that this momentous decision is emblematized by a letter that is written and then destroyed—an action that is done and then undone—seems even in its formal structure to privilege the coherence of intentions over the vagaries of actions.

It is the futility of Huck's commitment to Jim—a futility made visible in the destroyed letter—that has always angered the novel's detractors. The direct result of Huck's decision, after all, is not a serious attempt to free Jim but a game invented by Tom Sawyer. Yet, if Miss Watson's decision to set Jim free makes the final rescue attempt a mere game, it is a game only to Tom, who knows the truth from the moment he arrives at the Phelps farm. For Huck, the stakes of freeing Jim are just as high and the consequences just as real when Tom takes control of the rescue as they were when Huck agonized over sending the letter to Miss Watson. Only after the rescue fails does Huck discover what he and Tom have, in fact, been doing all along—not rescuing Jim but only pretending to: "And so, sure enough, Tom Sawyer had gone and took all that trouble and bother to set a free nigger free! and I couldn't ever understand, before, until that minute and that talk how he *could* help a body set a nigger free, with his bringing-up" (362). That Huck describes the evasion as Tom's action rather than his own is an issue to which I will return. For now, it is important to note that what Miss Watson's will reveals is the surprising fact that Huck could neither have succeeded nor failed to free Jim. Already free in the eyes of the law, Jim, it seems, can never be freer than he is.

This revision of the rescue enacted by the will provides a paradigm for the novel's representation of action more generally. Indeed, all of the central actions of the novel depend on the same kind of gap in knowledge: characters repeatedly come to know what they really did (or what their actions really mean) only after the fact, only retrospectively. Thus, Jim discovers that he has been not running away from enslavement but, as Tom tells him, simply running (361). Thus, Huck discovers that he has not been escaping from his father because, as Jim informs him, by the time they leave Jackson's Island his father is dead (365–66). The novel at once highlights intention (by focusing completely on the development of Huck's consciousness) and works to make intentions irrelevant to understanding certain kinds of action. No matter how deeply Huck is invested in his good intentions toward Jim or how powerful his decision to save Jim seems to the reader, this dramatic recasting of the rescue by Miss Watson's will already moves us well beyond an intentional model of action.

From a point of view that places the reader beyond intention, Huck's role in the evasion must be understood as an act essentially defined by other people. The game that Huck finds he is playing is not something he shares with Tom but rather something that is created by Tom. In the end, Tom's revelation neither enforces Huck's decision (as pure intention) nor invalidates it (as completely futile), but insists on the conflict between what Huck thinks he is doing and what he is told he has done. In thus recasting Huck's role in the rescue, *Huckleberry Finn* undertakes a project much more radical than imagining a self that can inhabit a variety of roles (after all, disguises and mistaken identities have always been central to the novel). Instead, the novel imagines what it would mean for someone to perform an action that can be narrated intelligibly only from outside the self, what it would mean, in other words, for Tom to understand what Huck is doing better than Huck can understand it himself. "It shows," as Huck puts it, "how a body can see and don't see at the same time" (293).

This retrospective account of action is so central to *Huckleberry Finn* that it ultimately comes to undermine the authority exercised by Huck's self-presentation. The novel thematizes this powerlessness over narration in its meticulous tracking of textual effects, in its exploration of how texts come to define and even transform what characters can do. That is, the novel is concerned with something more than a text's ability to represent; it is concerned with the ways that texts can determine what counts as someone's action. Miss Watson's will, for instance, casts a shadow over the entire plot, redefining what everyone has been doing to Jim. This power of texts to produce or to define action is emblematized early on by Tom's unshakable commitment to acting out his favorite adventure stories. In the evasion sequence, tales prompt adventures not so much by providing Tom and Huck with an intention as by standing in for intention, by becoming intention's substitute. To be more specific, the romance novel that Twain satirizes in Tom's devotion to adventure stories is defined not by the experiences it describes but by the experiences it can produce; it is defined, in other words, primarily in relation to its effects on the reader. Accordingly, much of the opening section of the novel details the way that Tom acts out the stories he consumes, turning text into adventure by trying to get the details just right. Tom's attempt to organize a band of highwaymen on the model of the adventure tale depends entirely on these details; what counts for him is only his gang's ability to perform a given script. Thus, he commands the gang to bring hostages to their hideout "and keep them till they're ransomed," even though no one in the gang (including Tom) knows what the word "ransom" means. Tom's response to this seemingly devastating objection is, tellingly, a blind commitment to the text: "Why blame it all, we've *got* to do it. Don't I tell you it's in the books? Do you want to go to doing different from what's in the books, and get things all muddled up?" (27). This determination to live up to a textual model suggests not simply that the romance produces a particular kind of effect but that it is something that one must put into effect: "Now Ben Rogers, do you want to do things regular, or don't you?—that's the idea. Don't you reckon that the people that made the books knows what's the correct thing to do?" (27). Far from exercises in improvisation, Tom's games are the products of textual blueprints.

If Tom's perfect commitment to enforcing the rules of the romance is satirized, however, the power he accords texts is never questioned. Beyond the innovative use of dialect, what seems to mark *Huckleberry Finn* as the first recognizably modern American novel—what might explain the kinship a modernist like Hemingway felt for Twain—is the way it experiments with the production of textual effects. Through steady adherence to the illusion of presentness, the novel works to enforce a kind of readerly retrospection, so that just as Tom and Jim withhold important pieces of information until the end of the "adventure," Huck withholds their revelation from the reader. Presentness is an illusion here because Huck, who claims to be narrating his tale after the fact, tells it as if experiencing it for the first time. As Holland points out, *Huckleberry Finn* presents itself as a historical novel, but it is narrated as if it were happening in the "here and now" (73). What he does not remark on is that this illusion enables *Huckleberry Finn* to enact its retrospection formally, forcing readers into the same kind of recognition that Huck and Jim experience in the world of the novel. It is only after the fact that readers understand the descriptions they have been reading: of a game rather than a rescue, of a free man rather than a slave, of an orphan rather than a runaway. This withholding of information, finally, makes it impossible for one ever to read the same story again by making it impossible for one to be the same reader the second time around. If one reads the novel the first time as Huck, one must read it the second time as Tom.

Such shifting positions and tenses might explain how a novel that purports to focus on the South of "forty to fifty years" before the time of its publication can be understood as a novel essentially about the post-Reconstruction era. Certainly, if the novel's setting has been read in terms of nostalgia—for boyhood, for the antebellum South, for the small town—the fact that Twain detaches Huck and Jim from a familiar context and sets them literally afloat already begins to suggest a concern with the chaos of postwar America. There could hardly be a better image of modernization than the move from the familiarity of the village to the anonymity of the city. Indeed, this interest in relations between strangers makes sense of Twain's decision to focus the sequel to *The Adventures of Tom Sawyer* not on Tom but on the outcast Huck. For Tom's rebelliousness is grounded in a respectability that works against and thus depends on the established hierarchy of St. Petersburg, so that even when Tom resurfaces far from home at the end of *Huckleberry Finn* he is still surrounded by the familiar world of Aunt Sally and Uncle Silas. Huck, on the other hand, without family or position, seems completely detachable from the relatively closed community of this small town, an ideal figure for an experiment in the modern picaresque. This interest in the relation between strangers connects the novel with the politics of the post-Reconstruction era, for it goes beyond questions about individual disorientation in a rapidly industrializing America to raise broader questions about accountability in a changing public sphere.

If all the actors in the evasion sequence misunderstand what they have, in fact, done to Jim—Huck imagines that he is freeing a slave, the Phelpses and their neighbors imagine that by catching Jim they are quelling a slave revolt, Tom imagines that Jim's freedom can be turned into a game, and even Miss Watson imagines that signing her will is enough to make Jim free—how are they accountable for the harms they cause him? What, in the end, are these willing and unwilling participants in the evasion responsible for? These questions are at the center of *Huckleberry Finn* and the novel attempts to answer them by reframing actions in terms of their consequences. If *Huckleberry Finn* is a novel about intention, then, it might best be read as a novel about the limits of intention, even at the moments when interiority rather than action is presented as the privileged form of self-relation. It is, finally, a novel in which one's effects on other people rather than one's feelings about them define what one has done and, more important, what one can be held accountable for.

"Nobody to Blame"

The problem with most critiques of *Huckleberry Finn* is that they assume Twain was invoking an intentional model of morality (thus the frequent allusions to Huck's decision to act, for better or worse, against the mores of the community and in accordance with his "heart"), when he was actually exploring a model of moral action in which any particular state of mind or change of attitude is finally irrelevant. This model did not originate with Twain or emerge full-fledged in nineteenth-century America. In fact, it resembles what Bernard Williams, examining classical texts, calls the "whole person response" to harm.[10] By this Williams means an understanding that the existence of a harm requires us to trace causation and to hold someone accountable, even if the harm was caused unintentionally. The relevant question about a harm, in other words, is not "whether the agent intended the outcome" but rather "what exactly his action may be said to have caused"

(63). Thus, in the *Odyssey*, Telemachus, having left open the door to the storeroom by accident, is nonetheless to blame—for this and for the fact that the suitors could subsequently get at the weapons. To hold persons responsible in this way, to insist that they are accountable for their accidents and mistakes, is to make certain assumptions about what constitutes individuality. It is, according to Williams, to concede that committing an action "unintentionally does not, in itself, dissociate that action from yourself" (54) and thus to know "that in the story of one's life there is an authority exercised by what one has done, and not merely by what one has intentionally done" (69). "Telemachus can be held responsible for things he did unintentionally, and so, of course, can we" (54).

As Williams points out, nowhere is this model of responsibility for unintended effects more powerfully expressed than in the law of torts. Virtually nonexistent in antebellum America, torts became one of the most important elements of common law in the late nineteenth century, when industrialization, urbanization, and improved systems of transportation forced masses of people into close proximity and thus gave rise to an increasing number of accidental injuries. What made such accidents unprecedented (aside from their numbers) was that they at once demanded some form of reparation for suffering and raised serious questions about accountability, including those about who should be held responsible for accidental harms and who should bear their costs. With the dramatic rise of such harms, what had been an insignificant branch of the law dealing with torts became an increasingly important remedy because it did not make intention the ground of liability.[11]

In *The Common Law* (1881), which advanced one of the first and most influential theories of tort, Oliver Wendell Holmes Jr. made explicit this model of responsibility for effects. He claimed, "It may be said that, generally speaking, a man meddles with [tangible objects] at his own risk"—that the owner of an object might be understood as responsible for harms caused by that object.[12] Antebellum American courts were basically committed to this model of strict liability, under which actors are held responsible for the harms caused by their actions no matter how blameless their conduct. By midcentury, however, legal scholars were concerned about the economic effects of such a system; strict liability threatened American industry (which would have to pay for the damage it caused) by promising a radical redistribution of wealth. Holmes, reacting to the ever-increasing demand for compensation, dismissed calls to continue the system of strict liability, denying that the state's role was to "make itself a mutual insurance company against accidents, and distribute the burden of its citizens' mishaps among all its members" (96).

In fact, the story that legal historians generally tell about tort in the nineteenth century is the story of its limitation, of the way that the promise of compensation was routinely undermined in the American courts. Through a number of different strategies, American courts created a patchwork system of limitations on damages designed to protect industry. The "fellow servant rule," for example, made it impossible for an employee to sue his employer if he was injured by a fellow worker. Under the fellow servant rule, employers could be held liable only for the harms they caused personally, a situation that rarely came about in large factories or other places of work where employees were most at risk of injury. According to Lawrence Friedman, the result of such limitations was clear: "The cost of industrial accidents was to be shifted from the entrepreneur to the workers themselves. Insofar as there was any responsibility toward destitute workers and their families, society as a whole, through its poor laws, would bear the burden, rather than leaving it to the most productive sector of the economy."[13]

More than anything else, the courts' growing insistence that there be a standard of negligence significantly limited liability. If under a system of strict liability persons are liable for every harm they cause, under a system of negligence they are liable for harms they cause only if they are at fault. According to Holmes, who was instrumental in establishing negligence as the general principle of liability in tort, persons are at fault when they act carelessly, when they cause a harm that anyone could have foreseen and avoided. "Unless my act," Holmes says, "is of a nature to threaten others, unless under the circumstances a prudent man would have foreseen the possibility of harm, it is no more justifiable to make me indemnify my neighbor against the consequences, than to make me do the same thing if I had fallen upon him in a fit, or to compel me to insure him against lightning" (96). Thus, the key distinction in a determination of guilt "is not between results which are and those which are not the consequences of the defendant's acts" but rather "between consequences which [the defendant] was bound as a reasonable man to contemplate, and those which he was not" (93). For example, "hard spurring is just so much more likely to lead to harm than merely riding a horse in the street . . . that the defendant would be bound to look out for the consequences of the one," while he would not be held responsible "for those resulting merely from the other; because the possibility of being run away with when riding quietly, though familiar, is comparatively slight" (93–94). By proclaiming the harmful consequences of some actions to be predictable and by making agents pay only for their mistakes, American law drew formal boundaries around how much agents would have to pay for the costs of the harms they accidentally caused.

As *The Gilded Age* (1873) makes clear, by the 1870s Twain was concerned about the consequences of such limitations on liability. This novel is, at least in part, a condemnation of the American courts for their failure to protect people from the damaging side effects of economic progress. Twain and his coauthor, Charles Dudley Warner, devote an entire chapter to an account of a deadly steamboat accident and its aftermath. While the painstaking depiction of this accident seems, at least initially, out of place in a novel satirizing Washington, the account of the explosion reveals a great deal about the general mechanisms of guilt and blame in the age of industry. The incident begins as a kind of game. Noticing that the *Amaranth* is quickly gaining on them, the captain of the *Boreas* orders his crew to prepare for a race: "Lord how she walks up on us! I do hate to be beat!"[14] While the challenger, becoming "locked together tight and fast" with the *Boreas*, ultimately wins the race, the strain on the engines proves deadly: the *Amaranth* explodes, killing almost everyone on board (49). If the captains and crews of the two ships were clearly responsible for the race that led to the accident—the head engineer of the *Amaranth* calls his second engineer a "murderer" for refusing to heed his warnings about stress on the engines—the "jury of inquest" on the case refuses to find anyone liable for the accident: "After due deliberation and inquiry they returned the inevitable American verdict which has been too familiar to our ears all the days of our lives—'NOBODY TO BLAME'" (52).

According to Nan Goodman, Twain represents in this verdict an "epistemological uncertainty," pervasive in late-nineteenth-century culture, that led to a radical transformation in the conception of responsibility for harm. By the second half of the century, Goodman argues, technological advances in transportation and communication produced "temporal and spatial dislocations" that, in turn, "contributed to the condensation and disarticulation of agency"; the result was a kind of cultural vertigo and a "shift" in agency "from the individual to the machine" that eventually helped overturn "traditional notions of personal responsibility."[15] Harnessed to the rising power of negligence, which made guilt contingent on proving an agent at fault, this "epistemological uncertainty," which led to the kind of verdict Twain critiques in *The Gilded Age*, became "both a cause and a symptom of a widespread erosion of responsibility" (66). Goodman finds evidence in a number of Twain's novels to suggest that he was deeply suspicious of these changes. His primary concern, she claims, is the loss of "agency" and the threat to individual "identity" for which he blames the "legal and social understanding of individual agency as hopelessly confused and distorting" (68). What he tracks in a series of novels that involve accidents is "the gradual disappearance of the morally responsible individual" (97).

Goodman is certainly right that the verdict of blamelessness in *The Gilded Age* registers the way in which the courts limited liability by favoring industry over the persons it injured. Yet we need not conclude from this evidence that Twain simply laments the inevitable "erosion of responsibility" caused by such limitations. On the contrary, this scene, in its sense of justified outrage over the verdict, dramatizes the important ways in which commonsense expectations about liability had been transformed. While it is true that legal devices like negligence limited liability and thus eased the burden placed on industry, the logic of negligence worked out by Holmes and other scholars actually succeeded (often despite their intentions) in articulating new forms of individual and corporate obligation.[16] Making carelessness the ground of responsibility implied that persons (even corporate persons) have at all times an obligation to act with caution. Formerly understood only as the failure to live up to a specific duty—the failure to fulfill a contract, say, or to perform a public office adequately—negligence began to be defined as the failure to meet a general standard of care. With the rise of negligence, not only were professionals like doctors bound by particular duties, but everyone was imagined to be bound by an obligation to others, an obligation not to cause harm. Negligence, designed to limit liability, ended up producing a much more expansive form of obligation owed to "all the world."[17]

Wai Chee Dimock has suggested that this sense of universal liability must be understood as an extension of contractual relations, the rise of which in the nineteenth century served "to enlarge not only 'the range of causal perceptions,' but also the range of assumed obligations."[18] In her view, these obligations are contractual, and thus products of the market, because they are subject to individual (or corporate) approval: one either feels obligated or one does not; one decides to compensate or one does not. To Dimock, the market that created new obligations to strangers—"strangers unknown, unloved, unconscionably numerous"—required, in turn, "an economy of pain," a way of deciding once and for all where one's responsibility ended (70). Yet to imagine that one could calculate responsibilities just as one calculates the benefits of entering a contract is to miss what is most important about the form of responsibility created by negligence: it is nonnegotiable. One cannot, generally speaking, contract out of liability.[19] As G. Edward White has pointed out, "by the close of the nineteenth century Torts . . . had become an entity distinct from the other private-law categories of Contract or Property: it was that branch of private law that dealt with universally imposed duties."[20]

The system of negligence installed by theorists like Holmes created a range of impersonal obligations. If one had a duty to "all the world," this duty had nothing to do with how one actually felt about one's fellows. The law, that is, did not require people to love their neighbors. Thus, while Holmes was adamant in his support of the fault principle's limitation of liability, arguing that "undertaking to redistribute losses" for injuries resulting from blameless action would not only hinder progress but also undermine any "sense of justice" (96), he nevertheless insisted that individuals were always acting under a general obligation to the public. If the move to a system of negligence meant that the law often failed to provide adequate compensation for the harms occasioned by industrialization, it nonetheless extended the reach of social obligation and thus transformed what it meant to act in public.

The Legal Imagination

The relation of the novel to the law has, in much recent criticism, been seen primarily in terms of opposition. Where the law is rigid, critics say, the novel is flexible; where the law is impersonal, the novel is committed to the human character; where the law fails in its mission to act justly, the novel provides a comforting form of "poetic justice."[21] Yet this vision of literature as law's supplement has perplexing implications. To claim that novels humanize the law is to suggest that novels in and of themselves are somehow more human than the law and thus inherently better at determining what is just. Moreover, it is to suggest that the legal concept of justice must be understood as "a formal universal," which "necessarily does violence to what it abstracts."[22] This apparent conflict between the formal and the quotidian, the abstract and the particular, prompts Martha Nussbaum, in her analysis of actual legal cases, to attribute all judicial attention paid to "history and social context" and all judicial expressions of empathy to "the literary" rather than the legal "imagination" (115). The novel, according to Nussbaum, not only describes but also creates sympathy by addressing "an implicit reader who shares with the characters certain hopes, fears, and general human concerns, and who for that reason is able to form bonds of identification and sympathy with them" (7).

Such defenses of the novel against the deadening abstractions of the law require us to concede that the novel, as a form, is always and inevitably devoted to the sanctity of individual experience and thus committed to the production of "bonds of identification and sympathy." But just as there is no reason to imagine that legal reasoning excludes the personal and the particular (after all, legal cases depend on individual stories of harm or damage), there is no reason to imagine that novels are limited to producing an experiential model of personhood. *Huckleberry Finn* attempts to move away from a model of responsibility that requires such bonds and changes of heart by disarticulating the meaning of individual and collective action from questions of sympathy or intention. This disarticulation is evident in the novel's investment in producing actions that can only be understood retrospectively. But it also emerges in Huck's failure ever to recognize his own role in the evasion—in his sense that it was Tom alone who "had gone and took all that trouble and bother to set a free nigger free!" (362). When it comes to describing the harm done to Jim and to assigning responsibility for it, the novel implies that Huck's experience and self-perception—what he recognizes or fails to recognize about himself—is irrelevant.

Precisely because it reconceives personal obligation, negligence is central to *Huckleberry Finn*'s fantasy of racial justice in post-Reconstruction America. The law, it is worth noting, works differently here than it does in both earlier and later stories by Twain (including those that describe the further adventures of Tom, Huck, and Jim) that involve overt intrusions of the law into the world of the novel.[23] In *Pudd'nhead Wilson* (1894), written as *Plessy v. Ferguson* was making its way through the courts, Twain relies on a form of retrospection that resembles the one he uses at the end of *Huckleberry Finn*. In this case, Tom Driscoll, having left for college believing himself white and free, returns home to find that he is in fact the son of one of his own slaves. But here, the reframing of action and identity works to a very different end. The revelation of Tom's race not only undermines the authority of Tom's self-perception but provides everyone with an explanation for his bad behavior. When he refuses to defend the "family honour" by fighting Count Luigi in a duel, for example, his mother Roxy blames his degradation on his blood: "It's de nigger in you, dat's what it is. Thirty-one parts o' you is white, en on'y one part nigger, en dat po' little one part is yo' *soul*. Tain't wuth savin'; tain't wuth totin' out on a shovel en throwin' in de gutter."[24] As becomes apparent in the final courtroom scene, when Tom is found guilty of murdering his uncle, the law's reliance on the new science of fingerprinting—the discovery of the permanent traces left behind by the body—allows it to establish the absolute inviolability of racial identity. David Wilson explains to the court the significance of these traces: "Every human being carries with him from his cradle to his grave certain physical marks which do not change their character, and by which he can always be identified—and that without a shade of doubt or question" (136). As set out by Wilson, the mouthpiece of law and "justice" in the novel, fingerprints not only connect Tom to his crime, but connect his crime to his black blood. In fact, one might say that the crime of being a murderer in this novel is overshadowed by the crime of being black. Given the way the law works here, the novel's attempt to highlight the contradictions of the "one-drop rule," with its commitment to race as a mere "fiction of law and custom" (13), is undermined by the race plot that upholds the legitimacy of this rule.[25]

In *Huckleberry Finn*, however, Twain derives from the law a different kind of power. He uses it to define a general model of responsibility for the consequences of action, one that might produce a form of racial justice. The advantage of the negligence model is that it is both impersonal (requiring no change in attitude or belief) and universally applicable (requiring no preexisting relationship between the agent and victim of the harm). In other words, the negligence model of responsibility is impersonal because it measures conduct not against an agent's intentions but against a general standard. As H. L. A. Hart argues, negligence "is not the name of 'a state of mind'" but the name of an action, a failure "to comply with a standard of conduct with which any ordinary reasonable man *could* and *would* have complied."[26] In negligence cases, the courts did not ask whether actors had in fact predicted the harm that would follow from their actions; the courts measured the actions against a general standard of behavior. And the model is universally applicable because it is not subject to individual consent. The law of negligence, as Holmes claimed, is grounded in "some general view of the conduct which everyone may fairly expect and demand from every other, whether that other has agreed to it or not" (77).

In the broadest terms, what Twain recognizes in the kind of obligation defined by negligence law is its potential to solve the problem of postbellum civil rights, a problem he conceives as structural rather than personal. If Jim's precarious position in the text—free in name but not in fact—represents the precarious political and economic situation of African Americans after Reconstruction, this position cannot be transformed by the power of sentiment because it is held in place by people who have the best of intentions. By the end of the novel, Huck's love for and commitment to freeing Jim become paradoxically essential to the game of humiliating him. The farce that ends the novel depends on Huck's willingness to defend Jim by raising endless objections to Tom's baroque plans, objections that become a central component of the game. Huck's dogged insistence on arguing about technique actually drives Tom to proliferate complications so that, in the end, Huck's arguments on behalf of Jim enable Tom's fantasy that they could play at freeing him indefinitely: "He said it was the best fun he ever had in his life, and the most intellectual; and said that if he could only see his way to it we could keep it up all the rest of our lives and leave Jim to our children to get out" (313).

I do not mean to claim that *Huckleberry Finn* simply replaces an intentional model of responsibility with one that disregards intention; it would be wrong to argue that Twain merely ironizes Huck's love for Jim. Rather, I am suggesting that the form of impersonal responsibility explored in the novel supplements an intentional model (just as negligence supplements the criminal law); it is a way of imagining remedies for different kinds of harms. One might argue that the sincerity of Huck's devotion to Jim only underscores how impossible it would be for him to single-handedly solve Jim's real problem. Twain, in other words, raises questions of sentiment in *Huckleberry Finn* in order to suggest that sentimental conversions go only so far to remedy wrongs that can be traced to no one agent. In the end, *Huckleberry Finn* is concerned less with the harms that individuals do to one another than with the harms done by systems.

Indeed, in *Huckleberry Finn* individual intention is consistently overshadowed by the problem it attempts to address, the problem of racial discrimination that is embedded in (to echo Smiley) American cultural, economic, and political systems. From this perspective, it makes sense to see each character's ignorance of the true meaning of his actions as a generalization about the unpredictable effects of individual action. Critics have been too quick to blame Tom for Jim's suffering, not acknowledging how the formal structure of the novel links Tom to much larger networks of action that include not only Huck but also Miss Watson and the widow Douglas, the Phelpses and their neighbors, the slave catchers, and the king and the duke. The narrative's enforced retrospection reveals that we have effects in the world that go beyond our intentions but for which we are nonetheless accountable. In drawing on a model of responsibility derived from the law of negligence, *Huckleberry Finn* enacts a fantasy of national responsibility for the bottoming out of black civil rights in postbellum America.

The Whole Body of the People

Twain was not alone in drawing on negligence to fantasize solutions to this racial crisis. In his argument before the Supreme Court in *Plessy v. Ferguson*, Albion Tourgée claimed that the Louisiana segregation law violated his client's rights under the Thirteenth and Fourteenth Amendments to the Constitution. Forcing African Americans to ride in a separate railroad car violated the Thirteenth Amendment because, as Justice Henry Harlan put it in his dissent, it served as a "badge of servitude wholly inconsistent with the civil freedom and the equality before the law established by the Constitution."[27] But when Tourgée approaches the question of racial justice in his novel *Pactolus Prime* (1890), he imagines a solution to de facto discrimination based in tort rather than Constitutional law.[28]

Given Tourgée's penchant for realism, *Pactolus Prime* is a strange novel of magical transformations and amazing coincidences. It recounts one day in the life of Pac, a black man who had passed for white in his youth and become a Civil War hero. Shot for his political activities after the war, Pac is treated for his injuries with nitrate of silver, which turns his white skin a deep shade of black. The plot of the novel—Pac's attempt to leave a fortune he has made as a boot black to his daughter (who thinks he is her guardian)—serves as little more than an excuse for Tourgée to motivate a series of conversations about the intractability of racial discrimination and arguments about how to alleviate the problem or compensate the victims. The novel takes place in Boston, but the lack of a legal system of segregation in no way lessens the severity of the discrimination experienced by the novel's black characters. Tourgée illustrates the pervasiveness of northern racism in a number of ways—the casual use of racial epithets, the indignities that Pac and his business partner Benny endure as they work, and Pac's incessant rage at these indignities.

One of the novel's earliest scenes unfolds as a series of arguments between the boot blacks and their white customers about what the nation owes the freedmen.[29] In Benny's argument, Tourgée goes beyond Twain by making the fantasy of legal compensation for racial injustice absolutely explicit. "Our case is in equity," Benny explains, echoing George Washington Cable's famous essay on the rights of the freedmen. Benny, however, is less concerned with the abstract rights and privileges of citizenship than with garnering concrete compensation both for the slaves' unpaid labor and for the profits reaped from that labor. His appeal to his listeners, then, is an appeal based in the logic of tort: " 'We do not ask to follow that which is ours, *in specie*. Our demand is for an equivalent, or a partial equivalent, for what has been wrongfully taken from us and converted to the use of the taker.' . . . 'In equity then,' the young man continued, 'those who received the labor of our people unjustly, became trustees for us by their own wrongful act, and it is not necessary that we should follow and designate our own. The trustee *de son tort* who mingles the trust fund with his own becomes a debtor to that amount' " (86–87). Having suffered, directly or indirectly, from someone else's "wrongful act," Benny demands compensation on behalf of his "people," an amount that Pac estimates at "*more than ten billions of dollars*" (76). This amount works as a retort to those who, as one customer puts it, would "like to have the account settled and be done with it!" because it makes the demands of African Americans simultaneously concrete and impossible to "be done with" (73).

For both Benny and Pac, the question of who is responsible for paying this debt is a relatively simple matter—it is the responsibility of the entire nation. Put more accurately, it is the responsibility of citizens who cannot themselves be understood as victims. Because, as Benny points out, the profits from slavery "have gone into the national wealth," the nation that profited must, he claims, "recompense our people, so far as may be, for the wrong done them in the past" (88). One listener, a judge, points out the obvious objection to such a claim, that "there is no means of making any distinction between the slaveholder or his descendants, and those who remonstrated against the injustice of slavery and opposed its continuance" (88). The judge's sense of individual responsibility here depends on the logic of genealogy as well as the problem of direct causation. Is it just, he asks, to make people pay for harms they did not themselves cause? Is it just to make people pay for harms that not even their ancestors caused? What about those who opposed slavery? Should they or their descendants be made to compensate its victims? For Benny and Pac (and, it seems clear, Tourgée himself), there are cases in which responsibility needs to be defined as public rather than private—a condition of corporate, rather than individual or even familial, action. When, as Benny points out, "the wrong is a result of some public act or neglect . . . the courts frequently hold the whole responsible for the resultant injury." Thus, "if a State takes a man's property, the whole body of the people is taxed to make the owner whole" (90). It follows that individuals can be held accountable for the harms of a corporate body of which they form part.[30]

In *Pactolus Prime*, the complaint of racial injustice works on the model of the class-action suit because the group it defines is united by common injury; the national collective, on the other hand, is united by shared profit and thus shared accountability. Indeed, Dr. Holbrook, who discovers the secret of Pac's black skin, seems to echo Benny when he explains his theory of natural justice to Pac's lawyer. To punish an entire nation is not, he claims, to "make the innocent suffer with the guilty": "There is no question of guilt or innocence in it, because it does not depend in the least degree upon intent. A law is violated: the penalty must be paid: that is all there is of it. Whether it is the doer of evil; those who profit by his acts; those who are sureties for his good behavior, or those on whom the heritage of his evil descends, it matters not. The penalty must be paid, and as the wrong is, such in type must be the expiation" (336). In this version of the debate, however, there is no call for action, no demand for compensation. Instead, the doctor tries to convince the lawyer that "doers of evil" are somehow naturally and inevitably punished for their crimes. "There is," he claims, "that mystical quality attached to the very act of wrongdoing that sets in motion the causes which produce retributory consequences of similar character. Sometimes they are physical, sometimes they are moral, sometimes economical" (335–36). And yet, strangely, the only one magically punished in the novel is Pac himself, whose black skin seems to be the novel's version of poetic justice. For his willingness to pass as white he is punished not only by the sudden emergence of black skin but by a job blacking boots. Just as Twain mocks Jim's freedom by having him kept in chains, Tourgée undercuts Pac's wealth and success by having him suffer the daily humiliations that go along with being marked out in a racially segregated city. In *Pactolus Prime*, Tourgée imagines what it means for an entire nation to "profit by" the wrongs of slavery and segregation. What he cannot imagine is how anyone might make the nation pay.

Forty Acres and a Mule

To suggest that novels, especially novels about race, might divorce collectivity from experience goes against a great deal of recent work that sees collectivity almost exclusively in terms of its effects on individual experience and individual identity. The collective, in other words, has been understood to extend the limits of experience, making it possible for individuals to imagine that they could, as part of a collective, remember things that they never experienced. Thus American Jews are enjoined to remember the Holocaust.[31] Such work often literalizes the metaphor of the social body by claiming that membership in an ethnic group gives one access to certain memories that then serve as the sign of one's ethnicity. From this point of view, collective memory and collective guilt look like two sides of the same coin: one is imagined to inherit guilt for ancestral crimes in the same way that one inherits a cultural past. But both *Pactolus Prime* and *Huckleberry Finn* refuse to make collective responsibility contingent on guilt or on ghostly notions of inheritance. Instead, they attempt to extend the logic of corporate responsibility (responsibility not simply for harms one has caused but for harms committed in one's name) to the nation.

What it would mean to hold an entire nation accountable for harm is articulated most compellingly in *Huckleberry Finn*'s final scene of compensation—the much-discussed moment in which Tom hands Jim forty dollars for playing the part of prisoner "so patient, and doing it up so good" (365). Almost all critics of *Huckleberry Finn*—proponents and detractors alike—are united in their condemnation of Tom's attempt to settle the score. Critics as diverse as Holland and Arac have suggested that this forty-dollar payment is, at best, condescending, and they have seen in Tom only the manifestation of postwar racism. Not only is this payment a paltry sum in comparison with Tom and Huck's wealth, the argument goes, but it is hardly enough to give Jim a fair chance to support himself or to buy his family out of slavery. That the number forty is something of an obsession in this text suggests, however, that it represents more than a pittance. Twain seems to insist on the symbolic weight of the payment by referring to the number with astonishing frequency in the evasion sequence. The duke, lying to Huck, tells him that Jim is being held "forty mile back here in the country, on the road to Lafayette" (275). Huck and Tom, plotting to sneak a ladder into Jim's cabin in a pie, claim that they had "rope enough for forty pies" (322). When Tom is injured,

Jim agrees to stay with him: "No sah—I doan' budge a step out'n dis place, 'dout a *doctor*; not if it's forty year!" (345). And the neighbors surveying the damage after the evasion imagine that the slaves have been plotting: "A dozen says you!—*forty* couldn't a done everything that's been done" (350).

This interest in the number forty gives Tom's payment an iconic quality; the payment appears as the culmination of a complicated circuit through the text, as a sum repeatedly given to and withheld from Jim. He first receives the money, indirectly, from the two slave catchers who offer Huck forty dollars after they refuse to help tow Huck's raft to safety. The money then resurfaces with the king and the duke (who sell Jim for forty dollars) and reverts back to Jim when Tom pays him for his patience at the end. Both payments to Jim, it should be noted, serve as damages for harm, even if the donor misunderstands the harm he has caused. If Tom's final gesture counts, then, it counts as an attempt to imagine what real compensation for a series of harms would look like. By linking these characters—Huck, the slave traders, the king and the duke, the Phelpses and their neighbors—through their relation to Tom's largely symbolic payment, Twain ties the scene of compensation that ends his antebellum tale to the post-Reconstruction era of failed national promises.[32]

Set against both the rise of negligence and the fall of the Freedmen's Bureau, Tom's offer begins to look like the antithesis of buying Jim off for a pittance and thus maintaining the fiction that he is property. It looks instead like formal, legal recognition of his personhood, of the obligation to compensate him for his injuries. Surely forty is meant to recall the promise of forty acres and a mule, which were to make the freedmen equal as well as free.[33] From this perspective, Tom's payment looks less like further injury to Jim—a refusal to see him as a man—than like a form of compensation much broader in its effects because it makes him representative of a group. In the post-Reconstruction era, Tom's payment would have recalled not only the promise of the Freedmen's Bureau to give support to freed slaves through the redistribution of confiscated or abandoned lands but also, and more forcefully, the government's total failure to fulfill its obligation. It was, at the time, the nation's most famous broken promise.[34]

This investment in collective forms of compensation also helps explain why Huck virtually disappears from the last third of the novel: Twain attempts to dissolve him, finally, not simply into Tom (whose name he takes) but also into the collective that Tom (always the mouthpiece for the authorities) has come to represent. Because Tom is the source of this collective voice, his final gesture, far from a dismissal of the economic problems faced by the freedmen, symbolically enacts the compensation that the nation withheld. And if, as I have been arguing, the force of the novel is to disarticulate accountability from intention, to make it possible to imagine guilt even in the absence of malice, then Tom's gesture is collective not because it stems from a shared experience of hatred reformed but because it offers Jim compensation for a series of systematic harms. To end the novel by recalling the promise of forty acres and a mule is thus to suggest a very different way of defining collective accountability. Instead, of imagining a spiritual connection among disparate individuals, it imagines, in Holmes's words, "some general view of the conduct which every one may fairly expect and demand from every other, whether that other has agreed to it or not."[35] Like the law of negligence, which created (even as it tried to limit) new forms of corporate responsibility, Twain's novel imagines extending this version of the collective—the corralling of actions for which no individual is to blame—to the entire nation.

Huckleberry Finn thus represents Twain's way of rewriting history or, more accurately, of fantasizing a new racial history of postwar America. What remains puzzling is that his biography suggests a much more ambivalent position on and within post-Reconstruction racism than this reading of the ending might seem to allow. Assessing the political and economic situation of African Americans in 1885, Twain remarked, "We have ground the manhood out of them. The shame is ours, not theirs, and we should pay for it."[36] This "brutally succinct comment on racism," according to Shelley Fisher Fishkin, "is a rare nonironic statement of the personal anguish he felt regarding the destructive legacy of slavery."[37] Of course, as Fishkin has pointed out, Twain had a habit of contradicting himself. "What would it take," she asks, "to acknowledge the complexity and diversity of this man?"[38] One thing it might take is a clear-sighted sense of Twain's equivocations on the subject of race: he was both a critic of political discrimination and a fan of minstrel shows and "darky jokes,"[39] a defender of both George Washington Cable (champion of black civil rights) and Joel Chandler Harris (creator of Uncle Remus).[40] *Huckleberry Finn* is full of these kinds of puzzles: why, for instance, does Jim reprimand Huck for his selfishness early in the novel and then silently bear his humiliations at the end? Tom Quirk, grappling with this problem, asks us to separate "Mark Twain, the imaginative artist" from "Samuel Clemens, U.S. citizen"[41] and thus attempts to rescue Twain from his own opinions. Smiley and Arac ask us to absolve the man by blaming the book.

The reading of the ending of *Huckleberry Finn* that I advance in this chapter depends on a recognition of Twain's commitment to black civil rights. But it would be a mistake, I think, simply to add *Huckleberry Finn* to the list of evidence in his favor. For the interest of the novel lies precisely in its attempt to think about the problem of American racism in structural rather than personal terms and thus to shift the focus (not permanently but, perhaps, strategically) from belief to practice, from intentions to effects. The fantasy enacted by the novel demands that the ascription of responsibility be seen as a formal rather than a moral question and that the world accordingly begin to see the problem of the freedmen as political rather than moral. What Twain recognizes is the poverty of treating racial justice as a question of sentiment (requiring a "change of heart") rather than a question of structure (requiring new political policies). Ultimately, the logic of Twain's novel—which fantasizes a political solution to Jim's troubles—works to override the deficiencies of its representations, in which Jim is often made a fool. Unlike Cable, who frames his own answer to the problem of postwar black civil rights in terms of "equity" by arguing that people must begin to judge their fellows on the basis of "the eternal principles of justice,"[42] Twain frames his answer in the context of negligence, so that the individual's blindness and petty prejudice might be replaced by a system that overrides the accidents of personal opinion.

It would be tempting then to argue that given *Huckleberry Finn*'s critique of Jim Crow America and its fantasy of racial justice, those who have argued so strenuously against its continued presence in the canon and curriculum are wrong and must stop. Indeed, if this reading of the novel is persuasive, it counters Arac and Smiley's arguments against the novel not only because it sees an interest in social effects where they see only liberal bad faith, but because it has the potential to change the way it is experienced by readers. At the same time, however, I have been arguing that taking the project of this novel seriously means taking effects seriously, and that must include the bad as well as the good effects that the novel has had on readers. To insist that either bad or good effects are merely irrelevant or based on misreading is, as the novel itself illustrates, to misread the way in which objects and actions can produce profound social consequences that cannot be explained in terms of intentions. *Huckleberry Finn* is about both the difficulty and the necessity of valuing effects over intentions. Thus, one of the implications of Twain's project is that no reading of the novel can put an end to the debate it has engendered. Taking effects on readers seriously means acknowledging that responses to the novel can be neither dictated nor replaced by a reading of the novel; even more importantly, it suggests that *Huckleberry Finn* itself provides the grounds for its own reassessment. Seen in this light, both proponents and detractors of *Huckleberry Finn* get the novel wrong. That Arac and Smiley have finally pointed us to the social effects of Twain's project should not, despite their best intentions, be understood as a dismissal of this project. For their use of *Huckleberry Finn* to oppose the politics of good intentions must count as a sign that we are beginning to get the novel right.

CHAPTER FOUR   # The Veil of Cedars:
Charles Chesnutt and Conversion

> But, as he said to himself, he had no intention of disamericanizing, nor had he a desire to teach his only son any such subtle art. It had been for himself so very soluble a problem to live in England assimilated yet unconverted.
> HENRY JAMES, *The Portrait of a Lady* (1881)

> The years of fraud—of passing for what thou wert not—I forgive, for thy noble husband's sake; but my confessor has told me, and I feel its truth, that if we allow thy return to thy people as thou art now, we permit a continuance of such unnatural unions, encourage fraud, and expose our subjects to the poisonous taint of Jewish blood and unbelief. A Christian thou must become.
> GRACE AGUILAR, *The Vale of Cedars* (1850)

In *Huckleberry Finn*, Twain imagines legal stipulation overriding the authority of individual intention, experience, and prejudice in the service of something like racial justice. Throughout the novel, Twain questions the ability of personal experience to define actions or identities in a world in which one's legal status can be directly contradicted by one's experience. Jim can be legally free while being held captive and threatened with death; the free black "p'fessor" vilified by Pap can be sold as a slave as soon as "he'd been in the State six months."[1] By the same token, Twain suggests that white Americans can be held accountable for the unintended effects of their actions on black Americans, for the harm they cause even with the best of intentions. Thus in *Huckleberry Finn*, legal stipulation both produces the race problem and solves it: African Americans might be free in law only, but they also might be compensated for the injuries inflicted by a racist culture, even when the individuals who inflict this harm are well meaning.

By the time Charles Chesnutt published *The House behind the Cedars* (1900), legal stipulation no longer represented a solution to America's racial crisis; it was too overtly a form of institutionalized racism in its own right. Although it is set "a few years after the Civil War,"[2] *The House behind the Cedars* was written in the wake of *Plessy v. Ferguson* (1896) and thus reflects a world in which the color line—the creation of a "caste" system based on racial classification—has moved from local custom to state law, and from state law (through the *Plessy* decision) to federally sanctioned law. As had Twain, Chesnutt makes a crucial section of his novel into an extended flashback; it returns to the moment "before the civil war" in order to trace the antebellum origins of postwar racism (104). Indeed, the novel begins with John Warwick's recollections of his childhood in slaveholding Pateville, North Carolina, including the memory of a white man who was imprisoned briefly for the murder of a "free negro" (3). If, at the time, the white man's sentence—less than a year in prison—barely qualified as punishment, the postwar years would make even this slap on the wrist seem like a version of racial justice. As the narrator acidly remarks, "Warwick was neither a prophet nor the son of a prophet," and thus "he could not foresee that, thirty years later," a commuted sentence for the murder of a black man "would seem an excessive punishment for so slight a misdemeanor" (3). Rather than emphasizing, as does Twain, what has not changed (former slaves, legally free, are still in fact enslaved), Chesnutt documents a horrifying change: the decimation of civil rights after Reconstruction and the beginnings of the Jim Crow South.[3]

The rise of negligence law was a response to accidental injury, a way of assigning responsibility for harms that seemed to be nobody's fault. Legal segregation might be understood as a similar attempt to organize the accidental. The "de jurification"[4] of racial segregation gave the state the power to invest the accident of birth with meaning, to transform it into a rigid legal identity and a permanent status and thus to divide the nation into "black" and "white." Accordingly, when Chesnutt demonstrates the ways in which the legal stipulation of identity—black or white—overrides the authority of individual opinion or control, he is exploring the power of the law to make the accidental essential. It is in relation to this de jurification of racial categories that John's sister Rena—Chesnutt's version of the tragic mulatta—can represent the power of assigned status to override individual will: "Since leaving the house behind the cedars, where she had been brought into the world without her own knowledge or consent, and had first drawn the breath of life by the involuntary contraction of certain muscles, Rena had learned, in a short time, many things; but she was yet to learn that the innocent suffer with the guilty, and feel the punishment the more keenly because unmerited" (51). Directed against a system that punishes "the innocent" for the fact of their birth, this description of Rena translates the relatively familiar sentiment, "I never asked to be born," into a critique of the kind of state power used to enforce arbitrary distinctions. But Rena's inability to consent, as Chesnutt makes clear, is not so much an existential as a social and political crisis.

In *The House behind the Cedars*, Chesnutt responds to this crisis with a meditation on the construction of willed identity. A novel about passing that never uses the term "passing," *The House behind the Cedars* is, in effect, a fantasy about the individual's power to turn the irrationality of segregation against itself. After all, segregation depends on distinctions of "color" that were often, as many historians have pointed out, impossible to see. In the language of Justice Henry Billings Brown's decision in the *Plessy* case, legal separation of the races is imagined to be based on self-evident physical distinctions: "A statute which implies merely a legal distinction between the white and colored races—a distinction which is founded in the color of the two races and which must always exist so long as men are distinguished from the other race by color—has no tendency to destroy the legal equality of the two races or reestablish a state of involuntary servitude."[5] But this suggestion that legal discrimination is based on color is undone by the existence of Homer Plessy himself, a man so light skinned that he had to announce his racial identity before he could be arrested.[6] Like Plessy, one could look white and yet be legally black. Against Brown's argument in *Plessy*, the authority of the "one-drop rule" had, by the turn of the century in much of the South, created a new racial category—"invisible blackness."[7] With respect to this conflict between blood and color, *The House behind the Cedars* poses a set of questions about identity under segregation. If the reliance on both skin and blood was a reliance on racial fictions, why couldn't one choose one arbitrary marker of identity over the other? In other words, why couldn't one derive one's legally stipulated identity from the fiction of skin color rather than the fiction of blood? What if the surface of the body—Rena's "ivory complexion" (47), John's "clean cut, high-bred features" (1)—really could, as Brown insisted, stipulate identity? Simply put, *The House behind the Cedars* asks what it would mean if one could be what one appeared to be.[8]

Granted, being what one appears to be means choosing between two "accidental" identities—the one assigned by fractions of blood (black) and the other assigned by appearance (white). What makes this choice significant for both John and Rena is the simple fact that it is a choice and thus requires their "knowledge" and "consent." As John's mentor Judge Straight puts it, "You have the somewhat unusual privilege, it seems, of choosing between two races" (115). Both the tragic mulatta genre that precedes *The House behind the Cedars* and the passing fiction that follows it take for granted that race is intrinsic, an attribute that must be hidden because it can never be changed.[9] Chesnutt's text diverges from this tradition most profoundly in its suggestion that what has come to be called "passing" is less about pretense than a self-determination so radical it can seemingly transform biology. If Rena has been born black "without her own knowledge and consent," she is reborn, voluntarily this time, as white. In *The House behind the Cedars*, Chesnutt fantasizes that one could turn the logic of the color line against itself by agreeing to be defined by color and thus imagines that the legal stipulation of racial identity in terms of color could lead to very different effects than the supporters of segregation envisioned.

As if to test the racial bonds that it will subsequently reject, the novel opens not with an escape from biological ties but with a return to them. After ten years of living as white among the social elites of Clarence, South Carolina, John returns to Pateville and to the home he has left but can never quite escape. The house, indeed, becomes the central figure of the novel; "shut off from the street by a row of dwarf cedars" (7), it comes to represent not only the "sins of the fathers" (51)—the secrets of race and illegitimacy—but the power of racial ties, and the allure of both affection and nostalgia. Described alternately as "a fit place to hide some guilty or disgraceful secret" and "an ideal retreat from the fierce sunshine and the sultry heat of the approaching summer" (7), the house serves as both refuge and prison. In much the same way John's mother, Mis' Molly, who bears what the novel calls "the mark of the Ethiopian" (122), stands in for both the domestic refuge of the house and the racial secret that her children hope to elude. The house is also marked as the site of a "private cemetery," where the body of Molly's dead son is buried "under a small clump of cedars" (107). The linkage of the hidden grave of Molly's unnamed son to the hidden house suggests that the house itself is a kind of grave, and that the son who is buried there might be the ghost of the son who has attempted to escape by leaving home and renaming himself Warwick.[10]

In this charged opening scene, the house organizes the movements of each of the central characters. John begins his stay by wandering aimlessly through the town but ends up following Rena home, not knowing she is his sister. In John's eyes, Rena is simply a "strikingly handsome" young woman (5). In fact, she is treated as a stranger by almost everyone during her walk through town: "Warwick observed, as they passed through the respectable quarter, that few people who met the girl greeted her, and that some others whom she passed at gates or doorways gave her no sign of recognition; from which he inferred that she was possibly a visitor in the town and not well acquainted" (5). John himself, although not exactly a "visitor" in his home town, travels about without being recognized by anyone, including Rena. Indeed, the entire scene unfolds as a series of rather troubling misrecognitions. John pursues Rena as a potential lover—"The sound of her voice gave Warwick a thrill" (6)—and Rena evades John as a potential seducer—"finding his glance fixed upon her, she quickened her pace with an air of startled timidity" (6). Mis' Molly invites John in without knowing who he is: "She . . . sat down facing him and looked at him closely. 'When did you last see my son?' she asked" (12). While Rena and John have changed enough to be unrecognizable, the house alone seems not to have changed at all: "Every detail of the house and garden was familiar" (8). And it is in relation to the house that familial ties are reasserted: Rena is transformed from lover to sister; John from seducer and stranger to brother and son.

One might be tempted, then, to read the house as the one place in Chesnutt's novel where a kind of natural order based on blood is restored. Equipped with a natural wall that shields the black family from the prying eyes of the street, the house seems to represent the white bodies of John and Rena, which allow them to hide their black identity. What undermines this reading, however, is that the house conceals not only the bodies of the black family but also the "inheritance" left behind by the unnamed white father: "In the 'hall' or parlor of his mother's house stood a quaintly carved black walnut bookcase, containing a small but remarkable collection of books, which had at one time been used, in his hours of retreat and relaxation from business and politics, by the distinguished gentleman who did not give his name to Mis' Molly's children" (107). Denied the "valuable heritage" (107) of the father's name, the children instead are given the valuable heritage of English high culture: a bookcase stocked with Shakespeare, Milton, Bunyan, Addison, Steele, and Paine, as well as novels by Richardson, Scott, and

Bulwer-Lytton. This description of the library appears in the flashback section of the novel, just after the young John Walden is forced to grapple with opposing accounts of racial identity—one provided by the mirror that "proved that God, the Father of all, had made him white" (107) and the other by the neighborhood children, who insist that he is black. The library stands as the promise of an escape not only from the drudgery of the "everyday," but from the burden of a racialized culture: John discovers in the library "the portal of a new world, peopled with strange and marvelous beings" (108). As the novel imagines it, the very fact that the house contains this hidden library changes its meaning; no longer exclusively the site of sentimentality and nostalgia associated with the black mother, it is also, and more crucially, the province of high culture associated with the white father. The house thus contains both the racial secret and the key to evading that secret.

The importance of this hidden library, which (in combination with pale skin) enables John and Rena to pass, has generally been overlooked by Chesnutt's critics. The few who mention the library have seen it in very much the same terms as John himself, who imagines the British novels he reads simply as a link to "the blood of his white fathers, the heirs of the ages" (109).[11] We might attribute this neglect of the library to the fact that its primarily European texts seem to be overshadowed by the relentlessly American political and social concerns of Chesnutt's project. In a novel that traces the devastating effects of segregation, in other words, Milton might seem to represent little more than a hopelessly vague desire for "cultural capital."

Yet in providing John with an English rather than American library, Chesnutt draws explicitly on the legacy of *Narrative of the Life of Frederick Douglass: An American Slave* (1845) (a book that, along with other works by African Americans, is conspicuously absent from the library). Douglass, after all, begins his political education not with *The Liberator* (he discovers this abolitionist journal after his escape) but with Richard Brinsley Sheridan's "mighty speeches on behalf of Catholic emancipation" in the *Columbian Orator* (1797).[12] Far from seeming exotic or alien, Sheridan allows Douglass to express his own thoughts and thus, for the first time, enables him to know his own mind: the speeches "gave tongue to interesting thoughts of my own soul, which had frequently flashed through my mind, and died away for want of utterance" (84). Sheridan "speaks" for Douglass, despite their racial and cultural differences, insofar as he provides him with a crucial historical analogue and a political vocabulary: "What I got from Sheridan was a bold denunciation of slavery, and a powerful vindication of human rights" (84). Like Douglass, Chesnutt imagines that British texts can provide valuable historical analogues for peculiarly American problems. But if a novelist like Walter Scott provides Chesnutt (if not John) with a political vocabulary, it is not the same one that helped produce the post-Reconstruction feudal revival in the South, which Chesnutt mocks in the tournament scene. Indeed *Ivanhoe* (1819), and by extension many of the texts that comprise the hidden library, is central to the political and cultural fantasy of *The House behind the Cedars* because it registers the British obsession with the problem of the Jews. One of the questions that drives *Ivanhoe*, a novel that charts the emergence of the English nation out of feuding Normans and Saxons, is the question of citizenship; specifically, how can the Jews, aliens by race and belief, become English citizens? In what follows I will suggest that what Chesnutt gets from Scott and a number of other writers (especially Grace Aguilar, whose novel, *The Vale of Cedars*, is alluded to throughout) is the idea of conversion.

One of my central claims in this chapter is that in creating a fantasy of self-transformation, Chesnutt was drawing on a series of British conversion narratives in which Jews have the power to transform themselves into Christians. Jewishness, in these texts, is at once racial and completely transformable. At the end of *Ivanhoe*, for example, Rowena does not dismiss the Jewish Rebecca but rather begs her to convert and thus become part of both her family and the new English nation: "O, remain with us; the counsel of holy men will wean you from your erring law, and I will be a sister to you."[13] Racial politics in the United States made such an offer—from a white woman to a black one—virtually unthinkable, a fact sustained by the passing fiction that often recuperates racial identity even as it questions racial purity or authenticity.

Yet Chesnutt, drawing on the logic of these British conversion tales—in which Jews do not merely pretend to be but actually make themselves into English citizens—creates characters who deny they are passing as white and insist that they actually are white. In this novel about the perils of legal segregation and the "one-drop rule," Chesnutt endorses an escape from a world where race is intrinsic and unalterable into the promise of something that resembles, in its emphasis on individual choice, a kind of religious conversion. The analogy Chesnutt draws between passing and conversion is not perfect; he simply disregards, for example, the fact that passing is a matter of racial identity while conversion is primarily a matter of belief. What is crucial about conversion, however, is that it makes identity (and, in the case of Jewish conversion to Christianity, even racial identity) into a matter of individual choice. Indeed, it is the power of conversion to make race a relatively straightforward question of belief that drives this analogy. That Chesnutt ends *The House behind the Cedars* with death and failure reveals not that he believed in the inescapability of race, but rather that he saw this kind of self-transformation from outcast to citizen (which he represents as the refusal to be racialized) routinely denied to African Americans. In Chesnutt's hands, British conversion fiction, with its suggestion that racial identity might be chosen or refused, proves to be a powerful vehicle for thinking about race precisely because the story that conversion narratives tell about the promise of self-transformation reveals the devastating absence of that promise in segregated America.

Thus Chesnutt does not view Europe as a place of refuge for African Americans (as does Pauline Hopkins in *Winona* [1902], which ends with its black characters fleeing Jim Crow America for liberal England).[14] Nor does he view European culture as an antidote to American racial politics (as does W. E. B. DuBois, who imagines in *The Souls of Black Folk* (1903) that European culture provides individuals with the capacity to "dwell above the veil").[15] Rather, Chesnutt sees England as a site of racial conflict in its own right, a conflict over citizenship that many Jews were able to "solve" by converting to Christianity. And while conversion was understood by many Victorian Jews (and continues to be read by many critics) as a threat to cultural identity, its premise that identity is not simply announced by blood but can be changed entirely by the force of individual belief looks like a solution to the problem of segregation, in which individual identity, imagined to be intrinsic and unalterable, keeps each individual in his proper place.

Indeed, the true secret of John's secret library—the books filled with "strange and marvelous beings"—might be its commitment, in the face of the restrictions imposed by segregation, to a radical freedom simply to move. When John escapes into the world of the library—"he penetrated with Richard the Lion-heart into Saladin's tent, with Gil Blas into the robbers' cave; he flew through the air on the magic carpet or the enchanted horse, or tied with Sinbad to the roc's leg" (108)—he discovers a world of magical mobility, not only on the part of the characters who populate it, but (as John's vicarious participation suggests) on the part of the reader as well. British conversion novels make this kind of mobility less magical by imagining it to be the product of perfectly ordinary self-transformations. These novels, then, form the subtext of *The House behind the Cedars*, which (through the very different careers of John and Rena) fantasizes its own version of willed identity and magical mobility in Jim Crow America.

Conversion in England

As Michael Ragussis points out in his invaluable study of the Jewish question in Victorian England, Scott inaugurates the peculiarly British tradition of the "conversionist novel."[16] The historical romance of *Ivanhoe*, he argues, documents both the hybrid nature of English national identity, derived from the merging of Norman and Saxon cultures and figured as a kind of natural process of cultural conversion, and the problem posed for this new identity by the exclusion of the Jews from such cultural blending—the requirement that they convert to Christianity before they can become truly English. According to Ragussis, "by depicting the persecution of the Jews, including the attempt to convert them, at a critical moment in history—the founding of the English nation—*Ivanhoe* located 'the Jewish question' at the heart of English national identity" (12). Jewish conversion is central to the construction of national identity in Victorian culture because it poses, in the starkest terms, the question of who is and who can legitimately become an English citizen. The question of conversion, in other words, depends less on a liberal model of citizenship, which requires certain civic responsibilities, than a cultural model of citizenship, which requires certain beliefs.[17] To insist that Jews convert in order to become English citizens is to assume that citizenship is not a question of political affiliation with a pluralist state but of personal rebirth into a kind of national family. *Ivanhoe*, as Ragussis suggests, illustrates the injustice of such a choice between citizenship and creed. To put the point slightly differently, the threat of conversion is that in order to be an Englishman one would have to stop being a Jew. Thus, according to Ragussis, Rebecca chooses death or exile to Spain over conversion in order "to preserve her racial identity" (112).

Certainly, the clash between the Normans and Anglo-Saxons figured in *Ivanhoe* is presented not merely as a question of culture but of race. As the opening of the novel asserts: "Four generations had not sufficed to blend the hostile Normans and the Anglo-Saxons, or to unite, by common language and mutual interests, two hostile races" (8); the marriage of Ivanhoe and

Rowena promises to link these two races figuratively if not literally. Yet, while race is central to English national identity, it is also (as the possibility of Jewish conversion makes clear) a much more fluid concept than the term would seem to imply; race is understood, at least in some instances, to be transformable because it is imagined to be subject to the will. Rebecca cannot be English, *Ivanhoe* suggests, not because she has Jewish "blood" but because she chooses to remain an outsider, a Jew. Rather than converting to Christianity at Rowena's urging, Rebecca leaves England for Spain at the end of the novel. While she insists, "I may not change the faith of my fathers like a garment unsuited to the climate in which I seek to dwell" (518), the repeated attempts to convert her (by Rowena, Bois-Guilbert, and the Grand Master at her trial for witchcraft) raise the possibility that her Jewishness might truly be a habit she can discard. Rebecca's analogy, although meant to deny the lure of conversion, actually reinforces the possibility of conversion. She does not, in other words, deny that she could if she chose transform herself into a new being: a Christian, an Englishwoman.

In the years that followed the publication of Scott's novel, a number of popular novels constructed historical "sequels" to *Ivanhoe* that, while tracking the bleak history of the Spanish Jews under the Inquisition, adhered to the belief that Jewish conversion to Christianity was not only possible, but desirable.[18] In *Leila; or The Siege of Granada* (1838), Bulwer-Lytton (from another of whose novels Chesnutt's John Walden takes the name Warwick) has his beleaguered Jewish heroine defy her father and embrace Christianity. In fact, the only question raised by Leila's captors and by her spiritual guide Donna Inez concerns the best method by which to convert her: "It was on this point [of the afterlife] that the quick eye of Donna Inez discovered [Leila's] faith was vulnerable: who would not, if belief were voluntary, believe in the world to come? Leila's curiosity and interest were aroused; she willingly listened to her new guide—she willingly inclined to conclusions pressed upon her, not with menace, but persuasion."[19] Unlike Rebecca, who sees faith more as a kind of skin that one must accept than as a kind of garment one might change, Leila's counselors see faith as, in fact, "voluntary." Throughout the novel, they remind Leila that her identity—Jew or Christian—is for her to decide. So effective are the tactics of her counselors, that Leila's conversion seems effortless; it happens as a natural and painless result of persuasion: "Leila was a Christian while she still believed herself a Jewess" (669). If this transformation from Jew to Christian looks very little like a choice—it happens even before Leila is aware of it—it is significant simply for the fact that it is imagined to be possible. Leila, born a Jew, is at the end of the novel no longer a Jew. Rather than arguing with the conclusion of *Ivanhoe*, novels like *Leila* seem to make explicit the subtext of Rebecca's refusal to convert by insisting that racial identity is indeed transformable.

As Ragussis explains, however, the culture of conversion that emerged in nineteenth-century England was not without its opponents. Institutions devoted to proselytizing work, like the London Society for Promoting Christianity amongst the Jews, were attacked both by the Anglo-Jewish community, who found the link between conversion and full citizenship unacceptable, and by those Anglo-Christians who imagined that Jews were racialized in a way that made them essentially unconvertible. By the 1870s, the racialization of Jewishness—part of the growing science of ethnology—would overshadow the ideology of conversion. The crises that grew up around Benjamin Disraeli's administration (1874–1880), for example, often focused on his tenuous position as a converted Jew. The conversion to Christianity that opened up social and political opportunities for him also provoked suspicion that Jewish conversion was merely instrumental. Not only did political opponents accuse Disraeli of "crypto-Judaism," an opportunistic conversion used to hide Jewish beliefs and Jewish practices, but more forcefully used him to represent a kind of racial essentialism that made the very idea of conversion (in good or bad faith) impossible. On this model of English citizenship, the nation is connected not so much by common beliefs as by common ancestry, and the converted Jew continues to "pollute" the nation—not through practice but through blood.

George Eliot's *Daniel Deronda* (1876), which poses similar questions about the possibility of Jewish conversion, registers the tension between the national desires to absorb and to expel the Jews. Deronda himself serves as a figure of the Jew so perfectly converted that he appears to have no memory of what the novel considers his true identity. The project of Eliot's novel is slowly to introduce him to Judaism and to his own Jewish roots, a process of "reeducation" (Ragussis's term, 274) that ends not with Deronda's merging of Jewish and English identities, but instead with his decision (much like Rebecca's) to leave England permanently. The fact that Deronda leaves England at the end of the novel in order to settle in Palestine with his new Jewish family has generally been taken as evidence of the novel's "proto-Zionism" and thus, by extension, of its "philo-Semitism." Ragussis, for one, reads

Deronda's departure very differently than Rebecca's. Rather than seeing this journey to Palestine as a kind of exile (and thus a critique of English anti-Semitism), he sees it as an assertion of Jewish identity (and thus a resistance to the pressures of assimilation): "The idea of the Jew (whether Disraeli or Deronda) working toward the liberation of his oppressed people is legitimated in *Daniel Deronda*, by the complete endorsement of the claims of Jewish identity, that is, by the endorsement of the need for a Jewish state" (289).

For Jews in Victorian England, however, this connection between the "endorsement" of Jewish identity and the desire for a separate Jewish nationality was troubling at best. Written at a moment when English Jews were deeply engaged in political battles for civil rights and social equality (a moment that predates the Zionist movement), *Daniel Deronda*'s celebration of Jewish nationalism works as a tacit critique of Jewish emancipation in England. Arguments for assimilation, voiced by Mordecai's detractors in the Philosophers Club, are raised only to be defeated. "But I am for getting rid of all our superstitions and exclusiveness," claims Gideon. "There's no reason now why we shouldn't melt gradually into the populations we live among." For Mordecai, the novel's proto-Zionist, this desire to inhabit a pluralist state, in which race is subordinate to national identity, is simply self-defeating: "What is the citizenship of him who walks among a people he has no hearty kindred and fellowship with, and has lost the sense of brotherhood with his own race?"[20] For Mordecai—and, I would argue, for the novel itself—nationhood does not create ties of "brotherhood" or "fellowship" but rather grows out of preexisting racial bonds. This sense of racial solidarity is exemplified by Deronda, who, despite the fact that he is raised an Englishman, seems never to feel quite at home in England and eagerly embraces the opportunity to settle in Palestine. As Susan Meyer points out, *Daniel Deronda* repeats Mordecai's argument against pluralism from the English perspective, using the health and prosperity of the Cohens (a counterpoint to the sickly Mordecai and exiled Deronda) to evoke the threat of Jewish emancipation: "This vulgar Cohen family is populating England with Jews, rather than refining and burning itself away into both death and a desire to leave England's shores forever."[21] In *Daniel Deronda*, the threat that Jews pose to the English nation—the threat of racial pollution—can best be solved neither by conversion nor by assimilation but by the establishment of a separate Jewish nation.

Against the example of Eliot, the power of the conversion narratives becomes even clearer. True, the premise of most of these novels is that Judaism, as an inferior religion and culture, must be supplanted by Christianity. Ragussis's point throughout *Figures of Conversion* is to highlight the troubling racism of this position. He ends the book by calling attention to what he sees as the historical connection between conversion and genocide: "It is important to recall that the ideology of Jewish conversion, whose institutionalization in the textual and cultural life of nineteenth-century England I have explored, has been viewed by historians of the Holocaust as a critical stage in the development of 'the final solution of the Jewish question' " (299). One might question whether such a connection is warranted without denying that, for many Jews, conversion was a high price to pay for access to civil, political, and economic rights. But from the perspective of a legally segregated society, the rhetoric of conversion, which at the very least holds out the possibility that individuals might gain access to those rights, looks strikingly less oppressive. Because *The House behind the Cedars* is essentially a fantasy about access—to wealth, to high culture, to political power, to middle-class respectability—it is no wonder that it draws on a model, however problematic, that enables such access.

Conversion in America

In 1905, Chesnutt gave a speech to the Boston Literary and Historical Association on the problem of "race prejudice." His speech concludes by returning to first principles: the role of skin color or "the still strongly marked difference . . . in physical characteristics" between blacks and whites in the perpetuation of racial discrimination.[22] Going well beyond his obsession with the disastrous effect of the color line on very light mulatto characters, Chesnutt makes a striking claim about the future of race prejudice: "I can look down into this audience and see how, in three or four generations, [this marked difference] has, with certain individuals and groups, almost entirely disappeared. Should it disappear entirely, race prejudice, and the race problem, would no longer exist" (231).

On one reading of this prediction, Chesnutt here makes the unsurprising claim that because race prejudice depends on physical differences, the eradication of those differences would make discrimination impossible: if everyone had the same skin color, no one would be able to recognize whom to despise. On another reading, however, Chesnutt is making a more radical claim about racial ontology: without distinctions of color, he suggests, race itself disappears. In either case, Chesnutt's goal is not tolerance, or even integration (in which different races mingle socially), but rather racial amalgamation, the literal blending of the races: "I not only believe that the admixture of the races will in time become an accomplished fact, but I believe that it will be a good thing for all concerned. It is already well forward, and events seem to be paving the way to embrace the Negro in the general process by which all the races of mankind are being fused together here into one people" (233).

Some scholars have seen this desire as evidence of the mostly white Chesnutt's own racism, his sympathy with the eugenics movement. Sally-Anne Ferguson has emphasized this aspect of Chesnutt's thinking, arguing that what Chesnutt wanted was "a wholesale racial assimilation achieved by the genetic dilution of the black race."[23] While it is true that Chesnutt—especially in "The Future American," the series of essays he wrote for the *Boston Evening Transcript* in 1900—advocated racial "fusion" and looked forward to a day when the races would be so mixed as to be indistinguishable, it isn't exactly true that this desire for racelessness stemmed from an embarrassment over blackness and a desire for whiteness. Indeed, given the predominance of the "one-drop rule" (in custom if not in law), one could argue that what Chesnutt describes in these essays is the production of an entirely black nation. But the ultimate goal, according to Chesnutt, is to make any such racial label impossible: "Why worry about what we shall be called, or what we shall call ourselves? It is enough that we are men and citizens and Americans; I think it might be well if we never called ourselves, or encouraged others to call us, anything else."[24]

Of course, the tone of this speech to the Boston Literary and Historical Association suggests that endorsing a system of race blending might have been as horrifying to his black middle-class audience as it would have been to the white racist opponents of miscegenation, integration, and civil rights. Acknowledging the power and popularity of race pride among African Americans, Chesnutt attacks not only the white but the black version of this argument: "Of what should we be proud?" he asks, referring to the "new doctrine ... of Race Integrity," according to which "we must so glory in our color that we must zealously guard it as a priceless heritage" (231–32). "Of any inherent superiority? We deny it in others, proclaiming the equality of man" (232). Because for Chesnutt this "new doctrine" is nothing but "a modern invention of the white people to perpetuate the color line," he demands to know "why and to what good end, should we wish to perpetuate this disastrous difference?" (231–32). The real problem, according to Chesnutt, is caste, the system that preemptively assigns individuals a place on the socioeconomic scale based solely on misguided assumptions about racial difference: "[Color] prejudice in the United States is more apparent than real, and is a caste prejudice which is merely accentuated by differences of race."[25] The kind of "color" prejudice that creates legal segregation is "more apparent than real" for Chesnutt because, as the *Plessy* decision demonstrates, discrimination often has little to do with any visible difference between the races. Thus, in much of his writing, Chesnutt demands that we see caste difference where others see only racial difference. Race then becomes nothing more than an excuse for retaining rights and privileges for a particular group of people; it is meant to rationalize a naked grab for power. "Once admit the right to classify people by any rule and limit or regulate their rights by that classification," he argues, "and we are on the verge of a system which will paralyze our liberty."[26] That Chesnutt thought about race in these terms might thus explain both his determination not to pass for white and his refusal to condone the sentimentalization of "race integrity" and "race loyalty."

Most of the critics of Chesnutt's fiction writing since the 1980s have ignored this aspect of his writing; they persist in seeing Chesnutt as a champion not only of black civil rights but of black culture and identity.[27] According to these critics, Chesnutt's point in representing characters who successfully cross the color line and are punished for this transgression is to deny the "naturalness" of racial categories while asserting his commitment to the black community and to black culture. William Moddelmog, for example, argues that *The House behind the Cedars* "genders blackness female to reveal post–Civil War legal history as a story of seduction and betrayal, in which yielding to the lures of whiteness (couched enticingly in terms of property rights) leads inevitably to a loss of 'home' in the form of racial identity."[28] Stephen Knadler refers to Chesnutt's "authentic voice of blackness or subversive signifying," even while suggesting that a novel like *The Marrow of Tradition* (1901) "positions its Anglo-American readers so that they would be compelled to ponder the unnaturalness of their race."[29] What is puzzling about these accounts is that not race but whiteness becomes the "unnatural" category: whiteness is "constructed," blackness is "authentic." Walter Michaels has criticized Chesnutt for exactly this commitment to "authentic blackness," arguing that *The House behind the Cedars* "suggests the seriousness of its growing hostility to miscegenation by transferring the responsibility of enforcing it to its newly blackened heroine. So if [Pauline] Hopkins's Jewel must die because her white lover was weak and hesitated before deciding to marry her, Rena must die lest *she* become weak and agree to marry Tryon."[30]

But Chesnutt's speeches (and, I argue, his novels) are absolutely opposed to race integrity and race loyalty in any form, black or white. And in fact, none of these readings of Chesnutt's work can account for his persistent advocacy of racial fusion, his desire to fight for black civil rights by attempting to overcome race itself. "Wherever the races meet," Chesnutt writes, "there will be, in a mixed race, a link to bind them into a common humanity and a greater efficiency. And in our own land, where all the races meet, will be tried first the experiment of what humanity, pure and simple, without regard to distinctions of race, can accomplish for the glory of God and the advancement of mankind. For we are all one people; we are all men and women" (234). Critics have read such sentiments as Chesnutt's way of opposing the doctrine of racial purity without dismissing a more nuanced account of racial identity, in which race is imagined in terms of culture and heritage rather than blood. But his argument here about the "disastrous" repercussions of enforcing racial differences, whether out of hatred or pride, undermines even this weaker version of racial identity. I do not mean to suggest that Chesnutt was not, in fact, committed to black civil rights, but rather that his commitment required him to deny completely the validity of racial distinctions.

To illustrate what it would mean to overcome rather than celebrate racial difference, Chesnutt, in his Boston speech, juxtaposes the realities of segregation with the myth of the melting pot:

> Every other people who come to this country seek to lose their separate identity and become Americans, with no distinguishing mark. For a generation they have their ghettoes—their residence quarters, their churches, their social clubs. In the second generation, when the differences of language and creed and culture and social custom have been modified, they still retain a sentimental interest in these things. In the third generation they are all Americans, and seldom speak of their foreign descent. They enter fully and completely, if they

are capable, and worthy, into the life of this Republic. Are we to help these white people build up walls between themselves and us, between our children and theirs? to fence in a gloomy back yard for our descendants to play in? (232)

In recounting the familiar story of immigrant acculturation for his predominantly black audience, Chesnutt highlights the contrast between the literal and figurative immobility imposed by segregation (the "walls" and "fences" that divide the world into white and black, both now and in the future) and the apparent fluidity with which immigrants move from the world of the ghetto to the "life of this Republic." Ethnicity, Chesnutt points out, makes no real difference if one is on the "white" side of the line, an anomaly that reverses the hierarchy of "alien" and "native," enabling "alien Italians, Portuguese, and Slavs of Europe" to "turn up their noses at the free-born citizens of a free country" (233). Thus, he argues in a 1928 public lecture, "there is practically but one race problem in the United States . . . the Negro Problem."[31]

If Chesnutt often used the assimilation of American immigrants as a powerful example of the irrationality of American racial discourse, he just as often proposed solutions to this racial crisis by describing the historical analogy between American blacks and European Jews. As early as 1882, in a speech in Fayetteville, North Carolina, Chesnutt suggests that Jewish success in Europe amid intense racial prejudice might work as a model for African Americans subject to similar legal and economic disadvantages: "I wish to call your attention to a peculiar people, a remarkable people. Two hundred years ago and less, the Jews were oppressed far worse than the colored people are anywhere. . . . Now they are the richest people on earth. How was it? . . . They are a steady, economical people. They work hard, after their way, and save what they make. They get money in their purse and they snap their fingers at prejudice."[32] Paradoxically, European Jews become models of success for Chesnutt because of their ability to participate fully in "the life of [their] Republic" despite social and legal barriers while maintaining a kind of cultural or even perhaps racial distinctiveness. They remain, despite their success, a "peculiar people."

In another speech given the same year, Chesnutt makes individual will rather than cultural distinctiveness the basis of Jewish success and thus uses Jews to make a rather different point about the possibility of racial amalgamation in the American scene: "Some of the greatest men of the century are those who have fought hardest for fame and fortune. Lord Beaconsfield, the late Prime Minister of England, and the great Tory leader, was a Jew—and during the last century a Jew in Europe was treated worse than a Negro in America. But he conquered the prejudice and rose to the head of the British nation. Gambetta, the leading, recently deceased statesman of France, was a Jew. Von Moltke the German Minister of War is a Jew."[33] If Chesnutt's point in this passage is clear, the strange thing about this list of exceptional Jews—who not only crossed the European version of the color line, but also managed to gain prominence and political power—is that not one of them was in fact Jewish. Both Gambetta and Von Moltke were born and remained Christians (although Gambetta was often rumored to be Jewish) and Disraeli had converted to Christianity as a child. Although we might dismiss as sloppy history Chesnutt's attempt to expose political leaders of all stripes as Jews, we might also see it as a fantasy of racial fluidity. From this perspective, individuals can convert so successfully that they are indistinguishable from the general population; no one (including those who wanted to celebrate such conversions) would be able to tell anymore who had started out as a Jew and who had not. Furthermore, Chesnutt here insists on the nonpermanence of Jewishness as a legal identity in Europe: the Christian Disraeli might forever be called a Jew, but that social custom could not stop him from taking on a new legal identity and legitimately assuming the political privileges of Christianity. And thus the subtext of Chesnutt's allusion to Disraeli (whose success depended on his conversion) is that one of the things that European Jews could do to overcome racial prejudice was stop being Jews.

The very existence of the novel of passing makes it clear that there was no such option for black Americans. Passing, after all, not only implies that one is hiding one's true identity—one pretends to be white when one is really black—it also registers the legal repercussions of blackness in America. If Jews, Chesnutt claims, suffer from social segregation, "it is a matter of their own choice or one of which the solution is in their own hands"; by contrast, American race segregation was a matter of law.[34] What British conversion novels like *Ivanhoe* and *Leila* represent for Chesnutt, then, is the promise of a willed identity—what we tend to think of as the stereotypical American promise of self-transformation. If *The House behind the Cedars* seems to follow the conventions of the tragic mulatta tale—the apparently white heroine, the star-crossed (and color-line-crossed) lovers, and a plot that ends in the heroine's suffering and death—it also reproduces the career of the Jewess in Victorian conversion novels: the seductive heroine who not only passes but is given the option of converting and intermarrying, and whose story, nevertheless, often ends in death or exile. Given that *The House behind the Cedars* was published amid a wave of Jewish American fiction about the vexed promise of assimilation, however, we might well ask why Chesnutt adopts the midcentury British novel of conversion as his model and forgoes the more contemporary American story of cultural and personal transformation.

One way of approaching this question is through the particular configuration of American racism and identity formation that existed at the turn of the century. According to John Higham, while "traditional American racism" had generally treated Jews as white, the "new racism" that emerged with the flood of central and eastern European immigrants at the end of the century lumped Jews in with the more amorphous groups of undesirable "ethnic" immigrants. Thus, Higham argues, "the new racism was intensely anti-Semitic, but not in a distinctive or exclusive sense."[35] The influx of eastern European Jews did foster a wave of increasingly severe social restrictions barring Jews from predominantly Protestant charitable organizations, social clubs, neighborhoods, and private schools.[36] But unlike African American segregation, which encompassed almost all areas of public space and which (after *Plessy*) became nationally sanctioned law, social restrictions on Jews remained a matter of custom. This is not to deny the debilitating effects of such customs, or the violence that sometimes accompanied and enforced these social divisions, but rather to suggest that for American Jews, unlike British Jews at midcentury and American blacks at the end of the century, legal "emancipation" was not the primary issue. As Arthur Hertzberg puts it, Jewish immigrants in the United States came to realize that, for the first time, "the law was not their enemy."[37]

Much of the scholarship on the Jewish experience of immigration makes clear that one result of this nonrestriction on Jews was an increasing pressure to assimilate. This desire to blend in by shedding cultural practices designed to isolate the Jewish community was seen as a threat not only to Jewish religious practice, but to Jewish identity itself. Thus Gerald Sorin describes the attempt to establish what he calls a "Jewish civil religion"—a set of secular practices designed to integrate Jews while preserving the uniqueness of Jewish identity—and Alan Silverstein describes the rise of Reform Judaism—an attempt to make the synagogue more closely resemble American Protestant churches.[38] Fittingly, when the Jewish American novel emerges at the turn of the century, it explores neither Zionism nor political emancipation in America but rather the problems posed by assimilation.[39] Indeed, the relative ease of assimilation, as Leslie Fiedler argued in one of the earliest accounts of the Jewish American novel, makes the perseverance of Jewish identity a "problem":

> It is self-evident that the Jewish-American novel in its beginnings must be a problem novel, and its essential problems must be those of identity and assimilation. The very concept of such a novel involves an attempt to blend two traditions, to contribute to the eventual grafting of whatever still lives in Judaism onto an ever-developing Americanism. One cannot, however, propose to lose himself without raising the question of what the self is which may be surrendered or kept; and the Jewish-American writer who is, of course, almost necessarily non-orthodox finds a riddle in the place where he looks for an answer. *Is* there a Jewish identity which survives the abandonment of ghetto life and ghetto beliefs, which for so long defined the Jew?[40]

The very fact that this question can be posed, regardless of the particular answers given by particular novels, reveals the perceived vulnerability of Jewish identity in the American context. If Jewish identity needs to be protected or reinvented in order to survive, the implication (nativist beliefs aside) is that Jews could in fact "melt gradually" into secular American culture.

In one strain of the Jewish American novel, intermarriage becomes the ultimate form of Americanization. While the Jew's desire to blend in by marrying "real" Americans is a familiar trope, it is crucial to note that the Jewish American novel changes considerably over the years in its evaluation of this desire. By the 1920s, according to Adam Sol, novels dealing with intermarriage—by such writers as Anzia Yezierska, Edna Ferber, Sidney Nyburg, and Ludwig Lewisohn—tended to reject "the benefits of complete assimilation" that accompanied intermarriage "in favor of continued identification with their ethnic heritage." In these later novels, in other words, although characters "experiment with cross-cultural romance," they "ultimately find that their lasting comfort and happiness depends on another member of their ethnic group who shares their memories, experiences, and challenges."[41] In an earlier generation of fiction both by and about American Jews, however, intermarriage is not a temptation that must be rejected but a rite of passage that must be celebrated.[42]

What links a number of these earlier novels of intermarriage is their shared impatience with what they see as a continued "clannishness" among American Jews. Thus in Eugene Baldwin and Maurice Eisenberg's *Doctor Cavallo* (1895), the eponymous Jewish hero lectures his religious uncle on the perils of "isolation": "What should be done by this people is to affiliate with their neighbors; to take hold of the questions of the day; to show that they are Americans, citizens of the great republic, and not caring for anything beyond."[43] It is his commitment to "affiliating" with his "neighbors" that leads, by the end of the novel, to Cavallo's marriage to his "gentle patient," the Christian Margaret. In Cavallo's estimation, although Margaret is not Jewish her "charity and benevolence" make her "a better Jew than the Jew who lives up to the dietary law, believes in the old ceremonies, hugs the old ritual, clings to the old dead husks of the superstitious ages, but is indifferent to the principles of humanity" (63). If in *Doctor Cavallo* the Christian becomes an honorary Jew, in Emma Wolf's *Other Things Being Equal* (1892), the Jewish Ruth Levice, in love with the Unitarian Dr. Kemp, proclaims herself an honorary Christian: "Ever since I have been able to judge . . . Christ has been to me the loveliest and one of the best men that ever lived." Thus, she admits, "so far as Christmas is concerned, I am a Christian also."[44] Despite Ruth's appeals, or perhaps because she puts her appeal this way, her father opposes the marriage until he falls ill during a trip to New York and undergoes an unlikely awakening. Suddenly repudiating "the old prejudices, the old superstitions, the old narrowness of faith," Mr. Levice begins to believe that "the rest of the world will be as nothing to these two who love each other" (251, 254). On his death bed, he openly rejects the "vanishing restriction" on intermarriage and asks to "bless [their] new life" (255).[45]

Henry Harland, who passed in print as a Jew under the pseudonym Sidney Luska, was famous (and controversial) for his support of just this kind of Jewish "amalgamation."[46] In *The Yoke of the Thorah* (1887), Elias Bacharach, brought up to believe that "nothing can be more intrinsically repugnant than the idea of marriage with a Christian," finds to his surprise that he has fallen in love with the aptly named Christine Redwood.[47] Elias's newfound liberalism is openly endorsed by the novel, which sees in his desire to marry Christine against his uncle's wishes a sign of enlightenment: "What had become of his Judaism? his race-pride? his superstition? Love, apparently, had swept them clean away. Not a vestige of them remained. At a touch, it seemed, love had converted Elias Bacharach from the most reactionary sort of orthodoxy, to a rationalism, the bare contemplation of which, a few days ago, would have appalled him" (83). If love can convert Elias so that "the man [gets] the better of the Jew" (83), the power of superstition (embodied in his villainous uncle) proves almost impossible to subvert. The novel can imagine nothing but misery for its Jewish hero (who is tricked into leaving Christine at the altar and then persuaded to marry a Jewish woman): after walking out on his wife, he freezes to death alone in Central Park. Harland's point, here and in a number of his Jewish novels, is not that Jews should be free to marry non-Jews, but that they must marry non-Jews: "I am glad that there is this tendency among the better educated Jews to cast loose from their Judaism," says Arthur Ripley, the hero of Harland's *Mrs. Peixada* (1886). "I want to see them intermarry with the Christians—amalgamate, and help to form the American people of the future. That of course is their destiny."[48]

Still, the endorsement of intermarriage in novels about American Jews does not, as Sol suggests, inevitably lead to conversion and an outright rejection of Jewishness. If Harland wants Jews to become Americans and thus "cast loose from their Judaism," most novels of intermarriage refuse to go so far. In *Other Things Being Equal*, Ruth Levice, although willing to celebrate Christmas with Dr. Kemp—"so far as Christmas is concerned, I am a Christian also"—receives from Kemp the same level of interest in her religious practice: "If my wife would permit me to go with her upon her holidays to your beautiful Temple, no one would listen more reverently than I. Loving her, what she finds worshipful could find nothing but respect in me" (195). And, in turn, Ruth claims, "As for my religion, I am a Jewess, and will die one" (194). Along the same lines, in *Dr. Cavallo*, the hero, in rejecting the "old ceremonies" and the "old ritual," does not, in the end, "deny [his] race and creed" but discovers in Reform Judaism a way of keeping, by compartmentalizing, his Jewishness. These novels imagine marriage as a kind of liberal state, in which the citizens of different backgrounds come together, committed at once to communal civic practice and to their own religious practice.[49]

In the British tales, by contrast, the rift between the lovers is created by precisely this difference in cultural affiliations and racial backgrounds and can therefore be resolved only when race and culture are aligned. In the British conversion novel, a non-Jew marrying a Jew is a scandal. No matter how much Rebecca loves Ivanhoe, her Jewishness makes their marriage impossible; no matter how devoted Deronda is to Mira, the assimilated Jew, he cannot marry her until he becomes a Jew himself. Conversion is central to these novels in which, as we have seen, identity comes down to the issue of choosing sides. Will Scott's Rebecca become part of the new English nation or will she remain a Jew? Is Eliot's Deronda an English gentleman or a Jew? In the American context, however, novels about Jewish identity somehow manage to maintain their commitment to racial difference even when they're endorsing assimilation. Another way of putting this point would be to say that while British conversion narratives see Jewishness and Englishness as mutually exclusive, American novels imagine that one could be a good Jew and a good American at the same time.

However progressive the Jewish American novel's openness to difference might seem, Chesnutt's various writings reveal an intense suspicion of this commitment to identity. After all, Jews in these novels stay Jews. And as we have seen, Chesnutt called for an end to racial distinctions and classifications rather than a tolerance of racial difference. Despite the arguments that critics have made about his desire to preserve a uniquely black heritage, Chesnutt's desire in much of his writing was to deracialize culture. In a 1908 speech, he argued that it is absurd to imagine that races inherit particular cultures. All individuals, in his eyes, stand in exactly the same relation to a more general cultural past: "The civilization of Europe was borrowed from Asia and Africa. Modern civilization was founded upon the ruins of ancient systems. Much of the wealth of the world was created in past generations. Our laws in large part are those of ancient Rome, and our language is largely composed of its fragments. Our religion is that of Palestine. Our art is but a feeble copy of that of ancient Greece. Why should the Negro be excluded from his inheritance[?] He is entitled to share in it upon the same terms as the rest of mankind."[50] Culture and history, in other words, are not transmitted through blood, nor are they the exclusive possession of those who have a certain kind of racial identity. In *The House behind the Cedars*, Chesnutt dramatizes his belief in the "birthright"[51] of all African Americans by imagining an escape (albeit a partial and personal one) from the American imperative to be racialized.

The Veil of Cedars

The House behind the Cedars bears a striking resemblance to Grace Aguilar's *The Vale of Cedars; or, The Martyr* (published in 1850 and frequently reprinted through the end of the century), so much so, in fact, that it would be tempting to claim that Chesnutt takes the title of his novel from Aguilar. In *The Vale of Cedars* Aguilar tells the tale of Marie, a Spanish Jew who, in order to survive in fifteenth-century Spain, passes as a Christian and lives with her family in "a small dwelling almost hidden in the trees" deep in the mountains, which serves as "a refuge and concealment from the secret power of the Inquisition."[52] Written as Aguilar's rebuke to the culture of conversion (she was Jewish herself), the novel begins with Marie revealing her true identity to Arthur, her English lover: "When the words were said, when with blanched lips and cheeks, and yet unfaltering tone, Marie revealed the secret which was to separate them forever, Arthur staggered back, relinquishing the hands he had so fondly clasped, casting on her one look in which love and aversion were strangely and fearfully blended, and then burying his face in his hands, his whole frame shook as with some sudden and irrepressible anguish" (20). Although Marie is the heroine of the novel, this scene focuses at first on Arthur's reaction to her secret—the "irrepressible anguish" that seems to leave him speechless—rather than her reaction to his sudden "aversion." While Arthur immediately overcomes his racial prejudice—"What to me is race or blood? I see but the Marie I have loved, I shall ever love"—it is Marie who insists on the "impassable barrier" that divides them: "There is a love, a duty stronger than that I bear to thee. I would resign all else, but not my father's God" (21).

In *The House behind the Cedars*, the scene in which Rena's white lover, Tryon, discovers her hidden identity, while told from Rena's perspective, nevertheless unfolds in uncannily similar terms: "When Rena's eyes fell upon the young man in the buggy, she saw a face as pale as death, with staring eyes, in which love, which once had reigned there, had now given place to astonishment and horror. She stood a moment as if turned to stone. One appealing glance she gave,—a look that might have softened adamant. When she saw that it brought no answering sign of love or sorrow or regret, the color faded from her cheek, the light from her eye, and she fell fainting to the ground" (94). In Chesnutt as in Aguilar, the revelation of the woman's racial secret is greeted with something like "astonishment and horror." And in both cases the revelation of the secret, figured as racial, is represented in the blood that drains from the heroine's face, in her changeable "color." For Chesnutt, however, there is (at least initially) no ambiguity in Tryon's reaction: love is not "blended" with "horror" but is instead replaced by it.

Aguilar, who begins by racializing Marie's Jewishness—"What to me is race or blood?"—ultimately transforms her identity into a question of creed. When Marie is publicly unmasked as a Jew, Queen Isabella rescues her from the Inquisition and (like Donna Inez in *Leila*) attempts to use persuasion rather than torture to "turn her from her abhorred faith, and so render her happy in this world, and secure her salvation in the next" (153). For Isabella, as the novel would have it, Marie does not need to be killed or exiled, only converted, in order to save Christian Spain from "the poisonous taint of Jewish blood and unbelief" (228). In the end, conversion is just as effective as death because the Jew's tainted blood is imagined to die with Jewish belief. Thus, Isabella's response to Marie's taint is to demand that it be transformed through conversion: "A Christian thou must become" (228). Marie is exiled, finally, because she refuses to give up her Jewishness; she suffers for the obstinacy of her beliefs rather than the poisonousness of her blood.

In *The Vale of Cedars*, Arthur insists both that Marie's Jewishness changes nothing essential about her—"I see but the Marie I have loved, I shall ever love"—and that she can transform herself at will. In *The House behind the Cedars*, however, the discovery of Rena's race seems, at least in Tryon's eyes, actually to transform her body. Discovering the racial secret is here akin to stripping off a mask. Having once proudly claimed that Rena "carries the stamp of her descent upon her face and in her heart" (57), Tryon now gives this image of descent "stamped" on the body a sinister new meaning: "He dreamed of her sweet smile, her soft touch, her gentle voice. In all her fair young beauty she stood before him, and then by some hellish magic she was slowly transformed into a hideous black hag. With agonized eyes he watched her beautiful tresses become mere wisps of coarse wool, wrapped round with dingy cotton strings; he saw her clear eyes grow bloodshot, her ivory teeth turn to unwholesome fangs" (98). For Tryon, Rena's white skin is an illusion that can no longer hide the "hideous black hag" within. For him, the black Rena is "worse than dead" because the "impassable barrier" between them cannot be lifted by a mere change of heart; the fact that she cannot help but carry "the blood of slaves" means that he can never see her as anything but a "hag." Accordingly, when Tryon decides in a fit of "liberality" that "he would make her white," his plan is to hide her—to move her far "beyond the old town" (140) where she is known to a place where she can again take up her old disguise.

The House behind the Cedars, however, asks the reader to think about racial identity in terms that are closer to Aguilar's. This desire to make identity submit to individual desire (rather than blood or "heritage") is made explicit in the young John Walden's attempts to prove that he is exactly what he appears to be. "You are aware of course," asks Judge Straight, "that you are a negro?" " 'I am white,' replied the lad, turning back his sleeve and holding out his arm, 'and I am free, as all my people were before me.'" "You are black," claims the judge, "and you are not free. You cannot travel without your papers; you cannot secure accommodations at an inn; you could not vote, if you were of age; you cannot be out after nine o'clock without a permit" (113). For the judge (and, by extension, most of the nation), the physical evidence of John's whiteness is overriden by the legal and cultural authority of the "one-drop rule." According to Judge Straight, John can both feel that he is white and appear to be white but still be "black as ink": "One drop of black blood makes the whole man black" (113). The judge's proposed solution to John's problem is not that he try to fight the law of North Carolina, nor even that he try to pass for white, but that he find a law that will accommodate his racial desires. This solution, surprisingly, involves moving farther south, where a shrinking white population makes the legal definition of whiteness more flexible: "As you have all the features of a white man," Judge Straight explains, "you would, at least in South Carolina, have simply to assume the place and exercise the privileges of a white man" (115). In South Carolina, according to the judge, John can be "white in the abstract, before the law" (115). The irony, as John has been arguing from the beginning, is that his whiteness is hardly "abstract": "A negro is black; I am white, and not black" (113).

Here Chesnutt explores the possibility of a racial "conversion" akin to the one that Marie contemplates (but ultimately rejects) in *The Vale of Cedars*. By drawing on the conversion narrative rather than the model of "invisible blackness" in which appearance belies one's true and unchanging racial identity, Chesnutt creates characters who "become" white and then insist that they are not pretending. According to Samira Kawash, "the problem signified by the ambivalent bodies of such passing characters as Rena and John is that legal, physical, and social identities might fail to coincide, leaving open the gaping question of where the truth of race in fact resides."[53] As *The House behind the Cedars* defines it, however, the problem with race is not the complexity that makes "visibility" an "insufficient guarantee" of racial "knowledge,"[54] but rather the more radical fact that there is no "truth of race" that one could either hide or uncover. Rather than destroying or denying his true racial identity, in other words, John understands that he and Rena have succeeded in transforming themselves: "You must take us for ourselves alone," John tells Tryon; "we are new people" (57).

Despite the explicitness of John's appeal, this desire for self-transformation has been, as we have seen, downplayed and dismissed by critics. In the best study to date of Chesnutt's career, Eric Sundquist reads his devotion not only to black civil rights but also to a coherent black culture as a commitment that overrides his desire for assimilation to a primarily white middle-class culture. Sundquist sees this commitment to a black cultural past as the central, if hidden, feature of Chesnutt's fiction:

> One could say that his exploration of class and color divisions produced in Chesnutt an uneasy adherence to a "subculture" that was part of, not separate from, the middle class; the lower class, the "folk," and the reminders of slavery itself were contained "somewhere in its consciousness," just as the folk beliefs of African origin were contained somewhere in Chesnutt's own imaginative reservoir. The tension between the two realms, and the signs of Chesnutt's honest recognition of his moral obligation to keep them united, appear throughout his fiction.[55]

Making this claim, however, requires Sundquist to weigh the early "conjure" stories, which draw on a folk tradition of storytelling in order to explore the conflicts between black and white culture, more heavily than the novels, which often explore tensions among African Americans. In both *The House behind the Cedars* and *The Marrow of Tradition*, Chesnutt denies this romanticized notion of racial identity by making class divisions within the black community signify a divide that looks more like an unbridgeable gap than a relation between "conscious" and "subconscious" cultural affiliations.

In both novels, Chesnutt focuses on a division between the black middle class and the black working class that cannot be covered over by "folk beliefs" that unite the entire community. Indeed, he makes this division tangible and seemingly unchangeable by marking class distinctions on the page as the difference between dialect and nondialect characters. Sundquist notes that by the end of *Marrow* both the more radical and the more subservient African Americans (Josh Green, Mammy Jane, and Jerry) have been "deliberately sacrificed" by Chesnutt.[56] What he does not remark on, however, is that the one thing that unites all the victims of the Wellington massacre is dialect.

This category, in fact, includes the white supremacist McBane (also killed in the massacre), whose speech is similarly marked as nonstandard: "Make has'e, charcoal," he tells Jerry, "for we're gettin' damn dry."[57] In the turn-of-the-century novel, Gavin Jones has argued, dialect becomes a kind of "black vernacular counterdiscourse capable of overturning racist conventions."[58] But in Chesnutt's novels, dialect marks the fine but seemingly "impassable barrier" between the assimilable and the unassimilable. The kind of reconciliation that Chesnutt envisions at the end of *Marrow*, for example, involves the families of the upwardly mobile, racially mixed Dr. Miller and the racist editor Major Carteret; it requires class rather than racial unity. Once Chesnutt moves from the tension between the white owner and the black storyteller, which organizes the "conjure" stories, to the tension between the black middle class and the black "folk," which drives *Marrow*, any commitment to the unity of black cultural heritage would appear to have broken down.

The House behind the Cedars is marked by the same suspicion of cross-class racial unity. Unlike Aguilar, whose hermitage "behind the cedars" is depicted as a space where Jewish identity is reinforced, Chesnutt depicts the Waldens' home as a conflicted space, marking both the vexed convergence of black and white (in the "mixed" characters who live there) and the caste system within the black community that divides dark-skinned, dialect-speaking characters like Frank Fowler from light-skinned characters like Rena and John. Indeed, the seemingly unbridgeable divisions within the African American community of Pateville began to supplant the easy division between black and white on which segregation depends. If, in Clarence, where Rena and John are white, they happily share their home with African American servants, in Pateville, where they are black, their house is closed to their dark-skinned neighbors: "The free colored people of Pateville," all of whom are "mulattoes," "were numerous enough before the war to have their own 'society,' and human enough to despise those who did not possess advantages equal to their own; and at this time they still looked down upon those who had once been held in bondage" (141). It's not surprising, then, that when Mis' Molly holds a party, almost all of the guests are "bright mulattoes," and "the only black man present occupied a chair which stood on a broad chest in one corner, and extracted melody from a fiddle" (141).

Even Frank Fowler, the devoted friend of Rena and a virtual servant of the Waldens, who is marked in the world of Pateville by his "dark brown" (25) skin and in the world of the text by dialect, is rarely allowed to cross the threshold of the Waldens' house. Instead, he is forever watching the family from across the street, waiting for Rena or Mis' Molly on their back porch or looking at them through their windows. While Frank's parents believe in equality, at least among African Americans—"since the slaves had been freed, was not one negro as good as another?"—Frank imagines with some satisfaction that Rena "had branded him her slave forever" (117). In the racial logic used by Frank's parents, the Waldens are merely masquerading, and Molly's "airs and graces," not to mention her "white face," only cover over the drop of blood that puts her, even against her will, on the black side of the color line: "After all, they argued . . . was she not a negro, even as themselves?" (116–17). Frank himself, hopelessly in love with Rena, acknowledges that "there would have been no legal barrier to their union" despite her apparent whiteness, for "the drop of dark blood bridged the chasm" (117).

To test this notion of white identity as mere masquerade, Chesnutt effectively divides in two the hero of his novel: John, who flatly denies the power of the "one-drop rule" (and thus denies, by extension, that he is passing), and Rena, who decides after Tryon's desertion that she is willing to accept it. For Chesnutt, John represents the antisentimental view of racial identity: "Once persuaded that he had certain rights, or ought to have them, by virtue of the laws of nature, in defiance of the customs of mankind, he had promptly sought to enjoy them" (53–54). Committed entirely to the future, in the shape of his son Albert, John lives out the racial philosophy embodied in so many of Chesnutt's essays and speeches—the demand that African Americans fulfill their "duty towards those who will come after" by denying the importance of color and promoting racial "fusion."[59] The fact that John, soon after Tryon discovers Rena's secret, simply disappears from Pateville, from Clarence, and indeed from the text itself, suggests that Chesnutt was willing to take his fantasy of racial conversion to its logical extreme. John's ability to leave without a trace is the result of truly magical mobility. His disappearance looks like an attempt to ignore conventional racial categories altogether by literalizing racial invisibility.

In Rena, on the other hand, Chesnutt imagines a less "practical," more sentimental sense of racial identity. He stages Rena's introduction to white society in South Carolina not as an assertion of her "natural rights," but as a literal masquerade. She has her debut at the "annual tournament of the Clarence Social Club" (31), in which participants dress up as characters from *Ivanhoe* and reenact the tournament of Ashby-de-la-Zouch. Rena, fresh from a northern finishing school, finds herself surrounded by women who, as if to mock her, are dressed up as her namesake: "There are six Rebeccas and eight Rowenas of my own acquaintance in the grand stand," claims one of the "knights," "but she throws them all into the shade" (35). (So white is Rena, it seems, that she makes the "rich, fine folks" [34] around her look black.) Despite the fact that Rena is crowned the "Queen of Love and Beauty," she imagines herself to be masquerading, not merely in representing the "fiction of queenship," but in her newly acquired social position as southern belle: "Her months in school had not eradicated a certain self-consciousness born of her secret" (40–41). One of Tryon's acquaintants later reveals, unknowingly, the essence of Rena's secret: "She should have been named Rebecca instead of Rowena" (92).[60]

This sense that Rena is in fact playing false, that race is something she can hide because, rather than a simple matter of skin color, it is (as Kawash has put it) a matter of "something deeper, something hidden in the invisible interior of the organism,"[61] is borne out by Rena's newfound racial loyalty. Once she is unmasked, Rena's reaction is to assert her connection to "her inalienable race" (130). Echoing Marie, who in *The Vale of Cedars* refuses to leave her father for Arthur, Rena claims, "I shall never marry any man, and I'll not leave my mother again. God is against it; I'll stay with my own people" (121). Her decision to devote her life to racial uplift is clearly meant to recall two very similar moments in well-known race novels of the 1890s. In Frances Harper's *Iola Leroy* (1892), the blonde, blue-eyed Iola, who discovers her black ancestry just before the Civil War, refuses to marry the white Dr. Gresham because she will not "enter [his] home under a veil of concealment": "I intend, when this conflict is over, to cast my lot with the freed people as a helper, teacher, and friend."[62] In William Dean Howells's *An Imperative Duty* (1891), Rhoda Aldgate refuses to marry the white Dr. Olney when she discovers that her mother was an "octoroon."[63] In Howells's version of the refusal scene, in which Rhoda tells Olney that she has decided to go south in order to "educate" and "elevate" her "mother's people," Olney simply dismisses her proposed self-sacrifice with "tender mockery": "All that I shall ask of you are the fifteen-sixteenths or so of you that belong to my race by heredity; and I will cheerfully consent to your giving our colored connections their one-sixteenth" (145, 143). Neither Harper nor Howells (for all of his irony) questions this account of racial identity, which imagines individuals to be the products of their divided blood. In *The House behind the*

Cedars, by contrast, the central problem is not that Tryon cannot accept Rena because she is black, but that he cannot see her for what she is. Magically reborn in Clarence, Rena has (unlike Iola and Rhoda) become a "new person," a white woman. If, by the end of the novel, Rena is punished (she dies before the reformed Tryon can reach her), this punishment should not be understood as Chesnutt's novelistic revenge for either her initial willingness or her ultimate refusal to pass. Instead, Chesnutt treats her death as a racial tragedy. Death is, after all, Rena's only chance to escape an obsessively racializing culture. In having Rena live out this racial tragedy, Chesnutt reveals the real limits of self-transformation in the era of Jim Crow.

The kind of conversion contemplated in *The House behind the Cedars* might be read as a disturbing form of self-hatred in that it seems to register a desire to be other than one is so powerful that it leads to the denial of one's past, one's family, one's "heritage." Jews in nineteeth-century England (like Aguilar) recognized the ideology of conversion as a thinly veiled form of racism. And Chesnutt himself does not overlook the high price of such self-transformations: the novel takes Rena's longing for her mother as seriously as her longing for Tryon. Yet we cannot simply dismiss the fantasy of racial conversion (more accurately described, perhaps, as a fantasy of nonracial identity) that Chesnutt examines in *The House behind the Cedars*. For in this fantasy, Chesnutt challenges the system of racial segregation not by refuting but rather by fulfilling its logic. If legalized segregation organizes the world according to color, characters like John and Rena reveal what it would mean to obey the letter of the law. Rather than passing (and thus acknowledging the truth of racialized blood) they simply become what they appear to be—and thus imply that one arbitrary marker of racial difference is as good as another. More crucially, in representing characters who can choose their own racial identity in a world ruled by racial segregation, Chesnutt acknowledges the narrowness of such a model. At the end of the novel, Rena is dead and John has disappeared, leaving behind Molly and Frank, characters who are distinguishable by color and dialect and are thus, like Rebecca at the end of *Ivanhoe*, unassimilable. Like Rebecca, they stand in the text as a rebuke to a nation that makes "whiteness" a requirement for the privileges of citizenship.

PART THREE The Public Life

CHAPTER FIVE   Addiction and the Ends of Desire

The striking thing about Miss Penelosa, the mesmerist in Sir Arthur Conan Doyle's short story "The Parasite" (1894), is not that she can make her subjects perform certain actions but that she can make them, against their will, experience certain desires. Engaged in a series of mesmeric experiments with Miss Penelosa, Professor Paul Gilroy discovers to his horror that she has made him fall in love with her: "Again, tonight, I awoke from the mesmeric trance to find my hand in hers, and to suffer that odious feeling which urges me to throw away my honour, my career, everything, for the sake of this creature who, as I can plainly see when I am away from her influence, possesses no single charm upon earth."[1] But to suggest that the problem of mesmerism is that it both enables and enforces an unaccountable desire in the victim only raises a more fundamental question about the nature of desire in "The Parasite." For the threat that Doyle illustrates in this text—that one could find oneself ("in a moment of reasonless passion" [124]) desiring something one wants not to desire—is not so much a frightening exception to the logic of desire as it is the fulfillment of that logic: as this story makes clear, one cannot decide whether or not to desire. Even before he meets Miss Penelosa, Gilroy acknowledges the fact that desire is, by definition, involuntary; confronted with the "rich, silent forces of nature" he experiences an echoing "ferment in [his] blood" that makes him, despite his position as a staid and respectable man of science, want to "dance about" in the sunshine "like a gnat" (111).

What is truly striking, then, about Miss Penelosa isn't that she can make her subjects feel desire against their will, but that she can make the ordinary mechanisms of desire seem like the terrifying effects of magic. Gilroy explains this magic as a kind of monstrous "influence," a condition he compares to being helplessly under the influence of a drug: "Perhaps," he thinks at one point, "there is a mesmeric craze as there is an opium craze, and I am a victim to it" (125). At the time that Doyle was writing, however, these two kinds of "crazes" were hardly synonymous. Mesmerism, which at midcentury had been considered a form of mind control (enabling unscrupulous practitioners to enslave their victims), had become by century's end a way of liberating the subject's true desires.[2] Taken up as a form of "mind cure," mesmerism promised to help individuals transcend what was inauthentic in themselves and discover their own "divine nature."[3] And yet, Miss Penelosa's version of mesmerism, far from bringing to light Gilroy's hidden self, makes possible a desire that can bypass the self altogether. While he begins by entertaining the possibility that his unaccountable desire stems from "something in [him], something evil, something [he] had rather not think of" (125), he discovers in the end that his love for Miss Penelosa cannot be understood as his at all: " 'If ever you heard me speak of love,' said I, 'you know very well that it was your own voice which spoke, and not mine' " (135). Rather than defining himself in terms of his desires, Gilroy here defines himself against a desire that he feels but cannot identify as his own. By imagining that Miss Penelosa replaces Gilroy's desires rather than uncovering their truth, "The Parasite" charts the emergence of a particularly modern form of desire, a desire better understood in terms of opium than in terms of mesmerism, the emergence of addiction.[4]

The Rise of Addiction

At the turn of the century, the term "addiction" actually encompassed both the desire ascribed to the victim and the desire ascribed to the drug itself. Our own notion of addiction as unbridled consumption is indebted to the first model, in which the user is imagined to suffer from an uncontrollable desire. This kind of excessive desire became known as a disease because the user was believed to be unable to act freely against his urges; the addict feels a desire so strong and has a will so weak that he is literally forced to continue using the drug: he is "a victim to it." As early as 1829, certain temperance workers were arguing that "drunkenness is itself a disease.... When the taste is formed, and the habit established, no man is his own master," and by the late nineteenth century addiction as disease had become the dominant paradigm.[5] As Virginia Berridge and Griffith Edwards have argued, by the last quarter of the nineteenth century the medical profession had successfully transformed habitual drug use into a disease "defined in terms of 'moral bankruptcy' " and "a paralyzed control over a craving for drink, or opium, or cocaine."[6] Although it is true that "moral bankruptcy" looks more like a version of sin than a version of disease, this idea worked at the time to highlight the unhealthy imbalance between the user's will and her desires. The turn of the century was, of course, an era noteworthy for constructing identities out of what were perceived to be illnesses (homosexuality is perhaps the best-known example). And it was in this context that the victim of a diseased will, the individual who is defined by her inability not to act on her own cravings for a drug, becomes known as the addict.

For most contemporary critics, this rhetoric of addiction as desire becomes especially relevant for turn-of-the-century culture because it perfectly emblematizes the workings of consumerism.[7] Just as the addict is enslaved to his endless desire for the drug, they argue, the consumer is enslaved to a system of advertising and merchandising that creates an endless desire to consume. According to Harry Gene Levine, for example, it is no accident that addiction was "discovered" and popularized as a disease at a time of unprecedented market expansion. By drawing an explicit analogy between the excesses of the addict and the everyday experience of the consumer, Levine claims that "the idea of addiction 'made sense' not only to drunkards, who came to understand themselves as individuals with overwhelming desires they could not control, but also to great numbers of middle-class people who were struggling to keep their desires in check—desires which at times seemed 'irresistible.' "[8] Mark Seltzer attempts to complicate this easy connection between consumerism and addiction by stressing the horrifying "permeability" of the addict's self: "From the turn of the century on, the living dead subject . . . is at once generalized and pathologized. And it is generalized and pathologized precisely as the subject, or quasi-subject, of addiction." But if Seltzer shifts the focus of analysis from the addict's excessive desire to his excessive drive for a kind of mindless repetition and substitution, he nevertheless concludes that the "substitution mania" that grips the addict is a kind of market relation that is "epitomized in . . . exchanges of money."[9]

Yet there was a very powerful, competing model of addiction at work at the turn of the century, one that cannot be understood in terms of the competition between the individual's desires and her will, one that in fact helped to create an identity that cannot at all be understood in terms of the subject-centered discourse of the market. Indeed, according to a common description of inebriety, alcohol, once ingested, does not evoke a monstrous desire in the drinker so much as replace the individual agent with its own monstrous agency. Benjamin Ward Richardson, speaking at the 1893 World's Temperance Conference in Chicago, compares alcohol with fire in its ability to devour the drinker: "But here is the difference. A man cannot swallow fire, and he can swallow alcohol, which latter being swallowed, he does cry out for more, until he is slowly or quickly consumed."[10] The substitution of desiring object for desiring subject is made even more explicit in Henry Cole's *Confessions of an American Opium Eater* (1895), in a passage in which the newly recovered Cole casts a critical eye on a confirmed opium user, a person who seems to him to have become merely the phantasmatic body of the drug itself: "A lean, wan face, belonging to a creature who is just arousing himself from his long drugged sleep, stares out upon us with terrible eyes. . . . This is the gaze of what is called an 'opium devil'—one who is supremely possessed by the power of the deadly narcotic on which he has leaned so long. Without opium he cannot live; though human blood runs in his veins, it is little better than poppy juice; he is no longer really a man, but a malignant essence in forming a cadaverous human shape."[11] On this account, the problem with the addict is not that he desires too much or too freely but that he stops desiring altogether. Because the user is actually replaced by the drug, addiction here is constituted not by the self that wants the drug but by the drug that wants itself.

It is this sense that one could experience addiction as a form of nondesire that underpins Jack London's understanding of his own alcoholism in *John Barleycorn; or, Alcoholic Memoirs* (1913). Indeed, London frames his memoir by insisting on the essential difference between the "microscopically unimportant excessivist, the dipsomaniac," for whom he has "no word to say," and "the other type of drinker," represented by his own story, the "normal, average man" who drinks "in the normal average way, as drinking goes."[12] The essential difference for London is the distinction between the dipsomaniac's mental absence and lapses of bodily control (he "falls frequently in the gutter") and the normal drinker's perfect control and heightened mental states; unlike the dipsomaniac, "whose brain is bitten numbly by numb maggots," the normal drinker suffers from the fact that he "knows just

Addiction and the Ends of Desire   145

where he is and what he is doing," an awareness signaling that "it is not his body but his brain that is drunken" (19). Drunkenness for the normal drinker provokes a change in perception. When drunk, the normal drinker "strips away the husks of life's healthiest illusions and gravely considers the iron collar of necessity welded about the neck of his soul" (20). This distinction between the dipsomaniac and the normal (if excessive) drinker allows London to make the remarkable claim that, although he drinks to excess, he hates alcohol: "The physical loathing for alcohol I have never got over. But I have conquered it. To this day I conquer it every time I take a drink" (35).

If it is tempting to read London's insistence that he hates and has always hated alcohol as a somewhat shameless attempt to deny his addiction, this reading misses the way in which his memoir attempts to articulate a different model of addiction. What looks from one perspective like denial, so that London can both describe his various drinking exploits and still claim that he experienced "no desire for alcohol, no chemical demand" (74), looks from a slightly different perspective like an attempt to divorce questions of habitual alcohol use from questions of desire. "What I am insisting upon all this time is this: in me was not the slightest trace of alcoholic desire, and this despite the long and severe apprenticeship I had served under John Barleycorn" (149). Despite "years and years of heavy drinking, drinking did not beget the desire. Drinking was the way of life I led, the way of the men with whom I lived" (74). In Cole's *Confessions of an American Opium Eater*, we see much the same attempt to divorce addiction from desire. The moment that reveals to the narrator his own addiction to morphine is not a moment of profound and inescapable desire but of total self-evacuation—not the absence produced by drunkenness or hallucination, but the absence provoked by a particular type of habitual action: "While lying and contemplating with a grateful heart in God's goodness for my deliverance [from addiction], and filled with that 'peace which passeth understanding,' I seemed suddenly to lose control of myself, or, rather, *an impulse unprovoked by desire* seized me, and I rose from my reclining position, and as calmly and collectedly as I have ever done anything in my life, I went deliberately to my bureau drawer, took out my 'hypo' and morphine, and baring my left arm plunged the hypodermic needle under the skin" (120; my emphasis). In *John Barleycorn*, London regularly ties a deep aversion to alcohol to scenes of repeated use. It is no wonder then that London not only personifies alcohol, but sometimes slips into the rhetoric of possession: "John Barleycorn heated his way into my brain, thawing my reticence, melting my modesty, talking through me and with me and as me, my adopted twin brother and alter ego" (44).

It is this model of addiction as substitution that Doyle takes up in "The Parasite." Like the addict whose desire has been replaced by the stronger desire of the drug for itself, Gilroy discovers that what he took to be his own love for Miss Penelosa is actually her own love acting through him: "It was your own voice which spoke, and not mine." What this discovery makes visible is the fact that this kind of substitution does not represent the horror of desire so much as it represents an escape from desire. Because what frightens Gilroy about his desires is that they create a "hideous" self—so that when he claims that his feelings for Miss Penelosa stem from "something evil in me," he in fact means some evil part of himself—this displacement of his desires turns out to be a boon rather than a curse. In other words, if Miss Penelosa's presence evokes the problem of desire, her ability to "[creep] into [his] frame as the hermit crab does into the whelk's shell" (127) effectively solves it by transferring the "hideous" responsibility from Gilroy to the mesmeric "parasite" and rewriting "something evil in me" as "something evil that has possessed me." Through the mechanism of Miss Penelosa's mesmerism, he becomes free—not free to indulge in his dangerous or forbidden desires but free not to have any desires of his own. As Gilroy admits, "There is some consolation in the thought, then, that those odious impulses for which I have blamed myself do not really come from me at all. They are all transferred from her, little as I could have guessed it at the time. I feel cleaner and lighter for the thought" (127). Thus, when Gilroy imagines that "a peculiar double consciousness possessed me," he describes not a single consciousness divided but a literal doubling: "There was the predominant alien will, which was bent upon drawing me to the side of its owner, and there was the feebler protesting personality, which I recognized as being myself" (131). Of course, this reading denies the possibility that Doyle's tale allegorizes the unconscious, representing a form of disavowal in which these alien desires turn out to be Gilroy's own hidden desires after all. In the context of the turn-of-the-century obsession with addiction, however, Doyle makes a much more radical assertion about the self: not that it can have unconscious desires (and thus a more complicated psyche) but that it can have desires that cannot be understood in terms of psychology at all.[13]

In elaborating the logic of substitution being worked out in the rhetoric of addiction, "The Parasite" transforms a social crisis into a cultural fantasy.

For, to revise my earlier formulation, addiction in this text doesn't create a new form of desire so much as it creates selves that are free of the burden of having any desires of their own. Rather than emblematizing the way that the subject is constituted in consumer culture, addiction becomes a way of exploding the subject of desire, a way of imagining modes of desire that neither require nor sustain subjectivity. If the ability to replace one's own desires is exemplified in stark terms by the addict, however, this logic of substitution is certainly not limited to the world of drug addiction. Indeed, as "The Parasite" suggests, this logic finds one of its most perfect expressions in the "possession" narrative, a genre that reached the height of its popularity during the period and that comprised a wide range of Anglo-American fiction from George du Maurier's wildly popular *Trilby* (1894) and Bram Stoker's *Dracula* (1897) to tales by Frank Norris and Pauline Hopkins. Moreover, by giving the role of the drug to a person with designs of her own—an evil mesmerist, a vampire—the possession narrative literalizes the mechanism of addiction, exploring what it would mean for an object of desire to enact the desire for itself. By representing desire as a circuit that bypasses the subject completely, the possession story creates a world in which it is possible to have a desire outside the organizing framework of the self and thus to experience a self without the burden of desire.

My point in examining this competing model of addiction is not to dispute the fact that turn-of-the-century Anglo-American culture created psychological and contractual subjects, individuals who thought of themselves as having wants and who thought of the social realm as the place where these wants could be fulfilled. Instead, I am arguing that there was, during this period, a significant discourse of desire that not only dismantled these modes of subjectivity but also enabled individuals to invent forms of identity that had nothing to do with their desires and to imagine social relations that had nothing to do with contract. In imagining individuals who could embody feelings or intentions that were not their own, the possession narrative invented a new kind of subject, one defined not by the depth of its desires but by its permeability.

In examining both British and American versions of the possession narrative, we find that the British version reveals the interest in replacing the individual's desire with an alien desire, while the American version's commitment to ancestry translates this form of self-erasure into a way of creating new social formations. In this regard, Pauline Hopkins's fantasy of racial identity in *Of One Blood; or, The Hidden Self* (1902–1903) is the most compelling example of the American possession narrative, for the novel's insistence on replacing the individual's desires with collective memory ultimately produces the modern racial subject. It is the path that leads from the British model of ghostly possession as supernatural fantasy to the American model of ghostly possession as social technology that I explore in the rest of this chapter.

Vampires in London

Like the addict, the vampire has typically been understood as a product of consumer culture. Of course, the reading of the vampire as capitalist goes back at least to Marx, and finds one of its most powerful expressions in Franco Moretti's well-known reading of *Dracula*.[14] But the real evidence of Dracula's modernity, according to a number of recent readings, is not that he represents the capitalist (or even capital), but that he represents the system of consumer culture itself. On this reading, the vampire stands in for the "cultural technologies" of desire encountered "in the department store, on the billboard, in the nickelodeon parlor, at the newsstand or the telegraph office"; he "consumes but thereby turns his victims into consumers," "directed by invisible longings and compelled by ghostly commands to absorb everything in sight."[15] Du Maurier's *Trilby*, another popular tale of "psychic vampirism," would seem to take the vampiric construction of consumerist desire one step further. For this novel about a mesmerist who creates a desire for himself in his helpless victim became a remarkably effective advertisement for itself. Indeed, the novel proved so popular when it was finally released in book form that it sparked its own "craze" in the United States—"*Trilby* mania"—which lasted until du Maurier's death in 1896.[16] One of the first modern best-sellers, *Trilby* unleashed an unprecedented wave of merchandising; fans of the novel saw productions of *Trilby* on the stage, bought ice cream and brooches in the shape of Trilby's famous foot, sang songs based on the novel, read parodies like *Thrilby* and *Drilby Re-Versed*, and participated in countless other *Trilby*-related activities. What the novel seems to make visible, then, is the truth of the vampiric metaphor found on its pages; in creating and perpetuating an insatiable desire for itself in the mass reading audience, *Trilby* enacts the vampiric construction of desiring subjectivity.

At the level of the narrative, however, *Trilby* has quite a different investment in the technologies of psychic vampirism. For it is not the job of the mesmerist/vampire Svengali to evoke Trilby's desires but rather to save her from them. Accordingly, the bohemian Trilby, an artist's model in the Latin Quarter of Paris, begins with a miraculous unconsciousness of desire, an unconsciousness that makes it possible for her to pose naked in front of an audience of men and still maintain her innocence. In the end, the party responsible for bringing her hidden desires to consciousness is the band of bourgeois artists led by Little Billee. It is only when she witnesses Little Billee's horrified reaction to seeing her in the "altogether" that Trilby begins to imagine intention where there had been none ("I never thought anything about sitting [for the figure] before") and to imagine a desire for Little Billee where there had been only a kind of unthinking affection for everyone ("in the caressing, demonstrative tenderness of her friendship she 'made the soft eyes' at all three indiscriminately").[17] Furthermore, if Little Billee and his friends rebuild Trilby on the model of the consumer, they also insist on the immutability of this desiring self; Trilby finds that she is imprisoned in a self made legible by desire. Thus every transformation she undergoes is read as "a new incarnation of Trilbyness"; every action, no matter how uncharacteristic, becomes evidence of her "irrepressible Trilbyness" (63–63). The central problem of the novel, then, is that Trilby's newfound desires at once require her to change ("to live straight for the future" [82]) and make it impossible for her to change (she is, after all, "irrepressible"). No wonder that Trilby, forced to leave Little Billee, complains that her character "can't be righted!": "Of course I could never be a lady—how could I?—though I ought to have been one, I suppose" (128).

If Trilby can only dream of becoming another person, however, it is Svengali who transforms this metaphor into reality. A practiced mesmerist, Svengali at first seems to be working squarely within the consumerist model. As the Laird warns Trilby, mesmerists can "get you into their power, and just make you do any blessed thing they please—lie, murder, steal—anything!" (50). But what gives Svengali (like Miss Penelosa) his real power over his subject is that he has no interest in "making" her do anything: he neither convinces his victim to act against her desires nor evokes her own hidden desires; rather, he makes her desires irrelevant by acting through her. To hear Trilby "sing the 'Nussbaum,' the 'Impromptu,' " was actually to hear "Svengali singing with her voice" (288). Thus the mesmerized Trilby becomes "the unconscious voice that Svengali sang with" (288). If this version of possession is at first understood to create a kind of doubling, so that "there were two

Trilbys" (287), the one who sings and the one who cannot, du Maurier's account of mesmerism ends up describing not the multiplication but the systematic erasure of Trilby: when La Svengali sang, "*our* Trilby had ceased to exist . . . *our* Trilby was fast asleep . . . in fact, *our* Trilby was *dead*" (289). Because Trilby is, initially, something akin to an empty vessel—Svengali describes her mouth as "the dome of the Pantheon; there is room in it for 'toutes les gloires de la France,' and a little to spare!" and her throat as "the middle porch of St Sulpice when the doors are open for the faithful" (48)—by the end she can literally contain other people.

Far from creating the ideal modern consumer, Svengali here initiates an opposing model of subjectivity, for insofar as the mesmerized Trilby becomes a desiring subject, she can only be understood as the subject—rather than the object—of Svengali's desire. Transformed into Svengali's "instrument" (288), Trilby is not only able to sing without actually singing but to love without actually loving: "He had but to say '*Dors!*' and she suddenly became an unconscious Trilby of marble, who could produce wonderful sounds—just the sounds he wanted, and nothing else—and think his thoughts and wish his wishes—and love him at his bidding with a strange, unreal, factitious love . . . just his own love for himself turned inside out—*à lénvers*—and reflected back on him, as from a mirror . . . *un écho, un simulacre, quoi! pas autre chose!* . . . It was not worth having!" (288). Whether or not Svengali loves Trilby, the fact that he has literally replaced her means that there can be no answering desire on her part. If their relationship is the most sexually charged in the novel, the charge is clearly autoerotic; Trilby is reduced to a "mirror," one component of the circuit of desire that begins and ends with Svengali. *Trilby* ultimately creates a fantasy world in which the subject/object relation is elided in favor of an object/object relation—the relation of an object to itself. Vampirism, then, cannot be understood to evoke the subject's own desires (or even to create a desiring subject); instead, it creates a hollow subject, a subject without desire. And thus the competition between Little Billee and Svengali over Trilby—one wins her love and loses her, the other replaces her love and keeps her—enacts in miniature the competition between the consumerist subject created by the novel as cultural artifact and the vampiric subject created by the narrative. Whereas one creates a version of market subjectivity by making the object irresistible to consumers, the other elides subjectivity altogether by making the object irresistible to itself.

At the same time, however, one might argue that Little Billee's "panic" when Trilby leaves him, far from representing the consumerist model of desire, is motivated by the Trilby-like desire to get rid of his desires. His panic grows out of his discovery that, after suffering a terrible shock, he no longer feels anything for anyone: "For some mysterious cause his power of loving had not come back with his wandering wits," a power of loving that "would never come back again—not even his love for his mother and sister, not even his love for Trilby—where all that had once been was a void, a gap, a blankness" (132). According to Eve Sedgwick, Little Billee functions here as one example of a late-nineteenth-century cultural stereotype—the "bachelor."[18] And if, according to Sedgwick, the bachelor "popularized by Thackeray," "felt no urgency about proving" he could love a woman, the bachelors that populate turn-of-the-century literature, a literature that was confronting the "ever greater visibility across class lines of a medicalized discourse of—and newly punitive assaults on—male homosexuality," find that "even that renunciatory high ground of male sexlessness had been strewn with psychic land mines" (194). The terrible feeling of "blankness" that Little Billee experiences is, in other words, the late-nineteenth-century version of male homosexual panic that is "acted out as a sometimes agonized sexual anesthesia that was damaging to both its male subjects and its female non-objects" (188).

Against such a reading stands the fact that Trilby is not exactly a "nonobject" to Little Billee. Indeed, he spends quite a bit of time in fetishistic admiration of her feet. At one point he notes, "with a curious conscious thrill that was only half-aesthetic," that their perfect form has "ennobled" her "shapeless" slippers "into everlasting classic shapeliness" (30). Thus, "reversing the usual process," Little Billee proceeds to "[idealize] from the base upward" (34). And yet this fetishistic desire for Trilby does not necessarily invalidate Sedgwick's claim about the novel's investment in homosexual panic because Trilby is meant to be, at the very least, androgynous—she has "a portentous voice of great volume, and that might almost have belonged to any sex"—and at times, unmistakably masculine—wearing "the grey overcoat of a French infantry soldier" and "a huge pair of male slippers," she, according to the narrator, "would have made a singularly handsome boy . . . and one felt instinctively that it was a real pity she wasn't a boy, she would have made such a jolly one" (12–13). In fact, given Little Billee's infatuation, it is more likely that what provokes the real sexual "panic" in the text isn't that he discovers that he feels nothing for Trilby, but that he feels too much for the boy-Trilby. His hysterical reaction when he sees her posing naked in an artist's studio—"I saw her, I tell you! The sight of her was like a blow between the eyes, and I bolted! I shall never go back to that beastly hole again!" (76)—seems to suggest that he is not, as his friends imagine, shocked by the impropriety of her action so much as he is shocked by the fact that she isn't a boy after all. Attempting to idealize "from the base upward," Little Billee suddenly discovers the ghastly truth of Trilby's anatomy—a "beastly hole." In light of such a shock, it seems more probable that his "sexual anesthesia" serves as one possible antidote to his sexual panic than that it serves as evidence of that panic. Little Billee, then, mirrors Trilby's problematic relation to desire as much as he counters it.

In *Dracula*, there is a very similar attempt to imagine the complete evacuation of the desiring subject. And yet the most interesting criticism over the past thirty years has seen this novel as an explicit fable of sexual repression, an attempt to come to terms with the desires that lurk beneath Victorian proprieties. In one famous scene, Jonathan Harker looks into his shaving glass, expecting to see Dracula standing behind him: "But there was no reflection of him in the mirror! The whole room behind me was displayed; but there was no sign of a man in it, except myself."[19] Critics have repeatedly turned to this scene, in which Dracula's reflection seems to take on the form of his victim, to argue that what the victim really fears in the monster are his own hidden desires; what the mirror reflects is not so much an absence as the presence of a "repressed" desire that "returns . . . disguised as a monster."[20] In such readings, scenes of vampires draining and sucking blood become "masked and symbolic" representations of, among other things, sexually predatory women, homosexuality, rape, group sex, forced fellatio, and incest.[21] More generally, critics claim that these "emanations of irresistible sexuality" that "break through into consciousness in fantastic and grotesque forms" perform a kind of cultural work in the late nineteenth century by creating "a fantasy world that would have provided escape from many of the sexual and psychic restraints prevalent in Victorian culture."[22]

If these readings have been set in opposition to the consumerist model (indeed Moretti, unable to reconcile the sexual reading and the economic reading, calls them "different signifieds"),[23] from the perspective of *Trilby* they look exactly the same. For, in terms of du Maurier's vampiric subject, what counts in such readings isn't the conscious or unconscious nature of the subject's desires but only that the desires are imagined to define the subject. To this way of thinking, the fact that Lucy Westenra's chaste exterior seems to hide a dangerous sexuality ("Why can't they let a girl marry three men, or as many as want her . . . ?" [76]) suggests that her emergence as a "wanton" and "voluptuous" vampire represents the monstrous truth of Lucy's self. But this kind of commitment to desire as the foundation of the self—the representation of Lucy's truth—cannot account for the radical mobility of desire in this novel, the fact that selves do not seem to produce desire so much as they come into relation with desire. Desire, in other words, comes from outside the self.[24]

Although the novel from the very beginning suggests that Lucy is not as demure as she appears to be, that she feels desires that are barely containable, Dracula's arrival does not so much liberate Lucy as herald a series of strange absences: her fall into her "old habit" (91) of sleepwalking, the beginning of her mysterious, "long spells of oblivion" (at one point she describes "the harsh sound that came from I know not where and commanded me to do I know not what" [164]). Indeed, when she finally confronts Van Helsing's army she is imagined to be dead. The most telling mark of her effective absence, however, is that the vampiric Lucy has become nothing but surface, a surface that the novel has already put in competition with any kind of interiority. As Lucy writes to Mina, "Do you ever try to read your own face? I *do*, and I can tell you it is not a bad study, and gives you more trouble than you can well fancy if you have never tried it" (71–72). Seward makes this distinction between surface and depth clear by calling the vampire "the foul Thing which had taken Lucy's shape without her soul" (256). In the terms the novel sets up, Lucy's ability to embody this "foul Thing" without becoming one herself suggests that if she is a cipher for repressed desires, these desires must have been repressed by someone else. Given the fact that Lucy has been transfused with blood from all of her suitors and the fact that blood is continually equated with desire in this text, it seems likely that her "wantonness" when she becomes a vampire does not represent her own hidden desires so much as it represents the sexual fury of this band of rejected lovers. And in fact, Lucy as vampire is more like a mirror image of her pursuers than their opponent; witnessing Lucy's "angry snarl," Seward admits that "had she then to be killed, [he] could have done it with savage delight" (253). What's interesting about Lucy, then, isn't the perverse content of the desires she figures but the hollowness that allows her to contain desires that are not her own. Like the mesmerized Trilby, Lucy in her vampiric state is not reduced to her desire but saved from it.

Dracula uses blood as a metaphor for desire precisely because of blood's mobility. Circulating from one body to another (from Lucy's suitors to Lucy, from Lucy to Dracula, from Dracula to Mina) and animating these bodies, blood marks the difference between the self and what is imagined to constitute it. Nowhere in the novel is this bloodlike mobility of desire made more explicit than in Seward's accounts of his mental patient Renfield: "My homicidal maniac is of a peculiar kind. I shall have to invent a new classification for him, and call him a zoophagous (life-eating) maniac; what he desires is to absorb as many lives as he can, and he has laid himself out to achieve it in a cumulative way" (90). Renfield defends his unusual practice of collecting, documenting, and eating the small creatures that populate his cell at the asylum (flies, spiders, even sparrows) by claiming that each one "was life, strong life, and gave life to him" (88). Yet Renfield's habit is not, as Jennifer Wicke would have it, simply "a pun on the tremors of consumption,"[25] a desire to consume for its own sake. Instead, according to Seward it follows a very curious pattern, "some scheme of his own" (87). That Renfield not only keeps meticulous records of the tiny ecosystem he has established (the flies eat the sugar, the spiders eat the flies) but is more concerned with creating the system than with eating any one individual within the system suggests that he doesn't want the flies or the spiders or the sparrows for themselves, for the "life" they offer; he wants them for their relation to one another. He swallows not the spiders but the spiders' desire for the flies, not the sparrows, but the sparrows' desire for the spiders. What is significant about Renfield, then, is that his odd eating habit is not an act of consumption so much as it is an attempt literally to *ingest* the process of consumption. More forcefully, the Renfield chapters provide a model of subjectivity in direct competition with that of the consuming subject, for in this account what one wants is not to fulfill one's desires but to replace them.

American Genealogies

American writers were just as interested as their British counterparts in writing tales of possession in order to investigate the ways in which one could experience a feeling or an impulse that seemed to originate outside the self. What they were not interested in, however, was writing vampire stories. And while this distinction might seem to be purely thematic, it actually signals a profound difference in the way that these structures of displacement were used in the American context. For when American authors from Henry James to Pauline Hopkins imagined possession, they did not imagine a self invaded by something as exotic as a vampire but rather by something much closer to home. If in British vampire stories the individual is typically replaced by a lover, in the American possession story the individual is, more often than not, imagined to be replaced by her grandfather. This insistence on the "sameness" of the possessor and the possessed (figured as the claims of ancestry) marks the crucial difference between American and British versions of the addiction allegory. When blood emerges in the British tales, it is not as a way of characterizing an individual's identity so much as it is a way of disrupting identity, a way of insisting on the difference between the individual and her desires. Thus whereas "The Parasite," *Trilby*, and *Dracula* all feature vampires who are racially "tainted"—Miss Penelosa is West Indian, Svengali is (in Taffy's words) "a filthy black Hebrew sweep" (46), and Dracula is not only eastern European but also "of criminal type" according to the classifications of "Nordau and Lombroso" (406)—their victims are unmistakably English. Or, to revise the point slightly, they are unmistakably white. The fact that Trilby seems to be as much French as she is English highlights the insignificance of actual ancestry in the British tales—what counts about Trilby is not the fact that her father was Irish (and a drunk) but that her "delicate, privet-like whiteness" (13) could never be confused with Svengali's "filthy" blackness.

These contrasts between black and white certainly can (and often have) been read in terms of England's own racial conflicts and the dynamics of empire. Stephen Arata, for example, explicitly connects English concerns with the fall of empire to the threat of racial difference depicted in Dracula's invasion of England. In his eyes, *Dracula* is an attempt to work through fears of the colonized as a potentially disruptive force, a force that works not through open hostility, but through covert forms of racial warfare. Dracula's victims "receive a new racial identity, one that marks them as literally 'Other.'" Miscegenation leads not to the mixing of races but to the biological and political annihilation of the weaker race by the stronger. Vampirism, in this account, represents "the intersection of racial strife, political upheaval, and the fall of empire."[26] But in terms of the problematics of desire I have been tracing, this contrast between black and white in the British version of the possession tale works as a purely formal difference, as a way of highlighting the noncoincidence of the self and the desire it embodies. Race is crucial here because the force of "possession" as an escape from the self depends on this rhetoric of absolute difference. It is, by contrast, the commitment to "sameness" that leads, in the American context, to the transformation of the possession narrative into a technology for producing new forms of identity. American tales of possession were interested not only in using race to evacuate subjectivity but also in creating, out of this permeable self, a form of racial identity.

One might argue that this interest in the vampire as the mirror image of his victim is not entirely absent from the British version of the possession tale.[27] Indeed, a kind of ambiguity about Gilroy's own racial identity, the repercussions of his trace of "foreign blood," surfaces repeatedly in "The Parasite." Gilroy calls attention to his "clear-cut Spanish face": his "black hair," "dark eyes," and "thin, olive face," as well as to the fact that as a boy he was "nervous, sensitive . . . a dreamer, a somnambulist, full of impressions and intuitions" (112, 130). In an age that obsessively connected "nervous" illness (especially feminine maladies like hysteria) to hereditary weakness, these qualities clearly mark Gilroy as racially suspect. Indeed, although Gilroy and Miss Penelosa could not be more different, the story begins to suggest that we should see them as mirror images. This mirroring becomes explicit when both Gilroy and Miss Penelosa threaten to "deface" the other. Gilroy promises to destroy the mesmerist, claiming that he "could have taken the crutch from her side and beaten her face in with it" (132). Miss Penelosa sees to it that he "loses face" during his public lectures at the university: "When she had once fairly mastered me, out would come the most outrageous things—silly jokes, sentiments as though I were proposing a toast, snatches of ballads, personal abuse even against some member of my class" (137–38). "The Parasite" literalizes this pun when Gilroy decides that because his own beauty has brought on the humiliation of being loved (and controlled) by Miss Penelosa, he wants nothing more than to be disfigured: "Ah, when I look in the glass and see my own dark eyes and clear-cut Spanish face, I long for a vitriol splash or a bout of the smallpox. One or the other might have saved me from this calamity" (130). These relentless images of facelessness threaten to make Gilroy and Miss Penelosa literally indistinguishable from one another.

In the American version of the possession story, however, the vampire is not merely similar to his victim—a ghostly double or horrifying mirror image. Rather, the vampire is imagined to have produced his victim. In "A

Reversion to Type," a story published in *The Wave* in 1897, Frank Norris tells a typical version of the American possession story. "Two months and a day after his forty-first birthday," a respectably employed man named Paul Schuster experiences an "unfamiliar" desire that "came upon him with the quickness of a cataclysm, like the sudden, abrupt development of latent mania."[28] Submitting to this impulse to "get drunk," to "bolt," the "respectable" Schuster is soon performing actions that are "counter to every habit, to every trait of character and every rule of conduct he has been believed to possess" (44).[29] Acting out this unfamiliar desire gives Schuster a new identity housed in a new, phantasmatic body: "At the beginning of that evening he belonged to that class whom policemen are paid to protect. When he walked out of the Cliff House he was a free-booter seven feet tall, with a chest expansion of fifty inches" (46). Yet unlike the actions of Lucy or Trilby, Schuster's actions actually reveal (as the title suggests) a continuity that runs even deeper than "character" or "habit"—the continuity of blood (44). As the narrator is quick to note, "Schuster, like all the rest of us, was not merely himself. He was his ancestors as well. In him, as in you and me, were generations—countless generations—of forefathers. Schuster had in him the characteristics of his father, the Palace Hotel barber, but also he had the unknown characteristics of his grandfather, of whom he had never heard, and his great-grandfather, likewise ignored" (45).

In taking on the phantasmatic body of his outlaw grandfather, Schuster cannot really be understood as acting because he only "[comes] to himself" (49) after robbing the superintendent of the Little Bear mine. But unlike the vampire's relation to his victim, the consciousness that possesses Schuster, that performs the robbery through him, cannot really be understood as another person's. His grandfather, although not exactly Schuster, is quite clearly imagined to be an integral part of him, both someone who helped create him and someone who is still alive in him. Thus the kind of heredity endorsed by Norris's story is only partially assimilable to the logic of substitution articulated by writers such as Stoker and du Maurier. Although it is true that in the model of heredity endorsed by Norris the victim experiences someone else's desire, the fact that this "someone else" is imagined to have produced the victim means, in "A Reversion to Type" at least, that the alien desire is not entirely alien after all. The desire, in other words, can be attributed not to the vampire that invades the self but to the grandparent who forms a part of the self.

This model of possession by an ancestor crops up in a surprising number of places. In *As It Was Written* (1885), Henry Harland tells a story of murder much like the one in "A Reversion to Type," even down to its suggestion that possession depends on a kind of racial taint. In this case, the protagonist Ernest Neuman, a Jewish musician, unknowingly acts out a revenge plot dreamed up by his father. Engaged to marry Veronika Pathzuol, a woman who turns out to be the daughter of his father's enemy, Ernest wakes up one morning with vague feelings of "anxiety and unrest," races to his fiancée's apartment and discovers to his horror that she has been brutally murdered.[30] Despite some alarming evidence against him (for instance, the fact that he has a key to her apartment), Ernest is acquitted of the murder. As in the case of Schuster, it is only after the fact, when he "comes to himself," that Ernest realizes he has killed Veronika. Years later, he discovers two things. First, that his father had left him a letter (long misplaced) in which he asks him to kill Veronika's father, Nicholas Pathzuol, the friend who had betrayed him: "The blood of Nicholas must be spilled, whether it courses in his veins or the veins of his posterity. The race of Nicholas must be exterminated, obliterated from the face of the earth" (205). Second, after being put into a kind of trance by a mesmerizing piece of music, he finds that he has written a confession. As he learns from his own confession, the night of the murder his body "began to act of its own accord! began to march briskly off in a direction exactly the opposite to that which I wished to follow!" (247). Arriving at Veronika's apartment, Ernest (like Gilroy) feels himself divided in two, the man who attempts to save his fiancée and the man who, controlled by an alien force that turns out to be the will of his own dead father, murders her: "I grabbed her wrist and led her down the hallway. If Veronika was terrified, her terror could not have equaled mine. What deed was I now bent upon committing? She followed me passively. The expression in her eyes made my soul ache within me. How I longed to speak to her and soothe her. How I longed to step between her and myself, to protect her from this maniac in whose power she was. To be obliged to stand by and see this thing enacted—imagine the agony I suffered" (250). Love and desire are, in this text, eclipsed by a power much stronger than either one—the racial possession that transforms Ernest Neuman into his own father.

Like both "A Reversion to Type" and *As It Was Written*, Jack London's *The Star Rover* (1915) centers on a man whose ancestors seem to live in and speak through him. Even as a child, Darrell Standing was aware of "other persons in [him]": "Yes, I, whose lips had never lisped the word 'king,' remembered that I had once been the son of a king. More—I remembered that once I had been a slave and the son of a slave, and worn an iron collar around my neck."[31] But unlike Norris and Harland, who are concerned with questions of biological inheritance and the claims of ancestry, London makes a point early on of disconnecting these "other persons" from Standing's actual ancestors. While Standing does offer an account of his family background—"A son of Alfred Standing fought in the War of the Revolution; a grandson in the War of 1812. There have been no wars since in which the Standings have not been represented" (13)—this story of his biological progenitors only establishes the vast difference between his family's identity and his own. Thus London attempts in *The Star Rover* to purify ancestry by divorcing it from biology. Standing, it seems, has never been born, only reborn. By marking the distinction between his own past and his family's, Standing rewrites ancestry as the series of his own past lives and heritage as the indestructible continuity of his personality: "The red wrath always has undone me in all my lives; for the red wrath is my disastrous catastrophic heritage from the time of the slimy things ere the world was prime" (11). Indeed, in one scene, Standing attempts to imitate the "experiments of Colonel de Rochas," who took his "hypnotic subjects" "backwards through time" to experience the lives of their "ancestors." Of course, these ancestors do not turn out to be the progenitors of his subjects but rather their own "previous personalities" (55). With this insistence on the absolute purity of inheritance (one inherits only from oneself) London radicalizes Norris's and Harland's conception of the family by imagining a chain of transmission in which each member of the group is literally the same person.

If British vampire stories like *Dracula* conceive possession as a radical escape from the self, and Norris's and Harland's versions of the possession tale still depend on a clear distinction between a man and his ancestors, London's attempt to make the self its own ancestor simply dissolves any possibility of self-transcendence. That Standing narrates his tale from solitary confinement in San Quentin only makes the point more emphatic: "In solitary," Standing claims, "one grows sick of oneself in his thoughts" (37). What he wants, accordingly, "was entirely to forget": "To be able to forget means sanity. Incessantly to remember means obsession, lunacy" (45). In one version of this "forgetting," Standing tries to sacrifice his conscious self to his "subconscious" through self-hypnosis. And initially at least, the experiment seems to produce the desired result, transforming the oppressive unity of the self into a "nightmarish madness, without coherence, without continuity of scene, event, or person" (51). But if the "problem" he confronts, according to Standing, "is the problem of forgetting," then the drawback of the subconscious is that it does nothing but produce memories that he cannot help but recognize as his own: "I knew afterward, when I awoke, that I, Darrell Standing, was the linking personality that connected all bizarreness and grotesqueness" (51). The absolute inescapability of the self is represented most strikingly by a game of chess. Realizing that "there could be no real contest when the same player played both sides," Standing explains, "I tried, and tried vainly, to split my personality into two personalities and to pit one against the other. But ever I remained the one player, with no planned ruse or strategy on one side that the other side did not immediately apprehend" (38).

And thus when Standing discovers a technique by which he can kill his body, he finds that even "death" cannot free him from himself. For, as his mentor Ed Morrell explains: "Once you get the dying started, it goes right along. And the funny thing is that you are all there all the time. Because your toes are dead don't make you in the least bit dead. By-and-by your legs are dead to the knees, and then to the thighs, and you are just the same as you always were. It is your body that is dropping out of the game a chunk at a time. And you are just you, the same [as] you were before you began" (71). Rather than enabling him to live out other lives, to escape from prison by escaping from himself, Standing's adventures in other times and places only extend the boundaries of the self. Awakening in medieval France, he knows that he is "not Darrell Standing" (who "was as yet unborn and would not be born for centuries") but insists nonetheless that he remains himself: "I was I, be sure of that" (85). Thus, when he finally frees himself from Darrell Standing's body (which is trapped in San Quentin) he does not visualize his prison collapsing, but expanding: "Without opening my eyes to verify, I knew that the walls of my narrow cell had receded until it was like a vast audience-chamber. And while I contemplated the matter I knew that they continued to recede. The whim struck me for a moment that if a similar expansion were taking place with the whole prison, then the outer walls of San Quentin must be far out in the Pacific Ocean on one side and on the other side must be encroaching on the Nevada desert" (81). If solitary confinement convinces Standing that he is trapped inside himself, then escape from solitary confinement makes it look as though this self is the system from which there is no escape.

In the context of the British vampire story, then, the American version of possession (in which the victim is replaced, but only by a version of himself) looks like a failed attempt to displace desire. This failure to get out of oneself seems to be the point of Henry James's unfinished novel *The Sense of the Past* (begun in 1900), in which Ralph Pendrel exchanges identities with one of his ancestors. He begins this adventure into the past by confidently claiming, "I'm not myself... I'm somebody else."[32] At first it does appear that taking on another identity might save him from his own failed relationship with Aurora Coyne by enabling him to live out his ancestor's successful courtship of Molly Midmore. What James ends up stressing, however, isn't the difference between the living man and the dead ancestor that makes this exchange worthwhile—Pendrel's desire for the "Past," his ancestor's desire for the "Future"—but the sameness that makes it possible; the ancestral portrait that sets this interaction in motion presents Pendrel with a face that "miracle of miracles, yes—confounded him as his own" (88). If the problem that James was working on at his death, then, was not how to get Pendrel back into his own identity but how to get him back to his "native temporal conditions,"[33] it is perhaps because Pendrel, in becoming his ancestor, had not completely ceased to be himself. Indeed, in this novel the ancestor is so much a part of the self that they are virtually indistinguishable. Thus when Pendrel ventures back into the past, it is not as if "he had lost himself, as he might have done in a deeper abyss, but much rather as if in respect to what he most cared for he had never found himself till now" (66). As Pendrel concedes, his ancestor is in his own right, "just exactly by the amazing chance, what I was myself—and what I am still, for that matter," so that "the strangest part of all" is that becoming his ancestor "doesn't interfere nearly as much as you might suppose" (99) with being himself. So long as becoming "somebody else" means becoming your ancestor, you are, as Pendrel discovers, "in fact not nearly so different" (99).

When possession moves from the exotic world of the vampire to the domestic realm of the family, then, it actually reproduces the subject-of-desire. In other words, if the vampire stories use blood to replace an individual's desires, the American possession tales use blood to recuperate them. In terms of Norris's project, this insistence on the sameness of the possessed self makes sense because he was setting out not to replace the self but to define it; not trying to displace desire but to explain it. To the question of how one can account for Schuster's unaccountable desires, Norris answers that he has those desires because he was born with them. But the American investment in blood as a form of possession did not necessarily lead to the continual reproduction of the desiring self. In *Of One Blood*, for example, Pauline Hopkins, unlike Norris, recognizes that the power of the possession model lies in its ability to produce a new kind of self. Thus, if Hopkins was interested in the model of possession based on blood, she wasn't concerned with the family that creates the individual but with the race that organizes individuals into the collective. Because the point of *Of One Blood* is to uncover the truth of the hero's identity, it is crucial to note that this identity is not based on the family into which the hero was born but instead resides in the race to which he belongs.

In Hopkins's novel, blood counts less because it connects individuals to their ancestors than because it makes possible a peculiar kind of collective memory. Thus Reuel Briggs, visiting Africa on an anthropological expedition, suddenly discovers that he can remember things he's never experienced: listening to the "musical language" of the people of Telassar, Reuel finds "to his own great surprise and delight" that he can speak their language "with ease." Looking out on the "hidden city," he claims, "I am surprised to find that it all seems familiar to me, as if somewhere in the past I had known just such a city as this."[34] At least initially, however, this interest in a kind of impossible familiarity appears merely to repeat Norris's sense of the power of ancestral inheritance. Revealed at the end of Hopkins's novel is the fact that the central love triangle is incestuous—Reuel, Dianthe Lusk, and Aubrey Livingston discover to their horror that they are long-lost siblings. Indeed, on one level the novel seems interested in literalizing familiarity, transforming it into the inevitable product of shared blood. Thus, the first time Reuel sees Dianthe—she is singing in a public concert—he realizes that it isn't the first time he's seen her. Having appeared to him as a vision in his solitary room, Dianthe is familiar to him before he meets her "in the flesh" (477). While Dianthe feels only a "slight, cold affection" (492) for Reuel after he befriends her, her attachment to him is based on the same kind of familiarity. Awakening from a brush with death to see Reuel for the first time, she seems already to know him: "Her eyes unclosed in a cold, indifferent stare which gradually changed to one of recognition. She looked at him—she smiled and said in a weak voice, 'Oh, it is you; I dreamed of you while I slept'" (470). On this account, the members of a family are, by definition, familiar to one another.

Unlike "A Reversion to Type," however, *Of One Blood* complicates this model of the individual as pure product of a family line by proposing that such familarity might organize something much bigger, might be the basis of a racial collective. Reuel and Aubrey are brothers, but the chapters that introduce the two men hint repeatedly that the link between them is, first and foremost, racial. Indeed, given the context of the novel (both the black middle-class audience it openly addresses and the history of race fiction it invokes), the opening chapters read like a series of in-jokes about passing. Reuel's skin is "white, but a tint suggesting olive" (444). Aubrey's "sculpted features did not inspire confidence"; in fact, they "engendered doubt" (447). Aubrey twice calls Reuel "son of Erebus," and then, mocking Reuel's obsession with his studies in mesmerism, suggests that he is known to "have a twist" (447). Reuel notices Aubrey sitting before an "ugly whitewashed wall" and then claims, "You have a greater gift of duality than I" (447). Aubrey, attempting to distance himself from Reuel's poverty, solicits the "shades of [his] fathers" (447). The lotus-lily birthmark that appears on Reuel, Aubrey, and Dianthe also marks the text's interest in moving from questions of familial to racial inheritance. At first, this birthmark merely confirms that all three are full siblings. Aunt Hannah proves to Dianthe that Aubrey is her "own blood brother" by pointing out that they share the same birthmark: "My Mira's children; by the lotus-lily on each leetle breast I claim them for de great Osiris, mighty god" (606). But in her attempt to fantasize both a better racial past and future, Hopkins transforms this birthmark into the sign of Reuel's connection to his subjects in Telassar; it becomes a racial emblem. Asked how the people would recognize their rightful king "after centuries of obscurity passed in strange lands, and amalgamation with other races," Professor Stone (the authority on African history) explains that "every descendant of the royal line bore a lotus-lily in the form of a birthmark upon his breast" (535). As the counselor Ai puts it, the lotus lily makes it possible to see the white-skinned Reuel as an African king; it is "God's mark to prove your race and descent" (555).

Whereas Reuel's relation to Dianthe—she is both his sister and his wife—underscores the power of family bonds by doubling them, this tie to Dianthe is finally (and, in the logic of the novel, inevitably) replaced by his tie to Candace, the queen of Telassar, a woman to whom he is not related but whom he also seems to remember: "She reminded him strongly of his beautiful Dianthe; in face, the resemblance was so striking that it was painful"

(568). That she appears to be the incarnation of Dianthe rather than, as Norris might have imagined, the reincarnation of her own grandmother, only emphasizes the way that in *Of One Blood* the sentimental bonds of family are systematically replaced by the mystical bonds of race. Candace herself is not so much a character as a placeholder for a character—she is the "virgin queen" who is embodied by a new woman "at intervals of fifteen years" (561). As a role filled by a series of seemingly interchangeable women, Candace becomes the perfect symbol of the racial collective. Inheritance, in other words, does not move diachronically from parents to children but rather synchronically, among the members of a group that it defines as racial.

From the perspective of race, Reuel's strange memories of places he has never been and languages he has never learned connect him to a whole racial community that comprises past and present, America and Africa. This insistence throughout the novel on blood as the creator of collective memory works against Hopkins's ostensible purpose—to demonstrate the irrelevance of blood to questions of identity and the injustice of the "one-drop rule": "Who is clear enough in vision to decide who hath black blood and who hath it not? Can any one tell? No, not one; for in His own mysterious way He has united the white race and the black race in this new continent" (607). After centuries of racial amalgamation, she argues, "no man can draw the dividing line between the two races, for they are both of one blood!" (607) In the end, however, being "of one blood" in this novel means not that individuals share a common humanity but that they belong to particular races.[35] Blood both emerges on the surface of the body (in the shape of the lotus-lily birthmark) and ultimately makes the appearance of the body inconsequential by announcing itself through memory. An outsider may not "know" that Reuel is black, but Reuel, surrounded by the evidence of racial inheritance, cannot help but know. In this novel, race—by which Hopkins means the blood ties that produce and enforce collective memory—becomes such a powerful indicator of identity that it actually assumes the burden of selfhood. According to the philosophy of Telassar, for example, the "Ego" not only "preserves its individuality" even "after the dissolution of the body," but is itself only the incarnation of the "One Supreme Being," the "great Unity" that is the racial collective (562). Thus Reuel's claim that "life is not dependent upon organic function as a principle" but "may be infused into organized bodies" (468) works not only as an account of the individual's relation to the body, but also as a more general account of identity itself. For identity in this text is collective before it can be individual; it organizes groups on the model of the self. From this standpoint, Hopkins's account of race is notable not for claiming that the self must always be understood within a system of "organized bodies," but for insisting that race be understood as one self, one "Supreme Being," one "organized body."

Several recent readings of *Of One Blood* acknowledge that Hopkins is working with notions of blood that were most often used in the racialist literature of the period. Susan Gillman argues that, by making the characteristics evoked by black blood positive, by "recovering the hidden self and history of the race, that is, both the kinship relations obscured by American slavery and an African ancestral spirit or race soul," Hopkins actually works against a racist American culture. In other words, "to make 'blood' thus speak out of school is to deconstruct an idiom by exposing the competing contexts and conflicting narratives, in which the term was regularly used."[36] Along the same lines, Thomas J. Otten claims that the "hidden racial self" that Hopkins describes enables "the self to move outside the bounds of its own consciousness and its own history," "describing [a] hidden 'power' that hearkens back to ancient Africa, and to a moment in African history centrally formative of Western culture," a power that "is here substituted for the savagery and degeneracy that many whites saw as the hidden self of the black personality."[37] And, although Cynthia Schrager notes that Hopkins embraces a "deterministic notion of racial identity by the end of the novel," she suggests that this reliance on "blood" enables Hopkins to "reestablish a network of kinship ties to family and ancestors that at least potentially may enable the formation of a Pan-African community capable of collective resistance and change."[38] Yet, while it is true that Hopkins makes African American identity into a positive force in this novel, she neither "deconstructs" the idea of blood that she shared with her racist adversaries nor imagines that she is freeing the self from its own "history" (a history she insists is racial). In order to reverse the affect of a particular racial identity, she must adhere to the same ideas of blood and racial history that produced and enforced the "one drop rule."

It is hardly accidental that Hopkins's implicit claim that blood has the power to enforce racial identity—that blood carries certain racial "markers" (like memory) that form the self prior to intentionality—also grounds the overt racism of Benjamin Rush Davenport's *Blood Will Tell: The Strange Story of a Son of Ham* (1902). In this novel, Walter Burton's "drop" of "negro blood" (one of his grandparents is black) eventually makes itself known as a kind of vampiric presence: "Sometimes there seems to come a strange, inexplicable spell over my spirit—a something that is beyond my control. A madness seems to possess my very soul. Involuntarily I say and do that, during the time that this mysterious influence holds me powerless in its grasp, that is so foreign to my natural self that I shudder and grow sick at heart at the thought of the end to which it may lead me."[39] But by the end of the novel, Davenport makes clear that it is this "mysterious influence" rather than the revulsion it provokes that reveals Burton's "natural self": "I have abandoned the useless effort to rehabilitate myself in the misfit garments of a civilization and culture for which the configuration of my mental structure, by nature, renders me unsuited. . . . My conduct, following natural inclinations, since my return to Boston, has demonstrated how little control civilization, morality, or pity have over my inherent savage nature" (250). The point of the novel, then, is to get Burton to admit to himself (and to the reader) that he "really" is, and has always been, "a negro" (301–302). The fact that *Blood Will Tell* was published in the same year that Hopkins began serializing *Of One Blood* thus indicates more than just, in Otten's words, "how prevalent the matter of African cultural origins was in writing about race at the time."[40] Rather, it reveals that both Hopkins's positive and Davenport's negative attitudes toward African American identity depended on the very same structure of possession. If Davenport's model of blood, unlike Hopkins's, does not produce something as coherent as racial memory, it nonetheless insists that racial identity is a "natural inclination," an inherited quality that counts as more truly individual than any actual experience.

Despite the fact that imagining blood as a carrier of memory is in direct opposition to the vampiric model (in which blood, figured as a kind of mobile, alien desire, replaces memory), it nevertheless ends up serving as an equally powerful displacement of desire. It is, after all, Reuel's blood ties to both Dianthe and Candace that make his desires irrelevant; one woman can easily replace the other because it does not matter, in the end, which he loves. By displacing desire with memory in this way, Hopkins produces a model of racial identity and racial experience that rivals the notion of racial double-consciousness made famous by W. E. B. DuBois in *The Souls of Black Folk* (1903): "It is a peculiar sensation, this double-consciousness, this sense of always looking at one's self through the eyes of others. . . . One ever feels his two-ness,—an American, a Negro; two souls, two thoughts, two unreconciled strivings; two warring ideals in one dark body, whose dogged strength alone keeps it from being torn asunder."[41] In DuBois's account, what marks the racialized subject is a sense of conflicted desire ("two unreconciled strivings"), the belief that race provides one self with "two souls." *Of One Blood* begins with a similar premise, with the suggestion that race constitutes the individual's "hidden self." Indeed, as the novel opens, Reuel is reading an article on the "new discoveries in psychology" called "The Unclassified Residuum" (442). (He attributes the article to Alfred Binet, known at the time for his important work on the unconscious and multiple personality; the actual quotations are taken from William James's essay "The Hidden Self," which Hopkins takes as her subtitle.) In the end, however, what distinguishes Hopkins's model from DuBois's is that the hidden self of race is, in her account, not established through the desires that divide the individual but rather through the memories that transcend him. If almost all of the characters in this novel experience a kind of double-consciousness, then, it is not because they are also their ancestors but because they are also part of the racial collective. The racial group emerges as a powerful organizing principle in Hopkins's novel precisely because it has nothing to do with what one wants or rejects; it replaces the burden of conflicted desires with the truth of memory.

Race, as Hopkins depicts it, reveals not only how possession works but, more important, what it can do; that is, that it can connect seemingly unrelated persons into a collectivity by inventing an identity that both transcends and defines them. Like addiction, which imagines a desire that originates outside the self, the racial collectivity that Hopkins imagines depends on a subject who cannot be understood in terms of what he wants. The intrinsic, involuntary nature of racial identity is then used to fuel a version of race pride. In thus casting race as a heritage that cannot help but claim the individual, Hopkins endorses the account of racial identity against which Chesnutt argued relentlessly and which *The House behind the Cedars* attempts to overcome. While Chesnutt's novel questions the power of blood ties (John initially desires Rena because he doesn't recognize her; Tryon desires her because he thinks she's white), Hopkins radically extends the reach of those ties (Reuel desires both Dianthe and Candace precisely because he does recognize them). In Hopkins's tale, characters find themselves, sometimes despite their best efforts to resist, collapsing into the racial collective that then redefines their place in a cultural hierarchy. For Chesnutt, this loss of control simply underscores the power of a segregated society to define and degrade African Americans; for Hopkins, it connects African Americans to a racial history intended to uplift them. A version of Hopkins's "law of affinity" (562) emerges in another of Henry James's "vampire tales" (which also makes use of supernatural powers, uncanny mirror images, and unpredictable desires). But for James, the political stakes are quite different. In *The Sacred Fount* (1901), as the next chapter will argue, it is not race but sexuality that claims an individual, and the mirror image that confronts and compels that individual is not the product of blood ties but rather of a formal correlative for same-sex desire. In James's account, the burden of conflicted desire cannot be replaced by memory but must be confronted through the formal traces of something like a text.

CHAPTER SIX   Homo-Formalism:
Analogy in *The Sacred Fount*

> In *The Sacred Fount* he attains form, perfect form, his form.
> EZRA POUND, *Make It New* (1934)

In *The Principles of Psychology* (1890), William James sets out to investigate the commonsense belief "that the thoughts which psychology studies do continually tend to appear as parts of personal selves." The primary question about experience, according to James, is why it seems "as if the elementary psychic fact were not *thought* or *this thought* or *that thought*, but *my thought*, every thought being *owned*."[1] In putting the question this way, James takes issue with Hume's empiricist critique of identity, his conclusion that persons "are nothing but a bundle or collection of different perceptions," and thus "whatever natural propension we may have to imagine that simplicity and identity" of the self, "there is properly no simplicity in it at one time, nor identity in different" (351–52). James's argument in the *Principles* is that this critique of the unified self ignores the most crucial evidence in its favor: what Hume identifies as our "natural propension" to imagine that we are so unified. For James, the fact that individuals continue to experience themselves as selves, despite all evidence to the contrary, suggests that this feeling of self must be more than a mere mistake. What holds the self together in his analysis is, in the end, a "feeling" of "warmth and intimacy" (331) with one's past thoughts, a recognition that they all belong to the same self. "And thus it is, finally," he claims, "that Peter, awakening in the same bed with Paul, and recalling what both had in mind before they went to sleep, reidentifies and appropriates the 'warm' ideas as his, and is never tempted to confuse them with those cold and pale-appearing ones which he ascribes to Paul" (334).

What is striking, I think, about this moment in the *Principles* is that the model for the routine way in which the self is constituted as a self in everyday life is an image of two men waking up in bed together. In calling attention to the strangeness of this image, however, I do not mean to suggest that the *Principles* is somehow "really" about homosexuality. In fact, it is precisely the asexual and unerotic nature of this image of Peter and Paul waking up together that interests me. One might argue that James relies on such an image here because the issue he is addressing is the issue of sameness, the way in which individuals inevitably recognize the sameness of their past and present selves. Given that (with their alliterative names) Peter and Paul are meant to work as mirror images of one another, James is asking how it is that Peter, on awakening next to Paul, has no problem recognizing that he is himself and not Paul. His answer is that while we make judgments of similarity all the time, some things are more the same than others. No matter how "warm and intimate" are Peter's feelings for Paul, no matter how like himself Paul seems to be, he could never, according to James, confuse those feelings with the even warmer ones he has for himself: "As well might he confound Paul's body, which he only sees, with his own body, which he sees but also feels" (334). I call attention here at the outset to James's use of this image of gender symmetry, his notion that the relation between two men could be used to illustrate the problem of self-relation, because it begins to suggest the way in which same-sex relations might be seen as a formal device, a heuristic used to produce or discover knowledge rather than a form of sexual knowledge that needs to be concealed.

Close to the end of Henry James's *The Sacred Fount* (1901) there is a scene that is in many ways the inverse of the one imagined in the *Principles*: two men confronting each other at a late-night meeting begin to wonder where each one ends and the other begins. The unnamed narrator, questioning his friend and coconspirator Ford Obert, suggests that his interlocutor has become a version of himself: "I said to myself that since *your* interest hadn't then wholly dropped, why, even at the worst, should mine? Yours *was* mine, wasn't it? For a little, this morning. Or was it mine that was yours?"[2] What is significant about this moment is not only its chiastic structure (which highlights the fact that the "me" and "you" are grammatically interchangeable) but the suggestion that these opposing terms have become so indistinguishable that the very structure of comparison, used consistently throughout the novel, seems on the verge of breaking down. It is fitting then that the narrator not only observes a striking similarity but phrases this observation as a question—is it "yours" or is it "mine," is it "me" or is it "you"?—as if the difference that would allow these terms to be opposed might simply have dissolved. Thus the narrator of *The Sacred Fount*, unlike William James's Peter or Paul, looks at his double and establishes the existence of "self" by seeing not difference, but sameness. For William James, the scene of self-recognition is imagined as the result of awakening—Peter, waking up with Paul, simply "reidentifies and appropriates" his own thoughts; for Henry James, the scene of self-recognition is imagined as itself a kind of awakening: "What," the narrator seems continually to be asking himself, "was the matter with *me*?" (75).

If this scene makes explicit the desire that the *Principles* simply ignores (an issue to which I will return), it raises the possibility that homosexuality might be put in the service of a very similar question about the mechanism of individual identity. To suggest that homosexuality might be used as a formal device rather than as the sexual secret that must be covered over or abstracted contradicts a great deal of the best recent criticism on the late works of James.[3] According to Eve Sedgwick's brilliant reading of "The Beast in the Jungle" (1903), for example, the famous silences and indirections of the tale register the "liminal presence" of "an embodied male-homosexual thematics," which is expressed as a thematics of "absence . . . specifically the absence of speech." In light of these telling "absences," Sedgwick argues two things about "The Beast in the Jungle" that also apply to James's late fiction more generally: one, that insofar as the "secret" produced by the text "has *a* content, that content is homosexual"; and two, that the secret really has no content at all—its content is itself a "lack," the "absence of a prescribed heterosexual desire."[4] More recent studies of James and sexuality complicate, but do not essentially challenge, Sedgwick's paradigm. Hugh Stevens, for example, while finding that no "consistent equation between secrecy and homosexuality can be made," nonetheless reads sexuality in the late work of James through the contest between the "official" text and the "unofficial subtext of desire," claiming further that "repression—a refusal to name the sexual—can operate as a productive value in James, creating pleasure, humour, generating narrative itself."[5]

One of the noteworthy features of *The Sacred Fount*, however, is that it does not refuse to name the sexual.[6] Indeed, the entire novel turns on the narrator's ability to trace from public signs the sexual liaisons of his fellow party guests, an investigation that leads him, in a surprising turn of events, back to himself. In *The Sacred Fount*, sex has visible effects in the world, so that, as the narrator puts it, "a great pressure of soul to soul" can make people grow noticeably older or younger or become uncharacteristically "clever" or "stupid" (23). What the narrator discovers early on is the intriguing fact that these effects form a pattern and that this pattern is traceable: "I was just conscious, vaguely, of being on the track of a law, a law that would fit, that would strike me as governing the delicate phenomena—delicate though so marked—that my imagination found itself playing with" (30). The law, it turns out, is the law of analogy. And what makes analogy so powerful a tool for the narrator and for Obert is that without "the detective and the keyhole" (57) it brings the unknown into visibility; it is a formal structure that not only organizes knowledge but enables the discovery of new knowledge. "Resting on psychologic signs alone," explains Obert, their spying becomes "the high application of intelligence" rather than the "ignoble" attempt "to nose about for a relation that a lady has her reasons for keeping secret" (57). And it is Obert who, in noting the connections between the transformed May Server and the transformed Grace Brissenden, names the "law" of sexual love that the narrator imagines he has discovered: "You've given me an analogy," says Obert, "and I declare I find it dazzling. I don't see the end of what may be done with it" (56). What this analogy allows Obert and the narrator to do, finally, is to discover the sexual intrigues of their fellow party guests: Mrs. Brissenden, vampirelike, seems to be draining her husband Guy of his youth just as Gilbert Long seems to be draining his mysterious lover of her intellect. In fact, the entire novel is structured around the narrator's attempt to discover Gilbert's lover by discovering the missing term of the analogy: if Mrs. Briss (as the narrator calls her) has acquired her newfound youth at the expense of her husband, from whom has Gilbert Long acquired his newfound wit? That the ravaged May is analogous not only to Mrs. Briss (in her startling transformation) but even more distinctly to Mr. Briss (in that this transformation looks like a kind of depletion) "gives" her to the vampire hunters as the final term in their equation: she is Gilbert Long's victim and the source of his newfound intelligence.

Generally speaking, it has been the question of interpretation (rather than sexuality) raised by the narrator in his musings on analogy that has dominated the criticism. Given *The Sacred Fount*'s obsession with art and "ambiguity," it should come as no surprise that it was particularly fashionable during the heyday of the New Criticism.[7] What is surprising, however, is that with the rise of sexuality studies the novel seems to have fallen out of favor. Despite the fact that the narrator thinks and talks about virtually nothing but sex, not one of the recent books on James and sexuality has addressed *The Sacred Fount*. Even (or especially) critics who have addressed the issue of homosexuality have ignored the novel, despite the fact that one could easily read it as a direct response to the revelations of the Wilde trials. To the narrator, after all, the interest of sexuality is not only that it must be revealed, but that it is, in itself, revealing. As a number of critics have pointed out, one profound historical effect of the Wilde trials was to help crystallize the image of homosexuality as a relatively stable (if, at the turn of the century, shocking or disruptive) form of identity.[8] The trials fostered the idea that sexuality could be registered not merely in acts but in identities. In *The Sacred Fount*, this relatively new linkage between homosexuality and identity is not merely a source of shame but of insight; far from hiding homosexuality, the novel depends on the formal specificity of what we would now call gay desire to illuminate more abstract issues of both personal and textual identity. In the wake of the Wilde trials, I will argue, James uses the logic of same-sex desire to represent the logic of identity in general.

Different from Herself

In *The Sacred Fount*, the country estate where the narrator has gone to spend the weekend turns out to be haunted by vampires. But James, in a slight variation on the conventions of the vampire story, does not make sexuality a tool of the vampire but rather makes vampirism a product of sexuality. The older Grace, in love with her husband, seems to incorporate him into herself, to glow with "poor Briss's" own youth; Guy Brissenden, in love with his wife, seems to have been drained by her (52). According to the narrator, the couple is "a fair, though a gross, illustration of what almost always occurred when twenty and forty, when thirty and sixty, mated or mingled, lived together in intimacy. Intimacy of course had to be postulated. Then either the high number or the low always got the upper hand. . . . 'One of the pair,' I said, 'has to pay for the other. What ensues is a miracle, and miracles are expensive'" (34). Because Grace Brissenden "*has*, by some extraordinary feat of legerdemain, extracted" from Briss "her extra allowance of time and bloom" (34), she has in some sense "become" her husband. Such a "law" of sexual love suggests that two persons do not, through love, become one, but that one person, in loving another, might become two; love enables Mrs. Briss to be both as young as her husband and "as old, as one might say, as herself" (136).

It is the power of sexual love to make people "different," according to the narrator, that might explain May Server's strange transformation, the fact that she seems to have multiplied herself, to be literally "all over the place" (63). Ford Obert's phrasing of the problem with May (as opposed to the problem with Mrs. Briss) suggests that with her an even more radical change has taken place: May Server is, on his reading, not only different from how she used to be, "from what she was when she sat to [him]" for her portrait, but different from how she is; she has become "different from herself" (55). Standing before the painting of the Man with the Mask, May is the only one who cannot see the resemblance between what she calls the "Mask of Death" and the person she has become: "That grinning mask?" she asks. "What lovely lady?" (51). It is in relation to these two paintings (the intentional and the unintentional portraits of her) that May begins to be understood not as one changed person but as two different persons. Posed in front of the Man with the Mask, the two May Servers seem to stand staring at each other, the "awful grimace" of the mask mirroring the "terrible little fixed smile" (109) of the woman, the mask, "blooming and beautiful," mirroring the woman who "might have been herself—all Greuze tints, all pale pinks and blues and pearly whites and candid eyes—an old dead pastel under glass" (63). She is, as Ford Obert points out to the narrator, "absolutely not the same person I painted. It's exactly like Mrs. Brissenden's having been for you yesterday not the same person you had last seen bearing her name" (57). In Wilde's *Picture of Dorian Gray*, the portrait stands as a marker of true individuality, so that Dorian's perversions leave traces not on his body (as they do for the characters in *The Sacred Fount*) but on the canvas. And yet, if *The Sacred Fount* presents the portrait in a much more conventional relation to its subject (so that the portrait captures a moment in time while the individual continues to change), it nonetheless proposes that the truth about individuality resides in the portrait rather than the person. May Server, it bears repeating, is not simply imagined to be "different" from Obert's portrait of her, she is imagined to be "different from herself," as if the changed May has somehow betrayed her own representation.[9]

When Edward Bellamy took up this same issue in a series of novelistic thought experiments in the 1880s he claimed that such transformations, rather than posing a problem for self-identity, in fact established the law of self-identity. In *Miss Ludington's Sister* (1884), Bellamy transforms Hume's notion of the self's inherent multiplicity into the idea that one necessarily becomes, at every moment, a "new being."[10] As Paul De Riemer informs his Aunt Ida Ludington, it makes no sense to imagine that a young man, "strong-winged and ardent," is in fact the same person, possessing the same "soul," as the "withered" old man he will one day become. This belief, that in "such utter diversity—physical, mental, moral—between infancy and manhood, youth and age" one could locate "a certain essence common to them all, and persisting unchanged through them all," makes the soul itself, according to Paul, only "a colorless abstraction" (30–31). Instead, Paul insists that one is at every stage in one's life an entirely new person with an entirely new soul. Thus persons are related to themselves (past and future) as the members of a family are related to one another: "The individual is no more the unit of humanity than is the tribe or family; but like them, is a collective noun, and stands for a number of distinct persons, related to one another in a particular way, and having certain features of resemblance" (26). While in the logic of Paul's theory, multiplicity replaces the individual with the family, in Miss Ludington's own account multiplicity itself produces an inviolable form of identity. Her belief that the individual has "no responsibility for her past self" but can become at every moment "a new being" (253) enables her to assert the absolute integrity of each of her past identities. She explains this idea to Ida Slater, whom she takes to be her earlier self reborn:

> "I suppose," said Miss Ludington, "everyone, in looking back upon their past selves, sees some whom they condemn, and perhaps, despise, and others whom they admire and sympathize with. . . . Those I don't like are some whom I remember to have lacked softness of heart, to have been sour and ungenerous; those for instance," indicating certain pictures. "But it is hardly fair," she added, laughing, "for us two to get together and abuse the rest of the family, who, no doubt, if they were present, would have something to say for themselves, and some criticisms to offer on us; that is, on me. None of them would criticize you. You were the darling and the pride of us all." (149).

Each of her past selves, captured in her old photographs, has her own unique personality; each has "something to say" for herself, each one "represented a person possessing a peculiar identity and certain incommunicable qualities—a person a little different from any one of those who came before or after her and from every other person who ever lived on earth" (145). Because Miss Ludington is herself no longer the youthful and beautiful Ida, she can transform this self into a "sister," preserve her unchanged and unchangeable, make her immortal. The theory of multiplicity that she and Paul share is, ultimately, an elaborate attempt to salvage identity by divorcing it from the idea of a changeable self.

In *Dr. Heidenhoff's Process* (1880), Bellamy takes the splitting of the self and the absolute difference of an individual's various identities to its logical conclusion. The novel creates both a situation in which the pain of remaining the same self becomes unbearable (the aptly named Madeline Brand is seduced and abandoned) and a phantasmatic solution to this terrible sense of the self's persistence. Madeline discovers an experimental procedure invented by a Dr. Heidenhoff that promises to surgically remove bad memories and thus to alleviate the pain of remorse. According to the doctor, if individuals are continually becoming new beings, then a later identity cannot be held accountable for the good or evil acts of an earlier identity: "I say that there is no such thing as moral responsibility for past acts, no such thing as real justice in punishing them, for the reason that human beings are not stationary existences, but changing, growing, incessantly progressive organisms, which in no two moments are the same."[11] For Heidenhoff there is no real justice, for its "only possible mode of proceeding is to punish in present time for what is done in past time," and therefore it "must always punish a person more or less similar to, but never identical with, the one who committed the offense" (121). Memory, in this schema, only enforces the same mistaken connection between past and present selves, producing both undeserved pride for past achievements and unwarranted guilt for past indiscretions. The surgical procedure, according to the doctor, is meant to correct this mistake "for those who can not attain to my philosophy" (125). And if, in the end, the doctor and his process turn out to be a dream (just as Ida Slater turns out to be an imposter rather than the reincarnation of Miss Ludington), the idea that persons are essentially multiple and thus have limited responsibility for their actions nonetheless gets the last word.

By the end of the century, this belief in the multiplicity of persons already had a certain amount of scientific support. Not only was there a growing interest in the "subconscious" among such psychologists as Boris Sidis,

F. W. H. Myers, and William James, but their investigations into the essential fragmentation of the mind made possible the invention of multiple personality disorder late in the century.[12] Thus for Morton Prince, a student of William James who became one of the leading authorities in the field of such disorders, the division of the mind into conscious and unconscious parts could produce, in certain "hysterical" individuals, a complete fragmentation of the personality. In Prince's *The Dissociation of a Personality* (1905), his famous account of the case of Miss Christine Beauchamp,[13] he reveals the strange consequences of James's theory that individuals can always and inevitably identify their own thoughts (based on their "warmth") from one moment to the next.

Soon after Prince begins hypnotizing Miss Beauchamp, to treat her for a range of hysterical symptoms, he discovers during one session that he is speaking to someone entirely different—a childlike, rebellious person (unlike his reticent patient) who calls herself Sally. Before long, he finds that he is dealing with three separate personalities or three different "Miss Beauchamps," whom he designates BI (the original patient, Christine), BIII (Sally), and BIV (dubbed the "Idiot" by Sally); BII refers to the original Miss Beauchamp when hypnotized. What makes Prince's book more interesting than the average psychology treatise, however, and what eased the transition from scientific discourse to the popular stage play that was based on it, is that Prince describes in some detail an amazing series of battles between these selves, incompatible persons who are quite literally stuck with one another. Here, for example, Prince describes a typical episode in which Sally tortures Christine: "Miss Beauchamp has a nervous antipathy to spiders, snakes, and toads; she abhors them to a degree that contact with them throws her into a condition of terror. One day she found in her room a small box neatly tied up, as if it were a present for herself. On opening it, six spiders ran out. 'She screamed,' said Sally, 'when she opened the box, and they ran out all over the room.' It turned out that Sally had gone out into the country and gathered these spiders as a treat for Miss Beauchamp. On other occasions, there is reason to believe that Sally provided snakes" (161). Miss Ludington can experience her "other selves," even those she doesn't like, as a harmonious family precisely because none of them (except her "darling" sister) are "present." Miss Beauchamp's selves, on the other hand, exist not serially but simultaneously, and are thus in a constant struggle for control of her body.

For someone like William James, who makes knowledge of thought the criterion of selfhood, there would be no way to determine which of these personalities is (as Prince puts it) the "Real Miss Beauchamp" (232): each one would have, by virtue of her unique relation to her own thoughts, an equal claim to selfhood and an equal right to exist. Indeed, what Miss Beauchamp's case seems to demonstrate is that this ability to "claim" one's thoughts can actually produce in one body many different selves, each of whom insists that she knows her own mind, thinks her own thoughts, and is therefore by this criterion a separate and independent person. It is not surprising, then, that Sally articulates a version of James's theory in her own defense when Prince challenges her use of the third person to refer to Miss Beauchamp:

> "Why are you not 'She'?"
> "Because 'She' does not know the same things that I do."
> "But you both have the same arms and legs, haven't you?"
> "Yes, but arms and legs do not make us the same." (27)

What is most significant about Sally's defense of self is not merely that she and the others think different thoughts (because it isn't difficult to imagine that one person might think, from one moment to the next, many different and unrelated things) but that they do not know the "same things" (because it is difficult to imagine one person not knowing from one moment to the next what she is thinking).

Prince's lengthy analysis of the problem of Miss Beauchamp's other personalities thus returns to the question that James ponders in *The Principles of Psychology*: namely, what holds the self together? In trying to integrate Miss Beauchamp's various personalities, Prince assumes that she has only one "real" self, "the real, original or normal self, the self that was born," "the self that she was intended by nature to be" (1). Indeed, his insistence that he can find a way to cure "poor Miss Beauchamp" (240) implies that multiple personality is a disease—a disorder of one mind rather than the "inconvenient" (2) arrangement of three. Because he cannot rely on her body or her thoughts to determine the boundaries of this one true self, he must finally rely on the kind of spiritualist explanation that James rejects. Self, in other words, is not phenomenal but transcendent; it is not derived from thought but makes thought possible. Accordingly, the barrier between Miss Beauchamp's various personalities do not strike Prince as proof of their autonomy but of their unreality. When he suspects that BIV is Miss Beauchamp's "real and original self" (245), he insists that each of the other three, despite her apparent individuality, "is not, properly speaking, a real person, but a dissociated personality, a quasi-somnambulist" (245). As such, each "must be made to disappear, to go back into the unknown whence she came" (245). If the dissociation of mental states produces "real characters," each of which "is as individual as any one of us" (244), the cure for dissociation requires that these characters be recognized for what they are—the mere fragments of a transcendent self. To imagine that the self is always dying is, according to Bellamy, to imagine immortality. The death of one's youth is in one sense as absolute as the death of the body in old age and in another it is simply meaningless: one dies only in order to become a "new being." But according to Prince, what seems to be the "psychical murder" (248) of BI and BIV marks instead the birth of the "Real Miss Beauchamp," the only legitimate heir to all of their experiences.

It is for this reason that making the self whole again does not involve awakening memories (because Sally, for instance, has no trouble remembering the minute details of Miss Beauchamp's childhood) but awakening the one self who already claims all of these memories as her own. Although Prince, when he finds that two of Miss Beauchamp's personalities (BI and BIV) become the same when hypnotized (BII), declares that this discovery "pointed to a way to synthesize all the memories of Miss Beauchamp . . . and to combine them in one person" (274), he makes clear that this synthesis is not something that he makes but something for which he must search. Thus, "according to the new hypothesis BII, hitherto, like Cinderella neglected and passed by, might be the very self for whom we had been hunting" (274). And BII, quite apart from the stability of her character and the fact that her existence forces the troublesome Sally "back to where she came from" (524), finally proves herself to be "the Real Miss Beauchamp" through her recognition of both BI and BIV as equally herself:

> "Who are you?" I asked.
> "I am myself."
> "Where is BI?"
> "I am BI."
> "Where is BIV?"
> "I am BIV. We are all the same person, only *now I am myself*." (520)

Following the logic of Prince's study, a more accurate statement would have been, "Now I *know* I am myself." Because the self, by this account, is the entity that transcends consciousness and makes consciousness possible, it cannot be reconstructed but only recovered—recognized as having somehow always been there. If multiple personality is marked by the limits of introspection, then, "normal" selfhood is marked by absolute self-transparency.

Ruth Leys has written the most comprehensive and insightful essay on Prince's treatment of Miss Beauchamp, in which she places Prince's work in a genealogy of psychoanalytic thought that culminates in the "revival" of the diagnosis of multiple personality disorder in the 1980s. For Leys, Prince's work exemplifies (and, in fact, inaugurates) a crucial mistake in the psychoanalytic account of trauma and its relation to the subject. The mistake, as she sees it, is to imagine that trauma "shatters" a preexisting subject rather than helping to create that subject. What Prince disavows in *The Dissociation of a Personality*, by insisting that Miss Beauchamp's original or normal self has been shattered by a traumatic event, is the extent to which her subjectivity (indeed all subjectivity) is essentially mimetic. In other words, the desiring subject does not in fact precede identification with another but instead grows out of such an identification; "The hypnotic rapport," according to Leys, "precisely exemplifies the workings of this 'primordial,' unconscious identification."[14] For Prince, to acknowledge the role of mimesis in subject formation would be to acknowledge that he had some role in creating Miss Beauchamp's various personalities (especially Sally, whom Leys reads as strongly "gendered male" [193]), that they were in fact products of his suggestions. Running this critique of nonmimetic identity through Freud, Leys claims that "what Freud finds uncanny or scandalous about hypnosis-suggestion, and what therefore he struggles to suppress, is the idea that in suggestion my thoughts do not come from my own mind or self but are produced by the 'imitation' or suggestion of another—the hypnotist or, in psychoanalytic practice, the analyst. Freud's theory of the unconscious is thus an attempt to solve the problem of the hypnotic rapport by *transforming suggestion into desire*" (172–73). The thoughts suggested to the subject by the therapist, in other words, are read as the subject's own, the symptoms of desire.

In *The Sacred Fount*, May Server is, like Miss Beauchamp, essentially multiple—she is "all over the place." Indeed, in light of the Miss Beauchamp case, we might read Gilbert Long, who seems to have stolen May's wit, as merely a new version of May, an alternate personality. And, following Leys's account of the Miss Beauchamp case, we might be struck by the moment in *The Sacred Fount* in which the narrator, unable to get May to speak for herself, begins to speak for her: "What could only, therefore, in this connection, strike me as indicated was fairly to put into her mouth—if one might do so without showing too ungracefully as alarmed—the words one might have guessed her to wish to use were she able to use any" (110). For Leys, the central question raised by Prince's treatment of Miss Beauchamp (and, by extension, the narrator's confession that he can speak for his fellows) is how we come to have our own thoughts. Could it be, Leys asks, that the thoughts we take to be primary, products of a transcendentally unified self, actually come from outside, products of an identification with another so strong that self cannot be distinguished from other? In *The Sacred Fount*, however, the central question for James is not how we come to have our thoughts but how we come to know them. If Leys suggests that the self is constructed only out of a mimetic relation to another, James suggests that the self comes to know itself only in analogous relation to others. Indeed, the obsession with analogy in *The Sacred Fount* might be read as an obsession with a formal structure that makes other people central to the construction of self-knowledge. What is striking about *The Sacred Fount* in this regard is that its attempt to undermine direct self-knowledge (the novel's epistemological foundation) in no way undermines the tyrannical unity of the self one comes to know (the novel's ontological foundation).

For example, while May Server's "difference from herself" initially marks her as tragic, it is, strangely enough, the fact that she cannot maintain this difference that finally constitutes her tragedy. The "horror" of her situation is not that she has been "abased" by her clandestine affair and subsequent dissipation but that "her abasement could be conscious" (101). As the narrator explains, the problem with May is that "her consciousness survived—survived with a force that made it struggle and dissemble" to cover up her "ravage[d]" state (101, 103). Unlike Miss Ludington and Miss Beauchamp, May experiences no abrupt "break" between different selves; she has only one self. The fact that May Server cannot become a new person, that her consciousness can neither be split in two nor destroyed completely but must continue to bind together a self, means that there is no escape from the horror of her abasement; no escape, in other words, from the self that is "responsible" for this abasement. And, as earlier critics never tired of pointing out, the narrator himself is consumed by the question of his own responsibility toward the guests he observes and out of whose lives he constructs his "perfect palace of thought" (214). As if to make explicit the analogy between the narrator and the novelist, Mrs. Briss takes the narrator to task for thus "using" her: "I cudgel my brain for your amusement" (200). It is this interest in individual responsibility that makes it possible to read *The Sacred Fount* as either a kind of detective novel or as a parable of the artist.[15] And yet, if his own responsibility is something that worries the narrator (he insists to Ford Obert that "our hands are not clean" [149]; Obert suggests that the narrator has "extraordinary notions of responsibility" [148]), this worry is, as we shall see, not limited to what he does as artist manqué.

Form and Homosexuality

In R. P. Blackmur's influential reading of the novel, *The Sacred Fount* becomes any one of a number of James's ghost stories that are fundamentally about self-division, attempts to give "rational form—knowledgeable form—to all the vast subjective experience of our 'other,' our hidden, our secret selves which we commonly either deny, gloss over, or try to explain away."[16] The appearance of ghosts in so much of James's late fiction is meant, according to Blackmur, to express an experience of "obsession," the way that the self can be "haunted" by its own thoughts. As he suggests, "James knew as well as any philosopher—and rather better than his brother—that we cannot master our knowledge until we have objectified it, and cannot objectify it until we have found conventions to give it form" (50). The vampires who populate Newmarch, then, rather than impinging on the narrator from the outside, might be understood as self-projections. Thus the novel becomes an allegory of novel writing, and the narrator (a stand-in for James) becomes the "conscience" of his "characters," while they, by the same token, become the objective form of his conscience (67).

One might extend Blackmur's argument by suggesting that this model of vampirism accounts not only for the narrator's relation to his own "hidden selves" but organizes the complicated social structure of Newmarch itself. On such a reading, the aristocratic vampires who populate the estate would perform a similar function for their fellow guests, providing them with a more terrible and accurate image of their hidden selves than any mirror could reflect. Mrs. Briss, growing younger at the expense of her husband, and Gilbert, slowly draining the intellect from May Server, are continually described by the narrator as "unconscious." Looking at Mrs. Briss, the narrator has "an almost intolerable sense of her fatuity and cruelty. They were all unconscious, but they were, at that stage, none the less irritating" (60). Characterized by nothing but their "selfish" but nevertheless unselfconscious desires—their complete obliviousness to their effects on other people—the vampires at Newmarch seem to embody the "hidden selves" of the respectable guests they simultaneously resemble and prey on. To put this slightly differently, the vampires are described as unconscious because they seem to stand in for the unconscious desires of those around them. The force of the ghost in this reading is that it makes visible the inherent fragmentation of persons by giving these disavowed parts of the self a human shape, an "objective" existence.

And yet, as other critics have noticed, the power of the novel's formal structure isn't so much that it fractures individuals into multiple selves as that it collapses many different individuals into one self. As Sharon Cameron has argued, *The Sacred Fount*'s restricted first-person narrative voice, which (in much the same way as *The Turn of the Screw*) makes it impossible for the reader to test the narrator's strange observations, raises the possibility that the story the narrator seems to be telling about others is really a story about himself:

> For the reader of *The Sacred Fount* there is no way to tell the difference between what the narrative mind thinks and whatever objective truth there may be to what the mind thinks. Criticism is subverted because there is no place outside the thinking mind (here the first-person narrator) where one could assess the status of what is being thought. Or, to put this in other terms, since the mind has effectively annihilated its own ability to ascertain the distinction between inside and outside, between what it supposes and what it knows, and has violated as well *our* ability to assess such a distinction from a reliable (that is other) place separate from that mind, then there is no story of the world but the one the mind tells. There is no place "outside" the mind.[17]

In this reading *The Sacred Fount* does not represent the eruption of internal difference so much as the complete failure of difference; rather than objectifying his own hidden selves, the narrator cannot judge the basic distinction between self and other. The novel not only depicts this radical extension of the self through a series of mirrorings and doublings but, as Cameron points out, enacts this extension through its formal structure. Because the world of Newmarch is seen only through the eyes of the narrator—"there is no place 'outside' the mind" that narrates—each character becomes a version of this lone observer.

The problem with both of these ways of reading James's vampire story, however, is that they rely on a model of subjectivity that the novel consistently undermines. The underlying assumption of both positions—that individuals have privileged access to themselves, to confront their own unconscious desires, or to know with any certainty their own thoughts—comes under repeated attack, most explicitly in the final exchange between the narrator and Mrs. Briss. During this debate, in which Mrs. Briss attempts to "save" herself by convincing the narrator that he has simply imagined the evidence of vampirism, she appears to be so uncertain of her own thoughts that she cannot report them to the narrator with any accuracy. Against his constant demand that she reveal to him the secret of her sudden change of mind—the moment when she decided that his theory no longer made sense, the "moment when the need of it—or when, in other words, the truth ... dawned upon you"—she can only plead ignorance:

> "*Won't* you understand—for you're a little discouraging—that I want to catch you at the earlier stage?"
> "To 'catch' me?" I had indeed expressions!
> "Absolutely catch! Focus you under the first shock of the observation that was to make everything fall to pieces for you."
> "But I've told you," she stoutly resisted, "that there was no 'first' shock."
> "Well, then, the second or the third."
> "There was no shock," Mrs. Briss magnificently said, "at all." (199)

It would be difficult to take seriously Mrs. Briss's report of her own state of mind at this moment (because it seems clear that she's lying), if not for the fact that what she suggests about self-knowledge is borne out by the rest of the novel. The claim that she can discover no "shock" of change is another way of saying that she can only discern her change of heart after the fact. It is, then, only in relation to the narrator's theory that she realizes she has changed at all: "I was not quite conscious at the time ... but when one has had the 'tip' one looks back and sees things in a new light" (62–63). Rather than imagining that one could objectify the self in order to know it (by taking what is internal and making it external), *The Sacred Fount* suggests that self-knowledge works in reverse: one comes to know what is internal to the self through what is external to it—through the intervention of something like analogy. In elaborating on his theory to a variety of different partners, the narrator realizes that he has, inadvertently, "tipped off" the vampires; he has, to use his words, "communicated to them a consciousness" (189). "Unconscious" of what they've done and what they are at the beginning of the weekend, the vampires acquire self-consciousness through "the torch of [the narrator's] analogy." If "Mrs. Brissenden and Long had been hitherto magnificently without it," he "was responsible perhaps for having, in a mood practically much stupider than the stupidest of theirs, put them gratuitously and helplessly *on* it" (131). Analogy mediates not only the relation between individuals—between observer and observed—but the relation between an individual and himself. The vampires require the intervention of a formal device like analogy in order to recognize what they are and what they have become. It is not introspection but analogy that finally gives the vampires and their victims knowledge of themselves.

The antiintrospective model of the self developed in *The Sacred Fount* is clearly at odds with commonsense accounts of what it means to have self-knowledge. And yet, even William James—who grounded his theory of selfhood in a commonsense notion of introspection, of our ability to know intuitively the difference between "my" thoughts and "your" thoughts—allowed himself to wonder, albeit briefly, about the limits of such intuition. At one point in the *Principles* he suggests that the stream of consciousness "might be better called a stream of *Scious*ness pure and simple," the product of a "Thinker" that is "only aware of its 'pure' Self in an abstract, hypothetic, or conceptual way" (304). In this schema, "the existence of this thinker would be given to us rather as a logical postulate than as that direct inner perception of spiritual activity which we naturally believe ourselves to have" (304). *The Sacred Fount*, then, might be understood as Henry James's attempt to dramatize what it would mean to experience oneself as a "logical postulate." In this way, the image of May Server staring at her portrait without recognizing it, far from asserting her difference from other characters, in fact radicalizes the peculiar nature of self-consciousness in the novel. Unable to see herself directly (or at least to see this reflection as herself) she relies on something outside of herself to voice her thoughts back to her. That Grace Brissenden uses a similar strategy—"when one has had the 'tip' one looks back and sees things in a new light"—makes it plain that this failure of direct insight is not a failure at all—that indirect knowledge is what continually "gives" individuals to themselves.

In *The Turn of the Screw* (1898), a similarly ambiguous ghost story from the same period, James explores the limits of introspection in almost the same terms. To the narrator of *The Sacred Fount*, the "opposed couples" he tracks with his law of analogy "balanced like bronze groups at the two ends of a chimney piece" (130). In much the same way, the unnamed governess who narrates *The Turn of the Screw* tracks two sets of opposed couples: Miles and the ghost of Peter Quint, and Flora and the ghost of Miss Jessel. Without ever being named explicitly, analogy guides the governess's investigation from the beginning. It not only helps her determine the facts (for example, that it must be Miss Jessel who is haunting Flora because it is Peter Quint who is haunting Miles) but, more important, provides her with a way of judging her own behavior. Seeing Miss Jessel appear by the lake (where she and Mrs. Grose have gone to seek the runaway Flora), the governess imagines that her own sanity depends on the objective existence of the ghosts: "She was there, so I was justified; she was there, so I was neither cruel nor mad."[18] If the ghosts are there, then Flora and Miles are not "innocent," and if they are not innocent, then she is heroic, "a remarkable young woman" (15). By the end of the novel, however, analogical reasoning has undermined not only the governess's certainty about her own perceptions, but her certainty about herself. When Miles tells her why he was sent home from school—because he "said things"—the governess is forced to confront a less appealing version of herself: "If he were innocent what then on earth was I?" (83).

The force of analogy in *The Sacred Fount*, celebrated as a "torch" in the "darkness" (57), is that it inevitably overrides the uses to which the vampire hunters put it. When analogy reemerges late in the novel, it begins to define the relation not simply between the guests that Ford Obert and the narrator have been tracking but between the two men themselves. Thus the confusion the narrator claims to experience in the smoking room: "Yours *was* mine, wasn't it? For a little, this morning. Or was it mine that was yours?" (147). Through the intervention of the sexual analogy, the two men are suddenly linked to the couples they've been tracking. Their intimacy is, on the one hand, flirtatious—"It was just the fact that you did wink, that you had winked at me, that wound me up" (149), says the narrator—and, on the other, all but explicitly sexual:

> I laid my hand on his arm and held him a moment with a grip that betrayed, I daresay, the effort in me to keep my thoughts together. . . . "It would take too long to tell you what I mean."
>
> The tone of it made him fairly watch me as I had been watching him. "Well, haven't we got the whole night?"

"Oh, it would take more than the whole night—even if we had it!"
"By which you suggest that we haven't it?"
"No—we haven't it. I want to get away."
"To go to bed? I thought you were so keen."
"I am keen. Keen is no word for it. I don't want to go to bed. I want to get away."
"To leave the house—in the middle of the night?"
"Yes—absurd as it may seem. You excite me too much. You don't know what you do to me."

He continued to look at me; then he gave a laugh which was not the contradiction, but quite the attestation, of the effect produced on him by my grip. If I wanted to hold him I held him. It only came to me even that I held him too much. (151)

By first inaugurating this conversation with Obert and then insisting that it end, the narrator enacts what has come to be a familiar turn-of-the-century scene of homoerotic desire that is indistinguishable in many ways from a full-fledged homosexual panic. Insisting, "I don't want to go to bed. I want to get away," the narrator attempts to escape from the man who evokes this desire. Directed at Obert, in other words, "I want to get away" becomes a way of saying "I want to get away from you."

Despite the intense scrutiny of the novel (the criticism has been scant, but incisive), this conversation has received surprisingly little attention. Adeline Tintner has argued that some of the difficulties of *The Sacred Fount* evaporate if we see that the novel is in some sense "about" homosexuality. But her argument focuses more on plot than on form and thus misses entirely the vexed relation between the narrator and Obert. Her claim is that the narrator has simply misinterpreted the evidence: it is Long who is having an affair with Mr. Briss while May Server is having an affair with Mrs. Briss.[19] The plausibility of both this reading and the one that sees the two "vampires" as the real lovers and the two "victims" as the rejected partners highlights the way in which symmetricality can produce false as well as true knowledge (the proposed situations are mutually exclusive). What neither reading can account for, however, is the way in which analogy comes to define not only the couples but the relation between the narrator and Obert, how it comes to explain the experience of desire rather than the existence of desire in others.

What I want to argue here is that the force of homosexuality in *The Sacred Fount* isn't so much that it reveals (through hints and indirection) a forbidden desire as that it rather openly reveals an analogous desire. The scene between Obert, the portrait painter, and the narrator (who, in a telling rhyme refers to himself as "a painter of my state" [75]) is not simply about desire but about desire between individuals who are consistently presented as mirror images of one another.[20] The other couples at Newmarch are analogous to one another in terms of each pair's exaggerated differences (the old Grace and the young Briss, for example, soon become the much younger Grace and the much older Briss: "It was he who was old—it was he who was older—it was he who was oldest" [29]); sexual love seems to transform one partner into a version of the other. The narrator and Ford Obert, on the other hand, are represented as analogous to one another, so much so, in fact, that they come to represent the form of analogy itself. Indeed, the attraction between Ford Obert and the narrator *literalizes* analogy by figuring it in the sameness of same-sex desire.

There is, of course, a long and controversial history of viewing homosexuality as a displaced desire for the self and thus a form of narcissism. In an early essay, Freud locates the perverse nature of homosexuality in the individual's inability to detach from himself, claiming that the "type of object choice" for "perverts and homosexuals" "may be termed narcissistic" because they "are plainly seeking themselves as a love object."[21] If all human beings, according to Freud, have two original love objects—the mother and the self—only homosexuals, he argues, continue to take themselves as the model object. In two essays that consider the legacy of this theory, Michael Warner examines the way in which gender difference has come to be understood as the one true mark of otherness. "Why," he asks, "is gender assumed to be our only access to alterity?" Why, in other words, is it assumed that there is "no other way of distinguishing between self and not-self?"[22] His larger point is to reveal the fallacy both of thinking that heterosexual love is not, to a great extent, a way of desiring the self and of thinking that the object of one's homosexual desire is not "different," in an important sense, from oneself. Warner explains: "Sexuality has any number of forms of the dialectic between identification and desire. But we do not say of people whose erotic objects are chosen partly on the basis of racial identity or of generation or of class that they have eradicated the distinction between self and not-self. We say that only of gender. The difference between hetero- and homosexualities is not, in fact, a difference between sexualities of otherness and sameness. It is an allegory about gender."[23]

But if gender difference is clearly not the only difference, the fact that *The Sacred Fount* takes such pains to identify Obert and the narrator not only as mirror images of one another, but mirror images that recognize one another as such (unlike, say, May Server, who cannot see her own face in the portrait of the Man with the Mask), suggests that gender difference might in fact figure as a crucial difference here. Indeed, James's interest in the commingling of identity and desire set him apart from one powerful strand of contemporary thinking on the subject, which took homosexual desire to be a form of "inversion" wherein a man who desires another man was imagined to have a "female soul." In such theories (promulgated by sexologists like Karl Heinrich Ulrichs) sexual desire depended on difference—the difference between the male body and the female soul that desires through that body—even when bodies superficially resembled one another.[24] Christopher Craft, in his description of the social utility of such theories, claims that this notion of inversion, if it did not exactly "normalize" homosexuality, at least made it comprehensible to a Victorian public. "What this account of same-sex eroticism cannot imagine," he claims, "is that sexual attraction between members of the same gender may be a reasonable and natural articulation of a desire whose excursiveness is simply *indifferent* to the distinctions of gender."[25] Surely, however, the anxiety that grew up around homosexuality at the turn of the century was not that individuals might be indifferent to gender, but that they might be far from indifferent to their own gender. In other words, the attempt to normalize homosexuality along heterosexual lines ("the female soul") suggests that the real scandal at the turn of the century was imagining that a person living in a male body could, without the intervention of a female soul, find another male body sexually desirable.

In *Homos*, Leo Bersani questions the way in which queer theory has attempted to divorce this notion of gender sameness from political theories of homosexuality. Writing against critics (like Warner) who want to deemphasize sameness, Bersani argues for an increased attention to the formal specificity of same-sex desire. For Bersani, the point isn't somehow to "get beyond" a restrictive (and normalizing) attachment to gender categories, to insist on "desexualizing" gayness, but instead to discover the "inestimable value of relations of sameness, of homo-relations."[26] His strongest claim is that sex with those of the same gender can become a model for new forms of sociality, a way of subverting the attachment to differences that always manifest themselves as disparities of power. This model of "homo-ness," if it is not meant to be a utopian form of democracy (in which hierarchies are dissolved in relations of political equality figured as gender equality), is meant at least to serve as a rejection of social worlds built on the assertion of essential differences. "Perhaps," Bersani claims, "inherent in gay desire is a revolutionary inaptitude for heteroized sociality," so that "the most politically disruptive aspect" of "homo-ness" can be read as "a redefinition of sociality so radical that it may appear to require a provisional withdrawal from relationality itself" (7). Rather than representing a form of social relation, gay desire looks like a form of self-relation in which the subject seeks out "inaccurate replications of himself, extensions of himself" (124). Bersani ultimately imagines a self-relation "that works against the narcissism of a securely mapped ego," and thus works to "block the cultural discipline of identification" (125). The sameness of same-sex desire is important for Bersani because it instigates both new ways of seeing the self and new ways of imagining what relations between selves might look like. Bersani's point seems to be that gender sameness is so closely connected to the very idea of human sameness that it becomes a model for new social relations built on the idea of nondifference. Homosexuality thus becomes a universalizing model for creating new forms of "connectedness to the world," for "an anticommunal mode of connectedness we might all share" (10). That is, it becomes a way of erasing difference, even homosexual specificity itself, by "bringing out and celebrating 'the homo' in all of us" (10).

But what is problematic about Bersani's attempt to mobilize the concept of "homo-ness" is that one aspect of his claim—the claim for homosexuality as a general model of sociality—appears to undermine the other—the claim for gay specificity. For Bersani's argument begins and ends with a recognition of the real differences in gay and straight desire, between gay and straight identity. He calls attention to the seemingly "obvious" fact that "gay men mainly go to bed with other men," a fact that is not meant to support "essentializing definitions of desire," but "to promote an active curiosity about the fantasies and identifications that have helped to constitute certain sexual preferences" (59). Indeed, for Bersani it is the insistence on the specificity of homosexual desire that enables gay politics: "The discrediting of a specific gay identity," he argues, "has had the curious but predictable result of eliminating the indispensable grounds for resistance to, precisely, regimes of the normal" (4). If asserting gay identity, then, means asserting the fact that "gay men, for all their diversity, share a strong sexual interest in other human beings anatomically identifiable as male," it is, in the end, the content of homosexual difference—this attraction to sameness—that leads to the slippage in terms (6). What makes homosexuality different, in other words, is that it is an identity built on sameness.

If Bersani's elaboration of a politics of sameness modeled on or exemplified by same-sex desire seems contradictory, his interest in the power of the formal symmetry of gay desire illuminates a crucial aspect of James's project. In the end, James's interest in the sameness of same-sex desire becomes an interest in a kind of surprising self-relation. Confronted by an analogous desire in the smoking room, the narrator attempts to flee the scene. In this light, the narrator's assertion, "I want to get away," might be more properly understood not as "I want to get away from you," but as "I want to get away from myself." Ultimately, the horror evoked in James's novel about vampires haunting a country estate is attached neither to sexual desire per se nor to the objects of such desire but rather to the self enforced by the analogous object of desire. Thus the ending of *The Sacred Fount* focuses on the narrator's attempt to escape from Newmarch—and from Obert—in terms that suggest a desire for an escape from his own thoughts: "It was on my way to [Newmarch] . . . that my obsession had met me, and it was by retracing those steps that I should be able to get rid of it. Only I must break off sharp, must escape all reminders by forswearing all returns" (142). That the narrator thinks he can escape from himself by escaping from those with whom he has come into relation is indeed a testament to the power of analogy. What he wants, in the end, is a physical distance from the formal system that enforces identity, as if he desires nothing so much as an escape from the novel itself. Because the novel is, in this instance, coterminous with the narrator's mind, the escape he longs for begins to look like a kind of erasure, the production of "blankness" rather than writing: "Was this now a foreknowledge that, on the morrow, in driving away, I should feel myself restored to that blankness? The state lost was the state of exemption from intense obsessions, and the state recovered would therefore logically match it" (137). If the escape the narrator longs for entails a radical break from his thoughts (because remembering the thoughts that he is trying to get rid of would count as continuing to think them), obsession by its very nature denies the possibility of a radical break; obsession names precisely this inability to escape from one's own thoughts or, in this context, to undo the knowledge produced by analogy. The narrator's continual postponement of his departure—"I *would* go, I was going; if I had not had to accept the interval of the night I should indeed already have gone" (142)—suggests both the absurdity of his imagining that a physical distance from the people he thinks about will restore him to "blankness" (will undo the work of the novel) and the intensity of his desire for such an escape.[27]

Same-sex desire figures in *The Sacred Fount* as a way both of literalizing the analogical relation with others through which individuals come to know themselves and of motivating (even more dramatically than vampirism) the terror of these analogies. Thus if homoerotic desire generates the "panic" in the smoking room scene, this panic is, according to the logic of the novel, not directed toward homosexuality alone but also toward the analogical relation it reveals. Rather than being displaced in this text, homoerotic desire is what displaces, motivating the fear that is directed at an object at once more abstract than same-sex desire and exemplified by its analogical form—the self made legible by desire. What I am suggesting, to revise Warner's formulation, is that homosexuality here does not become an allegory of gender but, through gender, becomes an allegory of analogy. Instead of imagining homosexuality as a kind of threat to sexual norms, James uses it to ground what the narrator sees as the "law" of sexual analogy: "It was of course familiar enough," he claims, "that when people were so deeply in love they rubbed off on each other—that a great pressure of soul to soul usually left on either side a sufficient show of tell-tale traces" (26). "Unconscious" at first of such passion and thus of such traces, the haunted characters in *The Sacred Fount* are, through analogy, brought into relation with themselves.

Public Traces

The "modernism" of *The Sacred Fount*—its experimentation with narrative form, its self-reflexiveness—has generally been read as a kind of preparation for the late fiction, which transforms its rather crude musings on aesthetic form into something that looks more like "art." But if my sense of *The Sacred Fount*'s linkage between sexuality and abstract form is right, then its interest in form is not necessarily detachable from large, essentially social concerns. We might, then, read *The Sacred Fount* not merely as prelude but as a kind of guide to the late fiction; it lays bare the formal conditions through which we come into relation with our own experience.[28] I would like to close, then, by considering the implications of the public "traces" codified or made to register by a formal system like analogy. If *The Sacred Fount* represents, through the formal symmetry of homosexuality, the fear generated by such indirect self-knowledge, James posits no necessary relation between the forms through which we come to know things and the things we come to know. James's prefaces to the New York edition, for example, treat the texts themselves as formal traces, as evidence of public action, and thus as vehicles of self-reflection. In looking back over his work in the preface to *The Golden Bowl* (1904), in which he describes the sexual intrigues of a very similar set of symmetrical couples, James makes the following claim: "Beset constantly with the sense that the painter of the picture or the chanter of the ballad (whatever we may call him) can never be responsible *enough*, and for every inch of his surface and note of his song, I track my uncontrollable footsteps, right and left, after the fact, while they take their quick turn, even on stealthiest tiptoe, toward the point of view that, within the compass, will give me most instead of least to answer for."[29] For James, it is the formalism of the novel itself, its status not merely as an object akin to a painting or a golden bowl, but as an abstract form that is essentially unbreakable, that enables what look like "uncontrollable footsteps" to be "tracked," illuminated, or explained.

James closes his preface, his testimony to the public trace of his earlier thought, by distinguishing between the ephemerality of the effects produced by routine social interaction and the endurance of the effects produced by aesthetic objects. "We are condemned," he claims, "whether we will or no, to abandon and outlive, to forget and disown and hand over to desolation, many vital or social performances—if only because the traces, records, connections, the very memorials we would fain preserve, are practically impossible to rescue for that purpose from the general mixture" (lxi). (This is, it seems worth noting, precisely what happens when Mrs. Briss cannot recollect the exact moment when she changed her mind.) With aesthetic objects, on the other hand, there is no such "general mixture" and thus no such loss: "Our relation to them is essentially traceable, and in that fact abides, we feel, the incomparable luxury of the artist" (lxi). And yet, if what looks like a horrifying encounter with form in *The Sacred Fount* becomes, in the prefaces, a kind of self-confirmation ("the incomparable luxury of the artist"), both of these scenes of self-knowledge depend on the mediation of abstract form. Analogy, I have suggested, serves as the condensed formal system embedded in *The Sacred Fount*. In the preface to *The Golden Bowl*, James imagines the novel itself to be an analogous formal system. Just as the analogy between the vampires and their victims requires the narrator to see himself reflected in Ford Obert, the novel, James is arguing, puts the author in relation to the unexpected effects of his own actions: "I track my uncontrollable footsteps, right and left, after the fact."

If the force of the deconstructive critique of the "trace" is that writing always escapes intention, always "acts" apart from its ostensible author, the force of James's interest in the aesthetic object is both that it escapes intention (in that it is uncontrollable) and that it is nonetheless traceable to an author: "Our literary deeds enjoy this marked advantage over many of our acts, that, though they go forth into the world and stray even in the desert, they don't to the same extent lose themselves; their attachment and reference to us, however strained, needn't necessarily lapse" (lx-lxi). Another way of putting this would be to say that for James, public traces may, in refusing to "lose themselves," become the source of surprising effects for which he is ultimately accountable. James, as I have been arguing, recognizes the novel itself as one of the more powerful forms of the public trace, an aesthetic object that does not transcend the world of action but becomes instead a testament to new forms of public "responsibility." After all, the novel is, in James's estimation, "conduct with a vengeance, since it is conduct minutely and publicly attested" (lxi).

To investigate James's interest in the unassimilability, the permanence, of the aesthetic object is, in a sense, to return to the New Critical interest in James's formalism—not to salvage this vision of James but to place this formalism in a new register.[30] For, as I have argued in relation to *The Sacred Fount*'s engagement with homosexuality, drawing attention to James's interest in a structure like analogy is not to evade questions of the "social" in favor of the "formal." Reading James's formalism requires us to recognize that the mundane details of sexual life are not necessarily opposed to aesthetic form, but become visible or comprehensible only through something like aesthetic form. It also requires us to recognize that abstract form is virtually inseparable from the materiality of the physical—the symmetrical bodies of Peter and Paul, Obert and the narrator. Thus, the narrator uses analogy to comprehend desire and identity just as the novel itself uses the imagined symmetry of homosexuality to represent analogy. If I have, in the preceding pages, strayed from persuasive recent accounts that see homosexuality as something the text must hide, I have also attempted to extend the line of argument (advanced in different ways by Sedgwick, Warner, and Bersani) that sees homosexuality as a kind of textual engine. One of the more interesting features of *The Sacred Fount*, after all, is its suggestion that homosexuality has a formal existence, that it does not simply inhere in identities or acts but that it can organize knowledge, can produce "a full-blown flower of . . . theory" (122).

More broadly, in thus musing on the power of the formal trace, James makes absolutely explicit the central problematic I have been exploring in the preceding chapters. James imagines, in his theory of the trace, a formal system that makes visible for the first time what common sense regards as obvious and unmediated knowledge—not only one's own thoughts and desires, but one's "vital or social performances." In this fantasy of the aesthetic object, these performances do not simply register the effects of social "discipline."[31] Instead, such public actions become the source of a very different process of individuation, a process that defines individuals in terms of their social effects. In *The Sacred Fount*, James seeks to represent, by way of sexuality, this world of effects; in the preface to *The Golden Bowl* he reflects on the sense in which the novel as a form might embody this world. It is in its attempt to attest to "the traces, records, connections, the very memorials we would fain preserve"—to examine the ways that effects could come to overshadow intentions—that the American novel transforms the simplest actions of daily life into "conduct with a vengeance."

Notes

INTRODUCTION: The Limits of Privacy

1. Edward Bellamy, *"The Blindman's World" and Other Stories* (Boston: Houghton Mifflin, 1898), 7.

2. I should note here at the outset my indebtedness to Jürgen Habermas's well-known account of the public sphere, especially his sense of its collapse in the face of an increasingly privatized, consumer-oriented culture. As I make clear in the following pages, however, my main interest is in the limits of this privatized, desiring subject regardless of whether that subject is oriented toward the market or rational debate. My concern here is with the idea of publicness as a condition of intelligibility for individual action. See Habermas, *The Structural Transformation of the Public Sphere: An Inquiry into a Category of Bourgeois Society*, trans. Thomas Burger (Cambridge: MIT Press, 1994).

3. Market critics make the economy the organizing principle of American culture, so that the novel creates contractual subjects endowed with desires they seek to satisfy in a burgeoning consumer society. At its most radical, market criticism imagines individuals reduced to their desires; character, from this perspective, denotes "an involvement with the world so central to one's sense of self that the distinction between what one is and what one wants tends to disappear" (Walter Benn Michaels, *The Gold Standard and the Logic of Naturalism* [Berkeley: University of California Press, 1987], 41). Those critics who deny the ubiquity of the market do not deny its central importance; instead, they imagine the novel less as an escape from its power than as an engine of "resistance" to it. The novel's critique of the market, on this account, depends on the subject of desire, albeit one who recognizes the limits of the market in satisfying those desires. Critics who, in very different ways, take the market—rendered as contractual or consumerist—as the defining feature of Ameri-

can culture in the nineteenth century include T. J. Jackson Lears, *No Place of Grace: Antimodernism and the Transformation of American Culture, 1880–1920* (New York: Pantheon, 1981); Michael T. Gilmore, *American Romanticism and the Marketplace* (Chicago: University of Chicago Press, 1985); Amy Kaplan, *The Social Construction of American Realism* (Chicago: University of Chicago Press, 1988); Mark Seltzer, *Bodies and Machines* (New York: Routledge, 1992); and Brook Thomas, *American Literary Realism and the Failed Promise of Contract* (Berkeley: University of California Press, 1997).

4. Feminist critics of the domestic make gender segregation the central organizing principle of American culture, so that women's fiction creates sentimental subjects endowed with feelings that are cultivated within the intimate sphere of the home. One version of this criticism sees the midcentury domestic women's novel as a critique of masculine culture, producing a world of intimacy and female power that counters the competition and acquisitiveness of the market, or a world of female rage that openly assails political and social oppression. Early and deeply influential accounts of this argument for the novel's depiction of women's power include Jane Tompkins, *Sensational Designs: The Cultural Work of American Fiction, 1790–1860* (New York: Oxford University Press, 1985); and Nina Baym, *Women's Fiction: A Guide to Novels by and about Women in America, 1820–70*, 2nd ed. (Urbana: University of Illinois Press, 1993). For recent extensions and refinements of this line of argument, see Shirley Samuels, ed., *The Culture of Sentiment: Race, Gender, and Sentimentality in Nineteenth-Century America* (New York: Oxford University Press, 1992); and Marianne Noble, *The Masochistic Pleasures of Sentimental Literature* (Princeton: Princeton University Press, 2000). Another version of domestic criticism sees the home created by women's fiction as a facet of market culture, which then in turn was shaped by it. The best articulation of this argument can be found in Gillian Brown's *Domestic Individualism: Imagining Self in Nineteenth-Century America* (Berkeley: University of California Press, 1990). More recently, Lori Merish has argued that the origins of "consumer subjectivity" are to be found in nineteenth-century idealizations of "domestic womanhood" (Merish, *Sentimental Materialism: Gender, Commodity Culture, and Nineteenth-Century American Literature* [Durham: Duke University Press, 2000], 2). It is crucial to note, however, that like market critics, domestic critics across the board imagine that it is interiority (whether rage or sympathy) that defines the individual and marks her relation to the world.

5. Louis Renza has recently argued that privacy, as it is constructed in the works of Edgar Allan Poe and Wallace Stevens, cannot be understood ideologically. His point, however, is that these writers pursue an even more radical conception of privacy—something that defies the conventional relation between reader and text—that cannot be understood in terms of solitude or autonomous personhood. See Renza,

Edgar Allan Poe, Wallace Stevens, and the Poetics of American Privacy (Baton Rouge: Louisiana State University Press, 2002).

6. Lionel Trilling, *The Liberal Imagination: Essays on Literature and Society* (New York: Anchor-Doubleday, 1957), 107. See also F. O. Matthiessen, *The American Renaissance: Art and Expression in the Age of Emerson and Whitman* (New York: Oxford University Press, 1941); and Richard Chase, *The American Novel and Its Tradition* (Baltimore: Johns Hopkins University Press, 1957).

7. Sacvan Bercovitch, *The Rites of Assent: Transformations in the Symbolic Construction of America* (New York: Routledge, 1993), 59.

8. There are countless histories of moral and social reform movements in America, especially the Progressive movement. A classic work on the bureaucratization of reform is Robert H. Wiebe's *The Search for Order, 1877–1920* (New York: Hill and Wang, 1967). For a recent instance, see Alan Hunt, *Governing Morals: A Social History of Moral Regulation* (Cambridge: Cambridge University Press, 1999).

9. William J. Novak, *The People's Welfare: Law and Regulation in Nineteenth-Century America* (Chapel Hill: University of North Carolina Press, 1996), 13. Novak's argument is directed against historians who have propagated both "the myth of liberal individualism" and "the myth of statelessness" in relation to nineteenth-century America (3). His claim is that the American regulatory state came into existence much earlier than anyone supposed—indeed, that regulation was fundamental to the early republic. In a real sense, however, the recent debate among historians about the individual's relation to the state in the nineteenth century seems irrelevant to literary critics, whose work suggests that if Americans neither inhabited a state with severely limited powers nor participated in an unfettered market, they were nonetheless subject to the ideology of the freely contracting individual. Here, however, I question the primacy of such an ideology. One of the most famous articulations of the argument for liberal individualism is Louis Hart's *The Liberal Tradition in America* (New York: Harcourt, Brace and World, 1955). Good examples of the argument of statelessness can be found in Morton Keller, *Affairs of State: Public Life in Late Nineteenth-Century America* (Cambridge: Belknap Press, 1977); and Stephen Skowronek, *Building a New American State: The Expansion of National Administrative Capacities, 1877–1920* (New York: Cambridge University Press, 1982).

10. Barbara Young Welke, *Recasting American Liberty: Gender, Race, Law, and the Railroad Revolution, 1865–1920* (New York: Cambridge University Press, 2001), 30, 123.

11. Ian Hacking, *The Taming of Chance* (New York: Cambridge University Press, 1990), 3, 6. Jackson Lears makes a related claim about statistics: "After acknowledging the existence of chance, statistical thinking aimed to rob it of its power" (Lears, *Something for Nothing: Luck in America* [New York: Viking Penguin, 2003], 21). His

larger point is to divide the nineteenth century into two opposing forces: "The rivalrous American cultures of chance and control" (6). And although he associates chance with spontaneity, freedom, and play (which are threatened by the ideal of a "perfectly managed society" [239]) his argument is similar to Hacking's in that the only possible response to chance he can imagine (aside from indulging in it) is the implementation of social control.

12. I address the history of tort law in America at greater length in chapter 3.

13. Nathaniel Hawthorne, *The Blithedale Romance* (New York: Norton, 1978 [1852]), 67.

14. Susan Warner, *The Wide Wide World* (New York: Feminist Press, 1987 [1850]), 296.

15. Henry Cole, *Confessions of an American Opium Eater* (Boston: J. H. Earle, 1895), 235.

16. In relation to race, see, for example, Eric Sundquist, *To Wake the Nations: Race in the Making of American Literature* (Cambridge: Harvard University Press, 1993); and Ross Posnock, *Color and Culture: Black Writers and the Making of the Modern Intellectual* (Cambridge: Harvard University Press, 1998). In relation to gender, see, for example, Lora Romero, *Home Fronts: Domesticity and Its Critics in the Antebellum United States* (Durham: Duke University Press, 1997); and the essays collected in Cathy N. Davidson and Jessamyn Hatcher, eds., *No More Separate Spheres!* (Durham: Duke University Press, 2002). Richard Brodhead's analysis of "social publics" organized around fictional texts, which moves easily from Hawthorne to Stowe to Chesnutt, served as a useful model for this project (see Brodhead, *Cultures of Letters: Scenes of Reading and Writing in Nineteenth-Century America* [Chicago: University of Chicago Press, 1993], 6).

17. Lauren Berlant, "Poor Eliza," *American Literature* 70 (1998): 641. For an extended analysis of sentimental politics that deals almost exclusively with the late twentieth century, see Berlant's *The Queen of America Goes to Washington City: Essays on Sex and Citizenship* (Durham: Duke University Press, 1997). For a related argument about sentimentality that deals with the early nineteenth century, see Bruce Burgett, *Sentimental Bodies: Sex, Gender, and Citizenship in the Early Republic* (Princeton: Princeton University Press, 1998).

18. In her examination of sentiment in the early American novel, for example, Julia Stern makes sentiment politically redemptive, arguing that "sensational" novels "contemplate the possibility that the power of genuine sympathy could revivify a broadly inclusive vision of democracy" (Stern, *The Plight of Feeling: Sympathy and Dissent in the Early American Novel* [Chicago: University of Chicago Press, 1997], 2). Stern's book is just one of a number of recent books on sentiment in American culture. See, for example, Elizabeth Barnes, *States of Sympathy: Seduction and Democ-*

racy in the American Novel (New York: Columbia University Press, 1997); Julie Ellison, *Cato's Tears and the Making of Anglo-American Emotion* (Chicago: University of Chicago Press, 1999); and Glen Hendler, *Public Sentiments: Structures of Feeling in Nineteenth-Century American Literature* (Chapel Hill: University of North Carolina Press, 2001). There have also been a number of recent polemics against the invasion of privacy in modern America. One example is Jeffrey Rosen's *The Unwanted Gaze: The Destruction of Privacy in America* (New York: Random House, 2000).

19. Berlant, "Poor Eliza," 641, 637.

20. Ibid., 646.

21. Michael Warner, *Publics and Counterpublics* (New York: Zone Books, 2002), 62.

22. Michel Foucault, "Politics and the Study of Discourse," in *The Foucault Effect: Studies in Governmentality*, ed. Graham Burchell, Colin Gordon, and Peter Miller (Chicago: University of Chicago Press, 1991), 59.

CHAPTER ONE: *The Blithedale Romance* and Other Tales of Association

1. Nathaniel Hawthorne, *The Blithedale Romance* (New York: Norton, 1978 [1852]), 5, 6.

2. Alexis de Tocqueville, *Democracy in America*, 2 vols., trans. Henry Reeve, ed. Francis Bowen (Boston: John Allyn, 1873), 1:243, 2:133.

3. Mary P. Ryan, *Cradle of the Middle Class: The Family in Oneida County, New York, 1790–1865* (Cambridge: Cambridge University Press, 1981), 105. According to Stuart Blumin, "the three decades preceding the Civil War ... may fairly be called an era of voluntary institutional innovation without parallel in American history" (Blumin, *The Emergence of the Middle Class: Social Experience in the American City, 1760–1900* [Cambridge: Cambridge University Press, 1989], 192). For other accounts of the rise of voluntary associations in the United States, see Daniel Feller, *The Jacksonian Promise: America, 1815–1840* (Baltimore: Johns Hopkins University Press, 1995); and Lori D. Ginzberg, *Women and the Work of Benevolence: Morality, Politics, and Class in the Nineteenth-Century United States* (New Haven: Yale University Press, 1990).

4. Sacvan Bercovitch, *The Office of "The Scarlet Letter"* (Baltimore: Johns Hopkins University Press, 1991), xxi, xx.

5. Lauren Berlant, *The Anatomy of National Fantasy: Hawthorne, Utopia, and Everyday Life* (Chicago: University of Chicago Press, 1991), 7, 6.

6. In much the same way, Donald Pease proposes that Hawthorne uses an idealized form of "collective memory" to critique contemporary American politics (Pease, *Visionary Compacts: American Renaissance Writings in Cultural Context* [Madison: University of Wisconsin Press, 1987], 47).

7. Nathaniel Hawthorne, *The Scarlet Letter* (New York: Norton, 1988), 4.

8. Jonathan Arac, "The Politics of *The Scarlet Letter*," in *Ideology and Classic American Literature*, ed. Sacvan Bercovitch and Myra Jehlen (Cambridge: Cambridge University Press, 1986), 253, 254. In *The Office of "The Scarlet Letter*," Bercovitch makes a similar point: "If we step outside the boundaries of intracultural debate, the difference between Hawthorne's 'natural' Democratic allegiances and the 'vivified' Whig platform he opposed reflects something else entirely: a series of no-longer-avoidable conflicts within a system whose principles and prejudices (including racism and American exceptionalism) were shared by virtually all parties and, though not equally, by Whigs and Democrats alike" (88).

9. Ronald Formisano, *The Transformation of Political Culture: Massachusetts Parties, 1790s–1840s* (New York: Oxford University Press, 1983).

10. For an engaging analysis of grassroots participation in nineteenth-century American politics, see Glenn C. Altschuler and Stuart M. Blumin, *Rude Republic: Americans and Their Politics in the Nineteenth Century* (Princeton: Princeton University Press, 2000). For accounts of the rise of the party system in the United States, see Richard Hofstadter, *The Idea of a Party System: The Rise of Legitimate Opposition in the United States, 1780–1840* (Berkeley: University of California Press, 1969); Richard L. McCormick, *The Party Period and Public Policy: American Politics from the Age of Jackson to the Progressive Era* (New York: Oxford University Press, 1986); Joel H. Silbey, *The American Political Nation, 1838–1893* (Stanford: Stanford University Press, 1991); and Jean H. Baker, *Affairs of Party: The Political Culture of Northern Democrats in the Mid-Nineteenth Century* (New York: Fordham University Press, 1998).

11. Nathaniel Hawthorne, *The Works of Nathaniel Hawthorne. Vol. 12: The Life of Franklin Pierce* (Boston: Houghton Mifflin, 1883), 416, 417.

12. For an interesting reading of the political context of Hawthorne's dismissal from the U.S. Custom House see Stephen Nissenbaum, "The Firing of Nathaniel Hawthorne," *Essex Institute Historical Collections* 114 (1978): 57–86.

13. Critics have generally recognized the connection between Fourier and *Blithedale* without analyzing it in any real detail. One exception is Lauren Berlant's essay on the novel, "Fantasies of Utopia in *The Blithedale Romance*" (*American Literary History* 1 [1989]: 30–62), which emphasizes Coverdale's fantasies of free love. For an account of Fourier's influence on American socialism, see Carl J. Guarneri, *The Utopian Alternative: Fourierism in Nineteenth-Century America* (Ithaca: Cornell University Press, 1991).

14. As biographer James R. Mellow points out, Hawthorne read Fourier only after he left Brook Farm, just as it was transforming itself into a Fourierist "phalanx" (see Mellow, *Nathaniel Hawthorne in His Times* [Boston: Houghton Mifflin, 1980], 248–49). Accounts of Brook Farm are numerous; among the best are Lindsay Swift, *Brook Farm: Its Members, Scholars, and Visitors* (Secaucus, N.J.: Citadel Press, 1973 [1900]);

Henry W. Sams, ed., *Autobiography of Brook Farm* (Englewood Cliffs, N.J.: Prentice-Hall, 1958); and Edith Roelker Curtis, *A Season in Utopia: The Story of Brook Farm* (New York: Thomas Nelson and Sons, 1961).

15. Albert Brisbane, *Social Destiny of Man; or, Association and Reorganization of Industry* (New York: Augustus M. Kelley, 1969 [1840]), 29.

16. Fourier uses the quoted terms frequently in his writings. For examples, see Jonathan Beecher and Richard Bienvenu, eds. and trans., *The Utopian Vision of Charles Fourier: Selected Texts on Work, Love, and Passionate Attraction* (Boston: Beacon Press, 1971), 222–23.

17. Charles Fourier, *Design for Utopia: Selected Writings of Charles Fourier*, ed. Frank Manuel, trans. Julia Franklin (New York: Schocken, 1971), 61.

18. Beecher and Bienvenu, *Utopian Vision*, 216.

19. Fourier, *Design for Utopia*, 107.

20. Ibid., 86.

21. Fourier, in Beecher and Bienvenu, *Utopian Vision*, 215.

22. Ibid., 98.

23. Fourier, *Design for Utopia*, 155.

24. Fourier, in Beecher and Bienvenu, *Utopian Vision*, 268, 355.

25. Brisbane, *Social Destiny*, 444. Brisbane's book is divided into chapters that are direct translations of Fourier's work and chapters that are Brisbane's own analysis, explanation, and amplification of Fourier's theories. This quotation is a translation of Fourier.

26. Fourier, in Beecher and Bienvenu, *Utopian Vision*, 225.

27. Fourier, *Design for Utopia*, 157.

28. Brisbane, *Social Destiny*, 17. This quotation is a translation of Fourier.

29. Fourier, in Beecher and Bienvenu, *Utopian Vision*, 229.

30. Roland Barthes, *Sade, Fourier, Loyola*, trans. Richard Miller (Baltimore: Johns Hopkins University Press, 1976), 114.

31. Parke Godwin, *A Popular View of the Doctrines of Charles Fourier* (Philadelphia: Porcupine Press, 1972 [1844]), 43.

32. Barthes, *Sade, Fourier, Loyola*, 112.

33. Brisbane, *Social Destiny*, 364.

34. Fourier, in Beecher and Bienvenu, *Utopian Vision*, 360.

35. Ibid., 361.

36. Recent discussions of the disciplinary function of visibility are too numerous to mention. All are extensions of Foucault's analysis of the prison. See Michel Foucault, *Discipline and Punish*, trans. Alan Sheridan (New York: Vintage, 1979).

37. "Meadow-Farm: A Tale of Association," *Knickerbocker*, April 1843, 330. Because pagination in the serialized version is not sequential, all further citations appear in the text by date and page.

38. Ralph Waldo Emerson, *The Journals and Miscellaneous Notebooks of Ralph Waldo Emerson*, vol. 7, ed. A. W. Plumstead and Harrison Hayford (Cambridge: Harvard University Press, 1969), 408.

39. Ralph Waldo Emerson, "The American Scholar," in *Selected Essays* (New York: Penguin, 1982), 104.

40. George Washington, "Farewell Address," quoted in Noble E. Cunningham Jr., ed., *The Making of the American Party System, 1789 to 1809* (Englewood Cliffs, N.J.: Prentice-Hall, 1965), 16.

41. Thomas Jefferson, letter to Francis Hopkinson, 13 March 1789, in *Thomas Jefferson: Writings* (New York: Library of America, 1984), 940–41.

42. *Vicksburg Register*, 25 December 1834, quoted in Silbey, *American Political Nation*, 25.

43. *Democratic Review*, March 1852, quoted in ibid., 61.

44. *The Log Cabin*, 13 June 1840, quoted in ibid., 101.

45. Hofstadter, *Idea of a Party System*, 247.

46. *New York Globe*, 19 April 1847, quoted in Silbey, *American Political Nation*, 48.

47. Quoted in Hofstadter, *Idea of a Party System*, 244.

48. Francis Lieber, *Manual of Political Ethics*, 2nd ed., vol. 2 (Philadelphia: J. B. Lippincott, 1911 [1839]), 260.

49. *Springfield Daily Republican*, 14 September 1853, quoted in Silbey, *American Political Nation*, 62.

50. Fourier, in Beecher and Bienvenu, *Utopian Vision*, 230.

51. Barthes, *Sade, Fourier, Loyola*, 114.

52. Frederick Grimke, *The Nature and Tendency of Free Institutions*, ed. John William Ward (Cambridge: Harvard University Press, 1968 [1848]), 174.

53. For example, see Monika Mueller, *"This Infinite Fraternity of Feeling": Gender, Genre, and Homoerotic Crisis in Hawthorne's "The Blithedale Romance" and Melville's "Pierre"* (Madison: Associated University Press, 1996).

54. This element of middle-class privacy coexisting with socialist "association" also characterizes Edward Bellamy's *Looking Backward* (Boston: Ticknor and Co., 1888), which offers a much more optimistic account of socialist reform.

55. Henry David Thoreau, *Walden* (New York: Oxford University Press, 1997), 121.

56. Gordon Hutner, *Secrets and Sympathy: Forms of Disclosure in Hawthorne's Novels* (Athens: University of Georgia Press, 1988), 106.

57. Gillian Brown, *Domestic Individualism: Imagining Self in Nineteenth-Century America* (Berkeley: University of California Press, 1990), 110.

58. Other critics who have approached Coverdale in these terms include Edgar A. Dryden, *Nathaniel Hawthorne: The Poetics of Enchantment* (Ithaca: Cornell University Press, 1977); Richard H. Millington, *Practicing Romance: Narrative Form and Cultural Engagement in Hawthorne's Fiction* (Princeton: Princeton University Press,

1992); Richard H. Brodhead, *Cultures of Letters: Scenes of Reading and Writing in Nineteenth-Century America* (Chicago: University of Chicago Press, 1993); and Harvey L. Gable Jr., *Liquid Fire: Transcendental Mysticism in the Romances of Nathaniel Hawthorne* (New York: Peter Lang, 1998).

59. Berlant, "Fantasies of Utopia," 53, 49.

CHAPTER TWO: The Rules of the Game: Punishment in *The Wide Wide World*

1. John T. Frederick, "Hawthorne's 'Scribbling Women,'" *New England Quarterly* 48 (1975): 235, quoted in Nancy Schnog, "Inside the Sentimental: The Psychological Work of *The Wide Wide World*," *Genders* 4 (1989): 12.

2. Susan Warner, *The Wide Wide World* (New York: Feminist Press, 1987 [1850]), 549.

3. Jane Tompkins, "Afterword," in Warner, *The Wide Wide World*, 598. See also Jane Tompkins, *Sensational Designs: The Cultural Work of American Fiction, 1790–1860*, (New York: Oxford University Press, 1985); and Nina Baym, *Women's Fiction: A Guide to Novels by and about Women in America, 1820–70*, 2nd ed. (Urbana: University of Illinois Press, 1993). Recent renditions of this line of argument include Susan K. Harris, *Nineteenth-Century American Women's Novels: Interpretive Strategies* (New York: Cambridge University Press, 1990); Isabelle White, "Anti-Individualism, Authority, and Identity: Susan Warner's Contradictions in *The Wide Wide World*," *American Studies* 31 (1990): 31–41; Grace Ann Hovet and Theodore R. Hovet, "Identity Development in Susan Warner's *The Wide Wide World*: Relationship, Performance, and Construction," *Legacy* 8 (1991): 3–16; Catherine O'Connell, "'We Must Sorrow': Silence, Suffering, and Sentimentality in Susan Warner's *The Wide Wide World*," *Studies in American Fiction* 24–25 (1996–97): 21–39; Suzanne M. Ashworth, "Susan Warner's *The Wide Wide World*, Conduct Literature, and Protocols of Female Reading in Mid-Nineteenth Century America," *Legacy* 17 (2000): 141–64; and Jennifer Mason, "Animal Bodies: Corporeality, Class, and Subject Formation in *The Wide Wide World*," *Nineteenth-Century Literature* 54 (2000): 503–33.

4. This is clearly part of a broader trend in the criticism of domestic fiction. For readings of the midcentury domestic novel as political critique that take other authors into account, see Barbara Bardes and Suzanne Gossett, *Declarations of Independence: Women and Political Power in Nineteenth-Century American Fiction* (New Brunswick: Rutgers University Press, 1990); Gillian Brown, *Domestic Individualism: Imagining Self in Nineteenth-Century America* (Berkeley: University of California Press, 1990); Lauren Berlant, "The Female Woman: Fanny Fern and the Form of Sentiment," in *The Culture of Sentiment: Race, Gender, and Sentimentality in Nineteenth-Century America*, ed. Shirley Samuels (New York: Oxford University Press, 1992), 265–81; and Joyce W. Warren, "Domesticity and the Economics of

Independence: Resistance and Revolution in the Work of Fanny Fern," in *The (Other) American Traditions: Nineteenth-Century Women Writers*, ed. Joyce W. Warren (New Brunswick: Rutgers University Press, 1993), 73–91.

5. Susan S. Williams, "Widening the World: Susan Warner, Her Readers, and the Assumption of Authorship," *American Quarterly* 42 (December 1990): 565–86; G. M. Goshgarian, *To Kiss the Chastening Rod: Domestic Fiction and Sexual Ideology in the American Renaissance* (Ithaca: Cornell University Press, 1992); Veronica Stewart, "The Wild Side of *The Wide Wide World*," *Legacy* 11 (1994): 1–16; Marianne Noble, *The Masochistic Pleasures of Sentimental Literature* (Princeton: Princeton University Press, 2000); and Jana Argersinger, "Family Embraces: The Unholy Kiss and Authorial Relations in *The Wide Wide World*," *American Literature* 74 (June 2002): 251–85. Earlier versions of the subversion argument include Helen Papashvily, *All the Happy Endings* (New York: Harper and Brothers, 1956); and Joanne Dobson, "The Hidden Hand: Subversion of Cultural Ideology in Three Mid-Nineteenth-Century American Women Writers," *American Quarterly* 38 (1986): 223–42.

6. Noble, *Masochistic Pleasures*, 96.

7. Indeed, much of the first half of the novel is taken up with her search for a teacher who could take the place of her mother. Aunt Fortune is shown to be a bad adopted mother not only because she cares little for religion but because she forces Ellen to replace schoolwork with housework: " 'If you are so tired of being idle,' said Miss Fortune, 'I'll warrant I'll give you something to do; and something to learn too, that you want enough more than all those crinkumcrankums. . . . It doesn't do for women to be bookworms' " (140). Conversely, Alice is shown to be a good adopted sister because she not only offers to teach Ellen Christian precepts but also languages, arithmetic, and natural science (complete with a cabinet of scientifically relevant "curiosities" [163]).

8. Richard Brodhead, *Cultures of Letters: Scenes of Reading and Writing in Nineteenth-Century America* (Chicago: University of Chicago Press, 1993), 21. For related Foucauldian accounts of the Victorian novel, see Nancy Armstrong, *Desire and Domestic Fiction: A Political History of the Novel* (New York: Oxford University Press, 1987); and D. A. Miller, *The Novel and the Police* (Berkeley: University of California Press, 1988).

9. Noble, *Masochistic Pleasures*, 97; White, "Anti-Individualism," 36; Shirley Foster and Judy Simons, *What Katy Read: Feminist Re-Readings of "Classic" Stories for Girls* (Iowa City: University of Iowa Press, 1995), 40.

10. Tompkins, *Sensational Designs*, 182.

11. Tompkins, "Afterword," 598.

12. Maria Susanna Cummins, *The Lamplighter*, ed. Nina Baym (New Brunswick: Rutgers University Press, 1995 [1854]), 50, 105.

13. Charles Kingsley, *The Water Babies* (London: Macmillan and Co., 1903), 174, quoted in Edward Haley Foster, *Susan and Anna Warner* (Boston: Twayne, n.d.), 48.

14. Tompkins, "Afterword," 597.

15. In addition to *The Lamplighter*, this tradition includes Augusta Jane Evans, *Beulah* (1859), Louisa May Alcott, *Little Women* (1868), Martha Finley, *Elsie Dinsmore* (1868), and Susan Coolidge, *What Katy Did* (1872). For more on the "girls' novel," see Gillian Avery, *Behold the Child: American Children and Their Books, 1621–1922* (Baltimore: Johns Hopkins University Press, 1994); and Anne Scott Macleod, *American Childhood: Essays on Children's Literature of the Nineteenth and Twentieth Centuries* (Athens: University of Georgia Press, 1994).

16. Martha Finely, *Elsie Dinsmore* (New York: Grosset and Dunlap, 1896 [1868]), 225.

17. Noble, *Masochistic Pleasures*, 110, 102.

18. Noble, for example, writes: "True womanhood makes the most basic experiences of the body so problematic for Ellen that pain seems alluring, simply because it affords the basic experience of embodiment" (*Masochistic Pleasures*, 95).

19. All of these texts went through a number of editions in the 1830s and 1840s.

20. Lydia Maria Child, *The Mother's Book* (Boston: Carter and Hendee, 1831), 20.

21. L. H. Sigourney, *Letters to Mothers* (Hartford: Hudson and Skinner, 1838), 14–15.

22. Mason L. Weems, *The Life of Washington*, ed. Marcus Cunliffe (Cambridge: Harvard University Press, 1962), xlix.

23. Other nineteenth-century works on Washington include Jared Sparks, *The Life of George Washington* (Boston: Little, Brown, and Co., 1860 [1839]); C. M. Kirkland, *Memoirs of Washington* (New York: D. Appleton, 1869 [1856]); and Morrison Heady, *The Farmer Boy, and How He Became Commander-in-Chief* (Boston: Walker, Wise and Co., 1864).

24. Garry Wills, *Cincinnatus: George Washington and the Enlightenment* (New York: Doubleday, 1984), 52–53.

25. Moreover, Washington himself came to be figured not simply as a founding father but as a kind of "national parent." According to Jay Fliegelman, the call in the eighteenth century for a system of common schools was represented in such a way that "Washington's example might ultimately be institutionalized" and "[a] national public school system serving in loco parentis to form the minds of Americans would eventually take Washington's place as a national parent" (Fliegelman, *Prodigals and Pilgrims: The American Revolution against Patriarchal Authority, 1750–1800* [Cambridge: Cambridge University Press, 1982], 199, 206).

26. Jacob Abbott, *The Mount Vernon Reader, A Course of Reading Lessons, selected with reference to their moral influence on the hearts and lives of the young, designed for the Middle Classes* (New York: Collins, Keese, and Co., 1840), 176–77.

27. E. D. E. N. Southworth, *Ishmael; or, In the Depths* (New York: Grosset and Dunlap, n.d. [1863]), 230.

28. This tract became the basis of a series of etiquette books for adults that ran from the late nineteenth through the late twentieth century. See, for example, Charles Moore, ed., *George Washington's Rules of Civility and Decent Behavior in Company and Conversation* (Boston: Houghton Mifflin, 1926); and Richard Brookhiser, *Rules of Civility: The 110 Precepts that Guided Our First President in War and Peace* (New York: Free Press, 1997).

29. It was Moncure Conway who published the first account attributing these rules primarily to one source: Francis Hawkins's *Youth's Behavior, or Decency in Conversation amongst Men. Composed in French by Grave Persons for the Use and Benefit of their Youth*, a 1640 translation of a sixteenth-century French source. See Moncure D. Conway, *George Washington's Rules of Civility: Traced to Their Sources and Restored* (New York: Hurst and Co., 1890).

30. Quoted in Horace E. Scudder, *George Washington: An Historical Biography* (Boston: Houghton, Mifflin and Co., 1889), 32.

31. Abbott is also the brother of Jacob Abbott, author of the popular Rollo books, which offered moral lessons for small children.

32. John S. C. Abbott, "George Washington," *Harper's New Monthly Magazine*, February 1856, 293.

33. One significant exception to this rule is *Queechy* (New York: G. P. Putnam, 1852), Warner's second novel, in which the young orphan Elfleda Ringgan, with her intuitive grasp of Christian duty, manages to convert her protector, Guy Carleton. In *The Wide Wide World* John is associated with his whip: "It was necessary," says Alice, "that either the horse or the man should give up; and as John has no fancy for giving up, he carried his point,—partly by management, partly, I confess, by a judicious use of the whip and spur" (377). In *Queechy*, however, it is Fleda who is associated with a weapon—in this case, a magic wand: "I wish," says Carleton, "you would make your wand rest on me, Fairy" (58).

34. Susan Warner, *Melbourne House* (New York: Robert Carter and Bros., 1864), 26; *My Desire* (New York: Robert Carter and Bros., 1879), 130; *The Letter of Credit* (New York: Robert Carter and Bros., 1882), 198.

35. In *The Old Helmet* (1863), Warner briefly tests a female mentor. The heroine's aunt (like Alice in *The Wide Wide World*) fosters the process of religious conversion (by both precept and example) without offering her charge the exhaustive attention she seems to require. Susan Warner, *The Old Helmet*, 2 vols. (New York: Robert Carter and Bros., 1863). All further references will be cited in the text by volume and page number.

36. The most famous articulation of this position is Nancy Armstrong's claim that

British domestic fiction "helped to produce a subject who understood herself in the psychological terms that had shaped fiction" (*Desire and Domestic Fiction*, 23). In the American context, Nina Baym makes a similar point, claiming that the function of domestic fiction was to "recommend and perform a middle-class, privately possessive and self-possessive way of being in the world" (*Women's Fiction*, xxii). For another important version of this claim, see Lora Romero, *Home Fronts: Domesticity and Its Critics in the Antebellum United States* (Durham: Duke University Press, 1997).

37. Elizabeth Barnes, *States of Sympathy: Seduction and Democracy in the American Novel* (New York: Columbia University Press, 1997), 12.

CHAPTER THREE: *Huckleberry Finn*; or, Consequences

1. Lionel Trilling, "*Huckleberry Finn*," in *The Liberal Imagination: Essays on Literature and Society* (Garden City, N.Y.: Doubleday, 1957), 102, 101.

2. Leo Marx, "Mr. Eliot, Mr. Trilling, and *Huckleberry Finn*," in "*Adventures of Huckleberry Finn*": *A Case Study in Critical Controversy*, ed. Gerald Graff and James Phelan, 2nd ed. (Boston: Bedford, 2004), 300.

3. For recent attacks on the ending that follow Marx's logic, see Evan Carton, "Speech Acts and Social Action: Mark Twain and the Politics of Literary Performance," in *The Cambridge Companion to Mark Twain*, ed. Forrest G. Robinson (New York: Cambridge University Press, 1995), 153–74; and Myra Jehlen, "Banned in Concord: *Adventures of Huckleberry Finn* and Classic American Literature," in Robinson, *Cambridge Companion*, 93–115. For defenses of the ending, see Richard Hill, "Overreaching: Critical Agenda and the Ending of *Huckleberry Finn*," *Texas Studies in Literature and Language* 33 (1991): 492–513; and Toni Morrison, "Introduction," in Mark Twain, *Adventures of Huckleberry Finn*, ed. Shelley Fisher Fishkin (New York: Oxford University Press, 1996 [1885]), xxxi–xli. All further references to *Huckleberry Finn* are to this edition.

4. Jonathan Arac, "*Huckleberry Finn*" *as Idol and Target: The Functions of Criticism in Our Time* (Madison: University of Wisconsin Press, 1997); Jane Smiley, "Say It Ain't So, Huck: Second Thoughts on Mark Twain's 'Masterpiece,'" *Harper's Magazine*, January 1996, 61–67.

5. The responses in *Harper's* were uniformly hostile to Smiley. Although they raised different objections, most were troubled by her insistence on using contemporary standards of political correctness to criticize Twain. One example: "It's too bad Smiley couldn't judge Twain for the book he wrote rather than for his failure to meet her 1990s political agenda" (James D. Pendleton, letter to the editor, *Harper's Magazine*, April 1996, 7).

6. Laurence Holland, "A 'Raft of Trouble': Word and Deed in *Huckleberry Finn*," in

American Realism: New Essays, ed. Eric Sundquist (Baltimore: Johns Hopkins University Press, 1982), 75. When Holland's essay first appeared in *Glyph* in 1979, James Cox had already made a version of this argument about the ending. Unlike Holland, however, who sees in the novel an attempt to grapple with the difference between legal and real freedom in the post-Reconstruction era, Cox sees the novel as an indictment of the complacent liberal reader: "If the reader sees in Tom's performance a rather shabby and safe bit of play, he is seeing no more than the exposure of the approval with which he watched Huck operate. For if Tom is rather contemptibly setting a free slave free, what after all is the reader doing, who begins the book after the *fact* of the Civil War?" (Cox, *Mark Twain: The Fate of Humor* [Princeton: Princeton University Press, 1966], 175). This tendency to read the novel in the light of post-Reconstruction politics has only gained steam in recent years, during which the imperative to historicize has been taken to mean addressing the moment in which the novel was written. One of the latest essays is by Christine Macleod, who interestingly extends Holland's claims without ever citing his essay; see her "Telling the Truth in a Tight Place: *Huckleberry Finn* and the Reconstruction Era," *Southern Quarterly* 34 (1995): 5–15. See also the essays collected in *Satire or Evasion? Black Perspectives on "Huckleberry Finn,"* ed. James S. Leonard, Thomas A. Tenney, and Thadious M. Davis (Durham: Duke University Press, 1992), especially Richard K. Barksdale, "History, Slavery, and Thematic Irony," 49–55; Charles H. Nilon, "The Ending of *Huckleberry Finn*: Freeing the Free Negro," 62–76; and David L. Smith, "Huck, Jim, and American Racial Discourse," 103–20.

7. Russell Reising, *The Unusable Past: Theory and the Study of American Literature* (New York: Methuen, 1986), 159.

8. Ralph Ellison, "Twentieth-Century Fiction and the Black Mask of Humanity," in *Shadow and Act* (New York: Random House, 1964), 22–44. In an essay on *Huckleberry Finn* published at about the same time as Arac's book and Smiley's article, Clara Claiborne Park takes a similar approach to a defender of the novel: "A critic such as D. L. Smith, brilliant, generous, and black, may try to save the appearances by reading Huck Finn as an allegory of Reconstruction. But the common reader must read with Hemingway and Doctorow a profoundly embarrassing novel, structurally fissured, ethically riven" (Park, "The River and the Road: Fashions in Forgiveness," *American Scholar* 66 [1997]: 58).

9. Actually, both Arac and Smiley share the impulse both to berate and, finally, to absolve Twain for these effects. Arac claims, "I am not holding Twain solely responsible for such use of his book" (*Huckleberry Finn*, 23). Smiley claims, "These are only authors, after all, and once a book is published the author can't be held accountable for its role in the culture. For that we have to blame the citizens themselves, or their teachers, or *their* teachers, the arbiters of critical taste" ("Say It Ain't So," 66).

10. Bernard Williams, *Shame and Necessity* (Berkeley: University of California Press, 1993), 61.

11. As Frances Ferguson has pointed out, "the tort law assigned a liability for possession that matched and perhaps overmatched its privileges as it came to hold persons responsible for their effects and for the effects of their objects" ("*Justine*; or, The Law of the Road," in *Aesthetics and Ideology*, ed. George Levine [New Brunswick: Rutgers University Press, 1994], 115). My discussion of tort law in relation to the novel is indebted to Ferguson.

12. Oliver Wendell Holmes Jr., *The Common Law* (New York: Dover, 1991 [1881]), 153. For another important contemporary text on torts, see Thomas M. Cooley, *A Treatise on the Law of Torts; or, The Wrongs Which Arise Independent of Contract* (Chicago: Callaghan and Co., 1880). For general legal histories of the period that include discussions of negligence, see Lawrence M. Friedman, *A History of American Law* (New York: Simon and Schuster, 1973); and Morton Horwitz, *The Transformation of American Law, 1780–1860* (Cambridge: Harvard University Press, 1977).

13. Friedman, *History of American Law*, 414.

14. Mark Twain and Charles Dudley Warner, *The Gilded Age: A Tale of To-Day* (New York: Oxford University Press, 1996 [1873]), 46.

15. Nan Goodman, *Shifting the Blame: Literature, Law, and the Theory of Accidents in Nineteenth-Century America* (Princeton: Princeton University Press, 1998), 66–67.

16. David Rosenberg argues that, despite critical consensus to the contrary, Holmes in fact supported strict liability in his treatise on common law. According to Rosenberg, the only model of strict liability Holmes rejected was "cause-based strict liability," under which a person is responsible simply because he caused a harm. For Holmes, Rosenberg explains, this rule violated "the prevailing norm of responsibility," which maintained that a person could not be held responsible unless he could have avoided causing the harm (Rosenberg, *The Hidden Holmes: His Theory of Torts in History* [Cambridge: Harvard University Press, 1995], 6). If Rosenberg is right and Holmes did in fact have a more liberal view of liability under tort than previously believed, it would further support my contention that the late nineteenth century saw the rise of a more expansive model of responsibility.

17. Oliver Wendell Holmes Jr., "The Theory of Torts," *American Law Review* 7 (1873): 660, quoted in G. Edward White, *Tort Law in America: An Intellectual History* (New York: Oxford University Press, 1980), 19.

18. Wai Chee Dimock, "The Economy of Pain: Capitalism, Humanitarianism, and the Realistic Novel," in *New Essays on "The Rise of Silas Lapham,"* ed. Donald Pease (New York: Cambridge University Press, 1991), 71.

19. As Horwitz has pointed out, in the mid-nineteenth century American courts, following English precedent, began to allow common carriers like railroads to con-

tract out of strict liability. This option, however, only rarely enabled carriers to limit liability for negligence. By 1873, "under the influence of the Granger Movement . . . the United States Supreme Court began to stem the tide by finally holding that a common carrier could not contract out of liability for negligence" (*Transformation of American Law*, 206).

20. White, *Tort Law in America*, 19. So powerful was this belief in a noncontractual obligation owed to "all the world" that the courts, initially responsible for ingeniously limiting liability, began to find ways around these restrictions.

21. Martha Nussbaum, *Poetic Justice: The Literary Imagination and Public Life* (Boston: Beacon, 1995).

22. Wai Chee Dimock, *Residues of Justice: Literature, Law, Philosophy* (Berkeley: University of California Press, 1996), 9.

23. Twain continues this pattern in such later works as *Tom Sawyer Abroad* (1894), "Huck Finn and Tom Sawyer among the Indians," and "Tom Sawyer's Conspiracy" (the last two of which were unfinished), in which Huck and Tom endanger Jim so that they might have adventures in rescuing him. It should be noted, however, that in the years following *Huckleberry Finn* (especially after the *Plessy* decision, when almost all hope for racial justice had evaporated), Twain does not address the problem of responsibility for harm in the same terms. The relevant legal context had changed. In "Tom Sawyer's Conspiracy," for example, Jim is falsely accused of murder and threatened with execution; he is thus no longer a victim in need of legal remedy but rather a victim of the criminal law. See "Huck Finn and Tom Sawyer among the Indians" and "Tom Sawyer's Conspiracy," in *"Huck Finn and Tom Sawyer among the Indians" and Other Unfinished Stories* (Berkeley: University of California Press, 1989), 33–81; and *Tom Sawyer Abroad*, in *Tom Sawyer Abroad, "Tom Sawyer, Detective," and Other Stories* (New York: Harper, 1904), 1–136.

24. Mark Twain, *Pudd'nhead Wilson* (1894) in *"Pudd'nhead Wilson" and Other Tales* (New York: Oxford University Press, 1992), 88.

25. Michael Rogin makes a similar point in "Francis Galton and Mark Twain: The Natal Autograph in *Pudd'nhead Wilson*," in *Mark Twain's "Pudd'nhead Wilson": Race, Conflict, and Culture*, ed. Susan Gillman and Forrest G. Robinson (Durham: Duke University Press, 1990), 73–85.

26. H. L. A. Hart, *Punishment and Responsibility* (New York: Oxford University Press, 1968), 147.

27. Brook Thomas, ed., *"Plessy v. Ferguson": A Brief History with Documents* (Boston: Bedford Books, 1997), 59.

28. Albion Tourgée, *Pactolus Prime* (Upper Saddle River, N.J.: Gregg Press, 1968).

29. As Brook Thomas has argued, this scene resembles nothing so much as a trial, in which "Benny and Prime interrogate prominent citizens occupying the shoe shine

chair as if it were the witness chair in court" (Thomas, *American Literary Realism and the Failed Promise of Contract* [Berkeley: University of California Press, 1997], 226).

30. This debate on compensation for the freedmen closely resembles the contemporary debate over reparations for slavery. Indeed, in a column in the online journal *Salon* in May 2000, David Horowitz provides "ten reasons" against the payment of reparations, one of which comes remarkably close to the judge's objection to Benny's proposal. Horowitz writes: "In terms of lineal responsibility for slavery, only a tiny minority of Americans ever owned slaves. This is true even for those who lived in the antebellum South, where only one white in five was a slaveholder. Why should the descendants of non-slaveholding whites owe a debt? What about the descendants of the 350,000 Union soldiers who died to free the slaves? They gave their lives. What possible morality would ask them to pay (through their descendants) again?" See Horowitz, "The Latest Civil Rights Disaster," *Salon*, 30 May 2000, http://dir.salon.com/news/col/horo/2000/05/30/reparations/index.html. Like Tourgée's judge, Horowitz views the public as a conglomeration of unique individuals, each of whom must be judged independently. Even the context of Horowitz's column resembles the scene in *Pactolus Prime*: just as the conservative white customers make their case against compensation on Benny and Pac's home turf—the shoe shine stand—a conservative writer makes his case in the liberal venue of *Salon*.

31. As Julia Epstein and Lori Hope Lefkovitz put it in the introduction to their collection, *Shaping Losses*: "Cultural memory refers to ethnic group consciousness of the past and provides the philosophical and historical foundations for ethnic, religious, and racial identities. It refers to the legacy of history as history retains the ability to affect everyday lives by the determining weight of the past" (Epstein and Lefkovitz, eds., *Shaping Losses: Cultural Memory and the Holocaust* [Urbana: University of Illinois Press, 2001], 1). There is, in fact, a vast archive that sees the Jewish relation to the Holocaust in terms of memory. Some of the most interesting recent examples are Miriam Bratu Hansen, "*Schindler's List* Is Not *Shoah*: Second Commandment, Popular Modernism, and Public Memory," in *Spielberg's Holocaust: Critical Perspectives on "Schindler's List,"* ed. Yosefa Loshitzky (Bloomington: Indiana University Press, 1997), 77–103; Geoffrey Hartman, ed., *Holocaust Remembrance: The Shapes of Memory* (Cambridge: Blackwell, 1994); and James E. Young, *The Texture of Memory: Holocaust Memorials and Meaning* (New Haven: Yale University Press, 1993). Peter Novick offers a powerful critique of this desire to sustain "collective memory," calling such memory "ahistorical, or even anti-historical" to the extent that it "simplifies; sees events from a single, committed perspective; is impatient with ambiguities of any kind; reduces events to mythic archetypes" (Novick, *The Holocaust in American Life* [Boston: Houghton Mifflin, 1999], 3–4). Walter Benn Michaels, on the other hand, critiques this position on the basis of what he sees as its

philosophical incoherence (see Michaels, "'You Who Never Was There': Slavery and the New Historicism, Deconstruction, and the Holocaust," *Narrative* 4 [1996]: 1–16).

32. Richard Gollin and Rita Gollin link Tom's claim that it would take thirty-seven years to free Jim to Lincoln's suggestion during the Civil War that the slaves be freed by the year 1900 (thirty-seven years after the end of the war). Their argument that this number ties Twain's text to the history it seems to be evading remains relevant to the current debate over the novel and to my account. See Gollin and Gollin, "*Huckleberry Finn* and the Time of the Evasion," *Modern Language Studies* 9 (1979): 5–15.

33. Carl F. Wieck notes this connection between the repetition of the number forty and the national promise to the freedmen of forty acres and a mule—without, however, explaining the terms in which Tom's payment could be understood as a form of compensation (see Wieck, *Refiguring "Huckleberry Finn"* [Athens: University of Georgia Press, 2000], 98–101).

34. For a history of the Freedmen's Bureau, see Eric Foner, *Reconstruction: America's Unfinished Revolution, 1863–1877* (New York: Harper, 1988).

35. Holmes, *The Common Law*, 77.

36. Quoted in Shelley Fisher Fishkin, "Racial Attitudes," in *The Mark Twain Encyclopedia*, ed. J. R. LeMaster and James D. Wilson (New York: Garland, 1993), 613.

37. Ibid.

38. Shelley Fisher Fishkin, *Lighting Out for the Territory: Reflections on Mark Twain and American Culture* (New York: Oxford University Press, 1997), 127.

39. Arthur G. Pettit, *Mark Twain and the South* (Lexington: University Press of Kentucky, 1974), 127.

40. For an interesting account of Twain's use of ethnic caricature, see Henry B. Wonham, "'I Want a Real Coon': Mark Twain and Late-Nineteenth-Century Ethnic Caricature," *American Literature* 72 (2000): 117–52.

41. Tom Quirk, *Coming to Grips with "Huckleberry Finn": Essays on a Book, a Boy, and a Man* (Columbia: University of Missouri Press, 1993), 74–75.

42. George Washington Cable, "The Freedman's Case in Equity," in *The Negro Question*, ed. Arlin Turner (New York: Anchor-Doubleday, 1958), 74.

CHAPTER FOUR: The Veil of Cedars: Charles Chesnutt and Conversion

1. Mark Twain, *Adventures of Huckleberry Finn*, ed. Shelley Fisher Fishkin (New York: Oxford University Press, 1996 [1885]), 49–50.

2. Charles Chesnutt, *The House behind the Cedars* (New York: Penguin, 1993 [1900]), 1.

3. Since C. Vann Woodward published *The Strange Career of Jim Crow* in 1955, historians have been debating whether the radical segregation instituted by southern

"Redeemer" governments at the end of the century was in fact a significant break with earlier social practices. Woodward's insight was to suggest that, while white supremacy dominated social life in the antebellum and Reconstruction South, it had not, until the 1890s, required the physical separation of the races: "Exploitation there was in that period, as in other periods and in other regions, but it did not follow then that the exploited had to be ostracized. Subordination there was also, unmistakable subordination; but it was not yet an accepted corollary that the subordinates had to be totally segregated and needlessly humiliated by a thousand daily reminders of their subordination" (Woodward, *The Strange Career of Jim Crow*, 3rd ed. [New York: Oxford University Press, 1974], 44). Woodward's arguments have been under attack almost since the moment he made them, as scholars have disclosed well-entrenched patterns of de facto segregation in both the North and the South that predate the Civil War. But while the evidence suggests that racial segregation was already well established in antebellum America, it was only at the turn of the century that segregation became an elaborate juridico-legal system. According to Joel Williamson, "This change represented no great revolution in physical arrangements.... It was a revolution, however, in declarations of intent by governments and the white constituencies they represented" (Williamson, *The Crucible of Race: Black-White Relationships in the American South since Emancipation* [New York: Oxford University Press, 1984], 253). In other words, by the 1890s segregation was not only the accepted social custom, it was the law. See also John W. Cell, *The Highest Stage of White Supremacy: The Origins of Segregation in South Africa and the American South* (Cambridge: Cambridge University Press, 1982); and David Delaney, *Race, Place, and the Law, 1836–1948* (Austin: University of Texas Press, 1998).

4. I take this term from Delaney, *Race, Place, and the Law*.

5. Brook Thomas, ed., *"Plessy v. Ferguson": A Brief History with Documents* (New York: Bedford Books, 1997), 43.

6. For a detailed discussion of this problem in *Plessy*, see Walter Benn Michaels, *Our America: Nativism, Modernism, and Pluralism* (Durham: Duke University Press, 1995), 114.

7. Joel Williamson, *New People: Miscegenation and Mulattoes in the United States* (New York: Free Press, 1980), 98.

8. One of the best accounts of *The House behind the Cedars*, William L. Andrews's very brief foreword to the University of Georgia Press edition of the novel, makes a similar claim about passing: "Why then, Chesnutt's novel seems to ask, should people who look as white as 'whites' and whose cultural affinities and socioeconomic goals mirror those of 'whites' be automatically condemned as racial imposters for simply being what to all appearances they actually are—white men and women?" (Andrews, "Foreword," in *The House behind the Cedars* [Athens: University of Georgia Press,

2000], xii). Andrews, however, provides no further explanation of Chesnutt's attempt to take on the problem of being what one is.

9. In such well-known novels of passing as Pauline Hopkins's *Of One Blood* (1902), James Weldon Johnson's *The Autobiography of an Ex-Coloured Man* (1912), and Nella Larsen's *Passing* (1929), crossing the color line is imagined both as transgression and as guilty secret. The narrator of Johnson's novel, for instance, feels compelled to tell his racial secret to the woman he wants to marry: "Then began the hardest struggle of my life, whether to ask her to marry me under false colours or to tell her the whole truth. My sense of what was exigent made me feel like there was no necessity of saying anything; but my inborn sense of honour rebelled at even indirect deception in this case" (Johnson, *The Autobiography of an Ex-Coloured Man* [New York: Knopf, 1951], 200). Even the language that the narrator uses here—"false colours" and "inborn sense of honour"—suggests his commitment to the truth of his black identity, the identity that is "inborn." Recent critics who have approached this fiction tend to see it as favoring antiessentialist accounts of race, a commitment to a racial identity that is shifting, unstable, or multiple. From Chesnutt's perspective in *The House behind the Cedars*, however, the point is not to underscore the instability of racial identity, but to imagine what it would mean if one's racial identity were voluntary. For antiessentialist accounts of racial passing, see Elaine K. Ginsberg, ed., *Passing and the Fictions of Identity* (Durham: Duke University Press, 1996); Samira Kawash, *Dislocating the Color Line: Identity, Hybridity, and Singularity in African-American Narrative* (Stanford: Stanford University Press, 1997); and Gayle Wald, *Crossing the Line: Racial Passing in Twentieth-Century U.S. Literature and Culture* (Durham: Duke University Press, 2000).

10. Giulia Fabi has argued that the first half of *The House behind the Cedars* deals with "passing" not only thematically but formally by refusing to reveal the race of the central characters: "Chesnutt undermines slowly and systematically, through indirect circumstantial clues, the impression he has created of the protagonist's whiteness and also reveals explicitly his mixed-race background half-way through the novel" (Fabi, *Passing and the Rise of the African-American Novel* [Urbana: University of Illinois Press, 2001], 73). But to read the novel this way is simply to misunderstand the text, which does not need to spell out the Waldens' background at the beginning of the novel in order to be "explicit" about their race.

11. See, for example, Richard Brodhead, *Cultures of Letters: Scenes of Reading and Writing in Nineteenth-Century America* (Chicago: University of Chicago Press, 1993).

12. Frederick Douglass, *Narrative of the Life of Frederick Douglass: An American Slave* (New York: Penguin, 1986 [1845]), 83–84. As Albert E. Stone has pointed out, Douglass was probably referring not to Sheridan but to Arthur O'Connor, whose speeches on Catholic emancipation, also included in the *Orator*, more closely resem-

ble those Douglass describes. See Stone, "Identity and Art in Frederick Douglass's *Narrative*," in *Critical Essays on Frederick Douglass*, ed. William J. Andrews (Boston: G. K. Hall, 1991), 62–78.

13. Sir Walter Scott, *Ivanhoe* (New York: Penguin, 1986 [1819]), 518.

14. Pauline Hopkins, *Winona* [1902], in *The Magazine Novels of Pauline Hopkins* (New York: Oxford University Press, 1988), 285–437.

15. W. E. B. DuBois, *The Souls of Black Folk* (New York: Penguin Books, 1996 [1903]), 90.

16. Michael Ragussis, *Figures of Conversion: "The Jewish Question" and English National Identity* (Durham: Duke University Press, 1995), 16.

17. For more on the question of liberal citizenship, see John Rawls, *Political Liberalism* (New York: Columbia University Press, 1993).

18. See, for example, Thackeray's *Rebecca and Rowena: A Romance upon a Romance* (Emmaus, Pa.: Story Classics, 1954 [1850]). In a recent novel, Noah Gordon attempts to single-handedly revive this tradition, although he views the Spanish Inquisition through the lens of American identity politics. In *The Last Jew*, Yonah Toledano, trapped in Spain after the expulsion of the Jews (and the murder of his family), passes as a Christian rather than converting to Christianity (Gordon, *The Last Jew* [New York: St. Martins, 2000]).

19. Edward Bulwer-Lytton, *Leila: or, the Siege of Granada* (Kila, Mont.: Kessinger Publishing, n.d. [1838]), 669.

20. George Eliot, *Daniel Deronda* (New York: Oxford University Press, 1984 [1876]), 449–50.

21. Susan Meyer, "'Safely to Their Own Borders': Proto-Zionism, Feminism, and Nationalism in *Daniel Deronda*," *ELH* 60 (1993): 747.

22. Charles Chesnutt, "Race Prejudice: Its Causes and Cures," in *Charles W. Chesnutt: Essays and Speeches*, ed. Joseph R. McElrath Jr., Robert C. Leitz III, and Jesse S. Crisler (Stanford: Stanford University Press, 1999), 231. All further references to Chesnutt's essays will be to this collection.

23. SallyAnne Ferguson, "Chesnutt's Genuine Blacks and Future Americans," *MELUS* 15 (1988): 109–19.

24. Chesnutt, "Race Prejudice," 234.

25. Chesnutt, "The Future American," 132.

26. Chesnutt, "Rights and Duties," 257.

27. One important exception is Ross Posnock, who has convincingly argued that the "resistance" to racial identity and the desire for "a cosmopolitan universalism" inspired not only Chesnutt, but a number of important African American intellectuals, including W. E. B. DuBois, Richard Wright, Ralph Ellison, and James Baldwin (Posnock, *Color and Culture: Black Writers and the Making of the Modern Intellectual*

[Cambridge: Harvard University Press, 1998], 21). William L. Andrews's account of *The House behind the Cedars* in his volume *The Literary Career of Charles W. Chesnutt* makes claims similar to mine about Chesnutt's essays and speeches. He writes, for instance, that "Chesnutt urged black people to be prepared and willing to give up their 'separate identity,'" in order "to accelerate the process of assimilation and the withering away of false racial distinctions" (Andrews, *The Literary Career of Charles W. Chesnutt* [Baton Rouge: Louisiana State University Press, 1980], 141). His argument has been virtually ignored by more recent critics.

28. William E. Moddelmog, "Lawful Entitlements: Chesnutt's Fictions of Ownership," *Texas Studies in Literature and Language* 41 (1999): 62. Dean McWilliams makes similar claims about Chesnutt's desire to reveal the dangers of passing. According to McWilliams, "Warwick comes, he believes, to rescue his sister from life as a Negro, but he brings instead another form of imprisonment—entrapment within white Southern ideology" (McWilliams, *Charles W. Chesnutt and the Fictions of Race* [Athens: University of Georgia Press, 2002], 135).

29. Stephen P. Knadler, "Untragic Mulatto: Charles Chesnutt and the Discourse of Whiteness," *American Literary History* 8 (1996): 427.

30. Michaels, *Our America*, 159.

31. Chesnutt, "Address before Ohio State Night School," 494.

32. Chesnutt, "The Future of the Negro," 31.

33. Chesnutt, "Self-Made Men," 34.

34. Chesnutt, "Address before Ohio State Night School," 494.

35. John Higham, *Send These to Me* (New York: Atheneum, 1975), 170–71.

36. The pattern for these exclusions was already in place by 1869, when Jewish banker Joseph Seligman was, in a famous incident, turned away from a Sarasota Springs hotel.

37. Arthur Hertzberg, *The Jews in America* (New York: Simon and Schuster, 1989), 175.

38. Gerald Sorin, *A Time for Building: The Third Migration, 1880–1920* (Baltimore: Johns Hopkins University Press, 1992), 235; and Alan Silverstein, *Alternatives to Assimilation: The Response of Reform Judaism to American Culture, 1840–1930* (Hanover, N.H.: Brandeis University Press, 1994).

39. For accounts of Jews in American literature (especially in the late nineteenth century and twentieth century), see Leslie A. Fiedler, *The Jew in the American Novel* (New York: Hertzl Institute Pamphlets, 1959); Sol Liptzin, *The Jew in American Literature* (New York: Bloch Publishing Co, 1966); Louise A. Mayo, *The Ambivalent Image: Nineteenth-Century America's Perception of the Jew* (London: Associated University Presses, 1988); and Louis Harap, *The Image of the Jew in American Literature: From Early Republic to Mass Immigration*, 2nd ed. (New York: Syracuse University Press,

2003). For a good account of the way in which assimilation in the twentieth century was fostered by Jewish involvement in popular culture, see Michael Rogin, *Blackface, White Noise: Jewish Immigrants in the Hollywood Melting Pot* (Berkeley: University of California Press, 1996).

40. Fiedler, *The Jew in the American Novel*, 16. Perhaps the most famous account of Jewish assimilation, Mary Antin's *The Promised Land* (1912), suggests that the answer is no. Antin's memoir tracks the way in which the claims of American identity quite easily begin to overshadow (rather than merely supplement) the claims of Jewish identity. To take one example, dietary laws, which had been strictly enforced in the European shtetl and celebrated as a sign of Jewish difference from gentile neighbors, become for her family in Boston an artificial barrier to their newly established national identity: "[My father] did not want us children to refuse invitations to the table of our Gentile neighbors. He would have no bar to our social intercourse with the world around us, for only by freely sharing the life of our neighbors could we come into our full inheritance of Amerian freedom and opportunity. On the holy days he bought my mother a ticket for the synagogue, but the children he sent to school." Once "ghetto life" and "ghetto beliefs" have been "abandoned," it seems, the particularity of Jewish identity vanishes. Just as the public school replaces the synagogue, the nation here replaces religion in what looks like a translation of the conversion narrative, so that (at least in Antin's account) if one must be reborn, it is as an American: "I was born, I have lived and I have been made over" (Antin, *The Promised Land* [Boston: Houghton Mifflin, 1912], 247, xi).

41. Adam Sol, "Longings and Renunciations: Attitudes Towards Intermarriage in Early Twentieth-Century Jewish American Novels," *American Jewish History* 89 (2001): 215.

42. Other works that might be included here, aside from those I discuss in detail in this chapter, are Ezra Brudno, *The Fugitive* (New York: Doubleday, Page and Co, 1904); Israel Zangwill, *The Melting Pot* (New York: Macmillan, 1909); and Elias Tobenkin, *Witte Arrives* (New York: Frederick A. Stokes Company, 1916).

43. Eugene F. Baldwin and Maurice Eisenberg, *Doctor Cavallo* (Peoria, Ill.: Press of J. W. Franks, 1895), 121.

44. Emma Wolf, *Other Things Being Equal*, ed. Barbara Cantalupo (Detroit: Wayne State University Press, 2002 [1892]), 196.

45. Similarly, in *Yetta Segal*, the Jewish Yetta sees her impending marriage with Alvarez Lanning as a "progressive" form of race blending: "Today, more fully than was possible in the past, the representative member of this or that race, the progressive inhabitant of this or that country, is a citizen of the wide world" (Horace J. Rollin, *Yetta Segal* [New York: G. W. Dillingham Co., 1898], 158).

46. Leslie Fiedler proposes, however, that the question of Harland's identity may

not be so simple: "There still exists in my own mind a vestigial doubt (unsupported by any fact I have been able to discover) that Luska-Harland may, after all, have been a Jew pretending to be a Gentile pretending to be a Jew" (*The Jew in the American Novel*, 10).

47. Henry Harland, *The Yoke of the Thorah* (Upper Saddle River, N.J.: Gregg Press, 1970 [1887]), 64.

48. Henry Harland, *Mrs. Peixada* (New York: Cassell and Co., 1886), 102.

49. From this perspective, the interest of Abraham Cahan's work is that it suggests (along slightly different lines) that marriage cannot work on this model. In one of Cahan's most well-known short stories, "The Imported Bridegroom" (1898), the thoroughly modern Flora gives up her dream of marrying "an educated American gentleman" in order to marry the Talmudic scholar (and immigrant) Shaya, when he agrees to study medicine rather than Torah: "Oh, won't it be lovely when everybody knows that you go to college and study together with nice, educated up-town fellows! We would go to theaters together and read different books" (Cahan, "*The Imported Bridegroom*" *and Other Stories of the New York Ghetto* [New York: Signet, 1996], 20, 64–65). And yet, rather than providing a link between Jews from two different cultures, this shared commitment to being American is what finally undermines their marriage; Shaya becomes even more of a stranger to Flora in his incarnation as an American intellectual than he was as a Yiddish-speaking Talmudic scholar.

50. Chesnutt, "Rights and Duties," 255.

51. Chesnutt, "Race Prejudice," 234.

52. Grace Aguilar, *The Vale of Cedars; or, The Martyr* (New York: D. Appleton and Co., 1880 [1850]), 16, 33.

53. Kawash, *Dislocating the Color Line*, 125.

54. Ibid., 130.

55. Eric Sundquist, *To Wake the Nations: Race in the Making of American Literature* (Cambridge: Harvard University Press, 1993), 298.

56. Ibid., 447.

57. Charles Chesnutt, *The Marrow of Tradition* (New York: Penguin, 1993 [1901]), 86. Even Sandy, a dialect character who is not killed, is nonetheless imagined to have mysteriously faded away at the end of the novel, "restored to the bosom of the church, and enfolded by its sheltering arms" (236).

58. Gavin Jones, *Strange Talk: The Politics of Dialect Literature in Gilded Age America* (Berkeley: University of California Press, 1999), 210.

59. Chesnutt, "Race Prejudice," 233.

60. For a detailed account of the parallels between Rena and *Ivanhoe*'s Rebecca, see Earle V. Bryant, "Charles Chesnutt's Southern Black Jew: Rena Walden's Masquerade in *The House behind the Cedars*," *American Literary Realism* 31 (1999): 15–21.

61. Kawash, *Dislocating the Color Line*, 130.

62. Frances Harper, *Iola Leroy; or, Shadows Uplifted* (New York: Oxford University Press, 1988 [1892]), 117, 114.

63. William Dean Howells, *An Imperative Duty* (New York, 1892 [1891]), 46.

CHAPTER FIVE: Addiction and the Ends of Desire

1. Sir Arthur Conan Doyle, "The Parasite" (1894), in *Dracula's Brood*, ed. Richard Dalby (New York: Dorset Press, 1987), 125.

2. In an anonymous pamphlet written in 1845, for example, a man who claims to be a mesmerist confesses to having used his powers to elicit desire in the attractive women he treated: "Reader, let me tell you that to be placed opposite a young and lovely female, who has subjected herself to the process for the purpose of effecting a cure of some nervous affection or otherwise, to look into her gentle eyes, soft and beaming with confidence and trust, is singularly entrancing. You assume her hands, which are clasped in your own, you look intently upon the pupils of her eyes, which as the power becomes more and more visible in her person, evince the tenderest regard, until they close in dreamy and as it were spiritual affection.—Then is her mind all your own, and she will evince the most tender solicitude and care for your good. Your will then becomes not only as law to her, but it is the greatest happiness to her to execute your smallest wish. . . . Self is entirely swallowed up in the earnest regard that actuates the subject, and they will stop at no point beyond which they may afford you pleasure should you indicate it by thought or word" (anonymous, *The Confessions of a Magnetiser, Being an Expose of Animal Magnetism* [Boston: Gleason's, 1845], 9–10).

3. Robert C. Fuller, *Mesmerism and the American Cure of Souls* (Philadelphia: University of Pennsylvania Press, 1982), 149. Of course, this transition was neither simple nor absolute. As many historians have shown, mesmerism was originally presented as a form of "cure," while later manifestations of hypnotism (as practiced by Freud, for example) were often feared as a form of enslavement as much as they were sought as therapy, especially for women who were, more often than men, the subjects of hypnotism. By the end of the century, however, there was clearly a shift in emphasis from a concern with coercion from outside the self to a concern with exposure of the self. For more on mesmerism and mind control, see Robert Darnton, *Mesmerism and the End of the Enlightenment in France* (New York: Schocken Books, 1970); Henri Ellenberger, *The Discovery of the Unconscious: The History and Evolution of Dynamic Psychiatry* (New York: Basic Books, 1970); Alan Gauld, *A History of Hypnotism* (New York: Cambridge University Press, 1992); Adam Crabtree, *From Mesmer to Freud: Magnetic Sleep and the Roots of Psychological Healing* (New Haven:

Yale University Press, 1993); Nina Auerbach, "Magi and Maidens: The Romance of the Victorian Freud," in *Reading Fin-de-Siècle Fictions*, ed. Lyn Pykett (New York: Longman Addison Wesley, 1996), 22–38; and Alison Winter, *Mesmerized: Powers of Mind in Victorian Britain* (Chicago: University of Chicago Press, 1998).

4. It would be wrong to assume, however, that Doyle is simply drawing on a much earlier model of mesmerism in which the mesmerist was imagined to "impress" his own desires upon the victim, for the form of desire he evokes in "The Parasite" was, by century's end, already being linked to the emergent technology of drug addiction.

5. Nathan Beman, *Beman on Intemperance* (New York: John P. Haven, 1829), quoted in Harry Gene Levine, "The Discovery of Addiction: Changing Conceptions of Habitual Drunkenness in America," *Journal of Studies on Alcohol* 39 (1978): 156. See also Levine's essay, "The Alcohol Problem in America: From Temperance to Alcoholism," *British Journal of Addiction* 79 (1984): 109–19.

6. Virginia Berridge and Griffith Edwards, *Opium and the People: Opium Use in Nineteenth-Century England* (New Haven: Yale University Press, 1987), 155.

7. Aside from the articles by Harry Gene Levine, see, for example, Eve Sedgwick, "Epidemics of the Will," in *Tendencies* (Durham: Duke University Press, 1993); and Mark Seltzer, "Serial Killers (I)," *differences* 5 (1993): 92–128. Avital Ronell's reading of Emma Bovary's addiction as "a kind of crash economy, an exorbitant expenditure with no reserve" also relies on the addict-as-consumer model (Ronell, *Crack Wars: Literature, Addiction, Mania* [Lincoln: University of Nebraska Press, 1992], 109). At the same time, a different school of criticism has claimed that addiction is not so much a generalizable pathology of market culture as it is kind of utopian transcendence of the market. Jacques Derrida, for example, claims that what scares us about the addict is that he flouts the logic of the market by liberating desire from the rhythms of exchange, becoming in the process a kind of pure consumer who refuses to make desire productive of anything except more desire. In an interview, "The Rhetoric of Drugs," he argues: "We do not object to the drug user's pleasure per se, but we cannot abide the fact that his is a pleasure taken in an experience without truth. . . . The drug addict, in our common conception, the drug addict as such produces nothing, nothing true or real." As a consumer who produces nothing, the addict, according to Derrida, empties out the model of identity built on possession in order to find the "ideal" self or "perfect body" that could resist "social oppression, suppression and repression" (Derrida, "The Rhetoric of Drugs: An Interview," *differences* 5 [1993]: 7–8, 14). Similarly, David Lenson argues that "what one is purchasing when one buys drugs . . . is the promise of a change in consciousness—and possibly an alternative to Consumerism" (Lenson, *On Drugs* [Minneapolis: University of Minnesota Press, 1995], 28). Of course, the fact that the addict in this model must purchase this "perfect body" with his endless desire for that body suggests that this

desire is, in fact, quite productive. In this reading, then, the addict doesn't escape the market so much as he manages to inhabit a "perfect" market in which he engages only in unalienated forms of consumption. From the perspective of the market, in other words, this utopian refuge from consumerism looks less like transcendence and more like a purification of consumerist logic.

8. Levine, "Discovery," 165.

9. Seltzer, "Serial Killers (I)," 111–14.

10. Benjamin Ward Richardson, "The Physical Benefits of Total Abstinence, or, Idiosyncrasy and Alcohol," in *Temperance in All Nations: Papers from the World's Temperance Congress*, vol. 2, ed. J. N. Stearns (New York: National Temperance Society Publications House, 1893), 217.

11. Henry Cole, *Confessions of an American Opium Eater* (Boston: J. H. Earle, 1895), 235.

12. Jack London, *John Barleycorn, or, Alcoholic Memoirs* (New York: Signet, 1990 [1913]), 19.

13. In other words, even something as disruptive as the unconscious still depends on a basic notion of unity in which each desire, intention, and thought must be understood as originating in and thus defining the self, whether or not this self is imagined to be transparent to itself. After all, the unconscious always works to define what the individual "really" wants. Mikkel Borch-Jacobsen makes a version of this argument when he claims that in Freud's theory of the unconscious "the *same* subject has and does not have access to a given representation, remembers and does not remember a given 'scene,' experiences and does not experience a given pleasure. In this scene, the cleavage or division of the subject that psychoanalysis keeps talking about takes place against a background of unity, a *unitary* subject" (Borch-Jacobsen, *The Freudian Subject*, trans. Catherine Porter [Stanford: Stanford University Press, 1982], 6). I am claiming that the model of addiction that Doyle draws on in "The Parasite" explodes this presumed unity by describing a desire that literally comes from outside the self—a desire, therefore, that cannot define that self.

14. Franco Moretti makes explicit the connection between his reading of *Dracula* and Marx's theory of how capital creates value: "'Capital is dead labour which, vampire-like, lives only by sucking living labour, and lives the more, the more labour it sucks.' Marx's analogy unravels the vampire metaphor. As everyone knows, the vampire is dead and yet not dead: he is Un-dead, a 'dead' person who yet manages to live thanks to the blood he sucks from the living. *Their* strength becomes *his* strength" (Moretti, *Signs Taken for Wonders: Essays in the Sociology of Literary Forms*, trans. Susan Fischer, David Forgacs, and David Miller [New York: Verso, 1988], 91).

15. Jennifer Wicke, "Vampiric Typewriting: *Dracula* and Its Media," *ELH* 59 (1992): 476–79.

16. L. Edward Purcell, "*Trilby* and *Trilby*-Mania: The Beginning of the Bestseller System," *Journal of Popular Culture* 11 (1977): 62–76.

17. George du Maurier, *Trilby* (New York: Oxford University Press, 1995), 78, 80, 63.

18. See Eve Kosofsky Sedgwick, *Epistemology of the Closet* (Berkeley: University of California Press, 1990), 189.

19. Bram Stoker, *Dracula* (New York: Penguin Books, 1979), 37.

20. Moretti, *Signs Taken for Wonders*, 103.

21. Stephanie Demetrakopoulos, "Feminism, Sex Role Exchanges, and Other Subliminal Fantasies in Bram Stoker's *Dracula*," *Frontiers* (1977): 106. Since the 1970s there has been an explosion of criticism on *Dracula*, focusing primarily on sexuality. What follows is a representative but by no means exhaustive list of essays that read *Dracula* in terms of sexual repression: C. F. Bentley, "The Monster in the Bedroom: Sexual Symbolism in Bram Stoker's *Dracula*," *Literature and Psychology* 22 (1972): 27–34; Phyllis A. Roth, "Suddenly Sexual Women in Bram Stoker's *Dracula*," *Literature and Psychology* 27 (1977): 113–121; Judith Weissman, "Women and Vampires: *Dracula* as a Victorian Novel," *Midwest Quarterly* 18 (1977): 392–405; Anne Williams, "*Dracula*: Si(g)ns of the Fathers," *Texas Studies in Literature and Language* 33 (1991): 445–63; and Kathleen L. Spencer, "Purity and Danger: *Dracula*, the Urban Gothic, and the Late Victorian Degeneracy Crisis," *ELH* 59 (1992): 197–225. For readings that argue that the novel represents the repression of a specifically homosexual desire, see Christopher Craft, "'Kiss Me with Those Red Lips': Gender and Inversion in Bram Stoker's *Dracula*," *Representations* 8 (1984): 107–33; Marjorie Howes, "The Mediation of the Feminine: Bisexuality, Homoerotic Desire, and Self-Expression in Bram Stoker's *Dracula*," *Texas Studies in Literature and Language* 30 (1988): 104–19; and Talia Schaffer, "'A Wilde Desire Took Me': The Homoerotic History of *Dracula*," *ELH* 61 (1994): 381–425. For a critique of the sexual repression model, see Robert Mighall, "Sex, History, and the Vampire," in *Bram Stoker: History, Psychoanalysis, and the Gothic*, ed. William Hughes and Andrew Smith (New York: St. Martin's Press, 1998), 62–77.

22. Demetrakopoulos, "Feminism," 106.

23. Moretti, *Signs Taken for Wonders*, 104.

24. In the work of Gilles Deleuze and Félix Guattari, the "body without organs" is imagined to be a circuit through which desire flows rather than desire's point of origin. While I am certainly indebted to their claims, I am not interested in making similar arguments against a strict oedipal model of subjectivity. I am arguing instead that this antiidentity model actually emerges at the same moment as the Freudian one and that it is not imagined to be an antidote to, but to be in competition with, this model. See Deleuze and Guattari, *Anti-Oedipus: Capitalism and Schizophrenia*,

trans. Robert Hurley, Mark Seem, and Helen R. Lane (Minneapolis: University of Minnesota Press, 1983).

25. Wicke, "Vampiric Typewriting," 478.

26. Stephen Arata, "The Occidental Tourist: *Dracula* and the Anxiety of Reverse Colonization," *Victorian Studies* 33 (1990): 630, 629. On *Dracula* and empire, see also Judith Wilt, "The Imperial Mouth: Imperialism, the Gothic, and Science Fiction," *Journal of Popular Culture* 14 (1981): 618–28; Judith Halberstam, *Skin Shows: Gothic Horror and the Technology of Monsters* (Durham: Duke University Press, 1995); Daniel Pick, "'Terrors of the Night': *Dracula* and Degeneration in the Late Nineteenth Century," in Pykett, ed., *Reading Fin-de-Siècle Fictions*, 149–65; and David Glover, *Vampires, Mummies, and Liberals: Bram Stoker and the Politics of Popular Fiction* (Durham: Duke University Press, 1996).

27. This mirroring is most obvious, perhaps, in the image of Harker looking at his reflection in *Dracula*, a scene that (as I have already mentioned) has typically been invoked as evidence for a psychoanalytic reading of the novel.

28. Frank Norris, "A Reversion to Type," in *The Third Circle* (New York: Doubleday, Doran and Co., 1928), 44.

29. In some respects, this image of a man overwhelmed by passion looks like a typical Naturalist dynamic. But in the context of my argument, this power of desire to overwhelm the personality is linked specifically to the personality of the ancestor—a model of identity that Norris shares, in varying degrees, with writers as different as Pauline Hopkins and Henry James.

30. Henry Harland, *As It Was Written: A Jewish Musician's Story* (New York: Garland, 1984), 43.

31. Jack London, *The Star Rover* (London: Journeyman Press, 1990 [1915]), 9–10.

32. Henry James, *The Sense of the Past* (1909), in *The Novels and Tales of Henry James*, vol. 26 (New York: Scribner's, 1945), 97.

33. This quotation is taken from Henry James's notes on the planned ending of the novel, reproduced in *The Sense of the Past*, 327.

34. Pauline Hopkins, *Of One Blood; or, The Hidden Self* (1902–1903), in *The Magazine Novels of Pauline Hopkins* (New York: Oxford University Press, 1988), 546, 551.

35. My reading of race at the turn of the century owes much to Walter Benn Michaels's account of racial identity in *Our America: Nativism, Modernism, and Pluralism* (Durham: Duke University Press, 1995). My argument differs from his, however, in that the model of possession I am describing is not uniquely racial but is a technology for creating identity in a variety of different ways. Indeed, race is only one example of a model that produces, among other things, addiction and celebrity. On the creation of the modern celebrity, see my "The Public Life: The Discourse of Privacy in the Age of Celebrity," *Arizona Quarterly* 51 (1995): 81–101.

36. Susan Gillman, "Pauline Hopkins and the Occult: African-American Revisions of Nineteenth-Century Sciences," *American Literary History* 8 (1996): 73–78.

37. Thomas J. Otten, "Pauline Hopkins and the Hidden Self of Race," *ELH* 59 (1992): 230, 248.

38. Cynthia Schrager, "Pauline Hopkins and William James: The New Psychology and the Politics of Race," in *Female Subjects in Black and White: Race, Psychoanalysis, Feminism*, ed. Elizabeth Abel, Barbara Christian, and Helene Moglen (Berkeley: University of California Press, 1997), 314, 322.

39. Benjamin Rush Davenport, *Blood Will Tell: The Strange Story of a Son of Ham* (New York: Books for Libraries Press, 1972 [1902]), 50.

40. Otten, "Pauline Hopkins," 255 n.38.

41. W. E. B. DuBois, *The Souls of Black Folk* (New York: New American Library, 1969 [1903]), 45.

CHAPTER SIX: Homo-Formalism: Analogy in *The Sacred Fount*

1. William James, *The Principles of Psychology*, vol. 1 (New York: Dover Publications, 1950 [1890]), 227, 226.

2. Henry James, *The Sacred Fount* (New York: New Directions, 1983 [1901]), 147.

3. Far from being a recent phenomenon, however, the exploration of sexuality and sexual repression in James was very much part of the mid-twentieth-century process of canonizing his late works of fiction. As early as 1934, Edmund Wilson not only read *The Turn of the Screw* as a representation of sexual repression and hysteria but also wondered "if the hidden theme of *The Sacred Fount* is simply sex again?" (Wilson, "The Ambiguity of Henry James," in *A Casebook on Henry James's "The Turn of the Screw*," ed. Gerald Willen [New York: Crowell, 1960], 125).

4. Eve Kosofsky Sedgwick, *Epistemology of the Closet* (Berkeley: University of California Press, 1990), 201, 202.

5. Hugh Stevens, *Henry James and Sexuality* (New York: Cambridge University Press, 1998), 15, 19. For a related account, see Wendy Graham, *Henry James's Thwarted Love* (Stanford: Stanford University Press, 1999).

6. William Bysshe Stein traces the "slang obscenities" of the novel in "*The Sacred Fount* and British Aestheticism: The Artist as Clown and Pornographer," *Arizona Quarterly* 27 [1971]: 163.

7. See, for example, Jean Frantz Blackall, *Jamesian Ambiguity and "The Sacred Fount"* (Ithaca: Cornell University Press, 1965); Dorothea Krook, *The Ordeal of Consciousness in Henry James* (Cambridge: Cambridge University Press, 1967); Ora Segal, *The Lucid Reflector: The Observer in Henry James's Fiction* (New Haven: Yale University Press, 1969); and Shlomith Rimmon, *The Concept of Ambiguity: The Example of James* (Chicago: University of Chicago Press, 1977).

8. For accounts of this transition in the understanding of homosexuality, see Michel Foucault, *The History of Sexuality*, vol. 1, trans. Robert Hurley (New York: Vintage Books, 1990); and Jeffrey Weeks, *Coming Out: Homosexual Politics in Britain, from the Nineteenth Century to the Present* (London: Quartet Books, 1977).

9. Obert's phrase, "different from herself," virtually asks to be read in either deconstructive or psychoanalytic terms. A deconstructive reading of May's "difference" would see her as a representation of the individual's irreducible internal difference—the structuring principle of the self—which is enacted and covered over through speech. As Jacques Derrida has argued, "the conscious and speaking subject . . . depends upon the system of differences and the movement of *difference*" so that "the subject is constituted only in being divided from itself" (Derrida, *Positions*, trans. Alan Bass [Chicago: University of Chicago Press, 1981], 29). A psychoanalytic reading would see this difference as an eruption of the unconscious. And, as I discussed in chapter 5, in the emergent field of psychology the notion that the mind might have an "unconscious," that it might be opaque to itself and thus be able to bear multiple "selves," was becoming increasingly influential. As will become clear in the following pages, however, neither one of these readings can account for the interest that the novel has in these transformations.

10. Edward Bellamy, *Miss Ludington's Sister: A Romance of Immortality* (Boston: J. R. Osgood, 1885 [1884]), 253.

11. Edward Bellamy, *Dr. Heidenhoff's Process* (New York: D. Appleton and Co., 1880), 121.

12. See, for example, Boris Sidis, *The Psychology of Suggestion: A Research into the Subconscious Nature of Man and Society* (New York: D. Appleton, 1909); and F. W. H. Myers, "The Subliminal Consciousness," in *Proceedings of the Society for Psychical Research* 7 (February 1892): 305–6. For a history of multiple personality disorder, see Ian Hacking, *Rewriting the Soul: Multiple Personality Disorder and the Sciences of Memory* (Princeton: Princeton University Press, 1995).

13. Pronounced "Beecham," as Prince informs us in *The Dissociation of a Personality* (New York: Longmans, Green and Co., 1910 [1905]), 1.

14. Ruth Leys, "The Real Miss Beauchamp: Gender and the Subject of Imitation," in *Feminists Theorize the Political*, ed. Judith Butler and Joan W. Scott (New York: Routledge, 1992), 172.

15. Indeed, beginning with Wilson Follett, the claim that the novel works as a satire (more or less successful) of the novelist has been a staple of the criticism. See Wilson Follett, "Henry James's 'Portrait of Henry James,'" *New York Times Book Review*, 23 August 1936, 2, 16. See also Laurence Holland, *The Expense of Vision: Essays on the Craft of Henry James* (Princeton: Princeton University Press, 1964); and Philip M. Weinstein, *Henry James and the Requirements of the Imagination* (Cambridge: Harvard University Press, 1971).

16. R. P. Blackmur, "*The Sacred Fount*," in *Studies in Henry James* (New York: New Directions, 1983 [1942]), 50.

17. Sharon Cameron, *Thinking in Henry James* (Chicago: University of Chicago Press, 1989), 160–61.

18. Henry James, *The Turn of the Screw* (New York: Norton, 1999 [1898]), 68.

19. Adeline Tintner, "A Gay *Sacred Fount*: The Reader as Detective," *Twentieth-Century Literature* 4 (1995): 1–9.

20. No wonder, then, that the key image evoked in this scene of mirroring and desire is a shared phallic object: the narrator passes to Obert "the torch of [his] analogy," which Obert explains, "I've blown on . . . till, flaring and smoking, it has guided me, through a magnificent chiaroscuro of colour and shadow, out into the light of day" (156).

21. Sigmund Freud, "On Narcissism: An Introduction," trans. Cecil M. Baines, in *Collected Papers*, vol. 9 (London: Hogarth Press, 1953), 45.

22. Michael Warner, "Homo-Narcissism; or Heterosexuality," in *Engendering Men: The Question of Male Feminist Criticism*, ed. Joseph A. Boone and Michael Cadden (New York: Routledge, 1990), 200.

23. Ibid. See also Michael Warner, "Thoreau's Bottom," *Raritan* 11 (1992): 53–79.

24. By the turn of the century, Havelock Ellis dismissed Ulrich's description of "the female soul" as merely a way of "crystallis[ing] into an epigram the superficial impression of the matter." For Ellis, the relevant question about homosexuality had become whether it was a natural, inborn propensity or a learned "perversion" (Ellis, quoted in Chris White, ed., *Nineteenth-Century Writings on Homosexuality: A Sourcebook* [New York: Routledge, 1999], 100).

25. Christopher Craft, "'Kiss Me with Those Red Lips': Gender and Inversion in Bram Stoker's *Dracula*," *Representations* 8 (1984): 112–14 (my emphasis).

26. Leo Bersani, *Homos* (Cambridge: Harvard University Press, 1995), 6–7.

27. Ross Posnock has argued that this escape from the self is realized in *The Ambassadors*, in which Strether chooses to "[let] his monadic self go to smash." What *The Sacred Fount* makes clear, however, is the impossibility of such a choice. The narrator can choose what to do—to leave Newmarch or to stay—but he cannot choose what to be—to remain himself or be restored to "blankness" (Posnock, *The Trial of Curiosity: Henry James, William James, and the Challenge of Modernity* [New York: Oxford University Press, 1991], 234).

28. Laurence Holland sees the exploration of form in *The Sacred Fount* as essential to understanding the project of the late fiction, although in his reading form is not merely essential but redemptive (Holland, *Expense of Vision*, esp. 224–25).

29. Henry James, "Preface," in *The Golden Bowl*, ed. Virginia Llewellyn Smith (New York: Oxford University Press, 1983), xlii.

30. For a different reading of James's aestheticism in relation to the New Criticism and to modernism more generally, see Jonathan Freedman, *Professions of Taste: Henry James, British Aestheticism, and Commodity Culture* (Stanford: Stanford University Press, 1990).

31. For a powerful example of the "social discipline" argument, see Mark Seltzer, *Henry James and the Art of Power* (Ithaca: Cornell University Press, 1984).

Index

Abbott, Jacob, 66
Abbott, John S. C., 67
Accident, 5–6, 9, 55, 108–10
Accidental harm, 85, 90–95, 97–98, 100–102
Addiction, 7, 9–10, 142–48, 155
Adventures of Huckleberry Finn, 4; and accident, 91, 93–94; and compensation for harm, 91–95, 99–104; and feeling, 81–86, 90, 95–96, 98, 105; futility in, 83, 86; and individual responsibility, 9, 14, 84–85, 90–107; and intention, 83–91, 96–98, 104–7; and national responsibility, 9, 85, 99, 102–5; and negligence, 8–9, 11, 14, 84–85, 92–99, 103–5; and racism, 8–9, 82–87, 96–107; retrospection in, 87–89, 96, 99; and social consequences, 82, 84–85, 90–93, 97–98, 105–7; and textual effects, 88–89; and tort law, 91–95, 99–101
Aesthetic form, 193–95
Affiliation, 7–8, 11, 17–50
Aguilar, Grace, 129–32
Analogy, 9–10, 49–50, 172, 181, 184–88, 191–94
Andrews, William L., 215 n.8, 218 n.27
Antin, Mary, 219 n.40
Arac, Jonathan, 20, 82–85, 105–6, 210 n.9
Arata, Stephen, 155
Armstrong, Nancy, 208 n.36

Assimilation, 118, 123–29, 133–35
Autonomy, individual, 4–6, 63–64, 70–72, 77

Baldwin, Eugene, 127–28
Barnes, Elizabeth, 77
Barthes, Roland, 28, 38
Baym, Nina, 209 n.36
Bellamy, Edward: "The Blindman's World," 1–2; *Dr. Heidenhoff's Process*, 176; *Miss Ludington's Sister*, 175–77; "To Whom This May Come," 1–3, 14
Bercovitch, Sacvan, 4, 19–20, 202 n.8
Berlant, Lauren, 12–13, 19–20, 38, 45
Berridge, Virginia, 143
Bersani, Leo, 189–91
Blackmur, R. P., 182–84
Blithedale Romance, The: and affiliation, 7–8, 11, 17–50; architecture in, 28–29, 31, 42; and Brook Farm, 18, 30, 34; contagion in, 8, 43, 46–47; and "The Custom House," 18, 20, 23; and Fourier, 24–31, 37–39, 41–42; free choice in, 22–24, 29, 38–41, 43; and individual opinion, 18, 23–24, 32–39, 46–47, 55; and intimacy, 20, 24, 28, 42–50; and *Life of Franklin Pierce*, 21–22; and "Meadow-Farm," 30–33, 36; and nation, 19–22; and partisanship, 8, 18–24, 30–39, 46, 55; and politics, 18–24, 30–39, 45–46; privacy

Blithedale Romance, The (continued)
  in, 17, 23, 29, 31–32, 38–39, 42, 44–47, 50
Blumin, Stuart, 201 n.3
Borch-Jacobsen, Mikkel, 223 n.13
Brisbane, Albert, 24, 28–30
Brodhead, Richard, 52–53, 57
Brook Farm, 18, 30, 34
Brown, Gillian, 45
Brown, Henry Billings, 109
Bulwer-Lytton, Edward, 116–17

Cable, George Washington, 105
Cahan, Abraham, 220 n.49
Cameron, Sharon, 183–84
Chesnutt, Charles: "The Future American," 120–23; *The Marrow of Tradition*, 133–34; speeches and essays on racism, 119–24. See also *The House Behind the Cedars*
Child, Lydia Maria, 62–63
Child-rearing literature, 6–8, 62–66
Civil rights, 83, 99–100, 105, 108, 118–22, 133
Cole, Henry, 10, 144–45
Compensation for harm, 91–95, 99–104
Confessions of a Magnetiser, The, 221 n.2
Consumer culture, 10, 40, 143, 148–51, 154
Contract, 4–6, 26, 94, 147
Conversion, religious, 9, 113–19, 124–25, 128–32, 137
Cox, James, 210 n.6
Craft, Christopher, 189
Cummins, Maria, 54–58
Cunliffe, Marcus, 64

Davenport, Benjamin Rush, 165–66
Deleuze, Gilles, 224 n.24
Demetrakopoulos, Stephanie, 152
Derrida, Jacques, 222 nn.7, 9
Desire, 9, 12; and addiction, 7, 10, 141–47; and group life, 22–29, 31, 34, 37–39, 41–50; same-sex, 171, 187–92; and supernatural possession, 147–58, 161, 163–64, 166–68

Dimock, Wai Chee, 94–95
Discipline, 2–3, 5–8, 13–14, 22, 29, 39, 49–50, 52–67, 76
Disraeli, Benjamin, 117
Domestic sphere, 4, 11, 23, 31–32, 41, 110–12. See also *The Wide Wide World*
Douglass, Frederick, 112–13
Doyle, Arthur Conan, 141–42, 146–47, 155–56
DuBois, W. E. B., 114, 166–67
DuMaurier, George, 148–52, 155

Edwards, Griffith, 143
Eisenberg, Maurice, 127–28
Eliot, George, 117–19
Eliot, T. S., 81
Ellis, Havelock, 228 n.24
Emerson, Ralph Waldo, 33–35
English conversion novel, 113–19, 128–32
Epstein, Julia, 213 n.31

Fabi, Giulia, 216 n.10
Ferguson, Frances, 211 n.11
Ferguson, SallyAnne, 120
Fiedler, Leslie, 126
Finely, Martha, 57–58
Fishkin, Shelley Fisher, 104
Fliegelman, Jay, 207 n.25
Follett, Wilson, 227 n.15
Formisano, Ronald, 21
Foster, Shirley, 53
Foucault, Michel, 2, 13–14, 29, 53, 62
Fourier, Charles, 24–31, 37–39, 41–42, 47
Freud, Sigmund, 188
Friedman, Lawrence, 92

Gillman, Susan, 165
Godwin, Parke, 28, 30
Gollin, Richard, 214 n.32
Gollin, Rita, 214 n.32
Goodman, Nan, 93–94
Gordon, Noah, 217 n.18
Grimke, Frederick, 38–39, 47
Guattari, Felix, 224 n.24

Habermas, Jurgen, 197 n.2
Hacking, Ian, 5–6
Harlan, Henry, 99
Harland, Henry (Sidney Luska): *As It Was Written*, 158; *Mrs. Peixada*, 128; *The Yoke of the Thorah*, 127–28
Harper, Frances, 136
Hart, H. L. A., 97
Hawthorne, Nathaniel: "The Custom House," 18, 20, 23; *The Life of Franklin Pierce*, 21–22; *The Scarlet Letter*, 18–19. See also *The Blithedale Romance*
Heredity, 157–64
Hertzberg, Arthur, 125
Higham, John, 125
Hofstadter, Richard, 35
Holland, Laurence, 83, 89, 228 n.28
Holmes, Oliver Wendell, 91–95
Homosexuality: as heuristic, 9–10, 170–71, 192–95; as identity, 173, 190–91; and "sameness," 186–95; as secret, 150–52, 171–72
Hopkins, Pauline: *Of One Blood*, 9–10, 162–68; *Winona*, 114
Horowitz, David, 213 n.30
Horwitz, Morton, 211 n.19
House Behind the Cedars, The: and assimilation, 118, 123–29, 133–35; and citizenship, 113–118; and civil rights, 108, 118–22, 133; and *Daniel Deronda*, 117–19; and English conversion novel, 113–19, 128–32; high culture in, 111–12; and *Ivanhoe*, 113–117, 135–36; and Jewish American novel, 125–29; and Jewish identity, 113–118, 123–131, 137; and racial passing, 8–9, 109–13, 124–25, 130–137; and religious conversion, 9, 113–19, 124–25, 128–32, 137; and segregation, 108–10, 113–15, 119–25, 130–37, 167–68; and skin color, 109–12, 119–21, 131–37; and tragic mulatta, 108, 110, 124
Howells, William Dean, 136
Hutner, Gordon, 45

Ideology, 4–5, 12, 19–22, 76
Intention, 2–3, 6–9, 55, 83–91, 96–98, 104–7

Interiority, 1–4, 7–9, 29, 47–50
Introspection, limits of, 2, 38–39, 50, 53–54, 68–69, 177–80, 184–86

Jackson, Andrew, 46
James, Henry: preface to *The Golden Bowl*, 193–95; *The Sense of the Past*, 161; *The Turn of the Screw*, 185–86. See also *The Sacred Fount*
James, William, 169–71, 177–78, 185
Jefferson, Thomas, 35
Jewish American novel, 125–29
Jewish identity, 113–18, 123–31, 137. *See also* Racial identity
Johnson, James Weldon, 216 n.9
Jones, Gavin, 134

Kawash, Samira, 132, 136
Kingsley, Charles, 55
Knadler, Stephen, 121

Lears, Jackson, 199 n.11
Lefkovitz, Lori Hope, 213 n. 31
Lenson, David, 222 n.7
Levine, Harry Gene, 143
Leys, Ruth, 180–81
Liberal individualism, 4, 7, 12, 77
Lieber, Francis, 36
London, Jack: *John Barleycorn*, 144–46; *The Star Rover*, 158–60
Luska, Sidney. *See* Harland, Henry

Marx, Leo, 81, 86
McWilliams, Dean, 218 n.28
"Meadow-Farm," 30–33, 36
Memory, racial, 102, 148, 162–67
Merish, Lori, 198 n.4
Mesmerism, 141–42, 146–50
Meyer, Susan, 118
Michaels, Walter Benn, 122, 197 n.3, 213 n.31, 225 n.35
Moddelmog, William, 121
Moretti, Franco, 148, 152, 223 n.14
Multiple personality disorder, 177–82

Negligence, 8–9, 11, 14, 55, 84–85, 92–99, 103–5
Noble, Marianne, 52–53, 59
Norris, Frank, 156–57
Novak, William, 5–6, 199 n.9
Novick, Peter, 213 n.31
Nussbaum, Martha, 95–96

"One-drop rule," 109, 113, 120, 132, 135, 164–65
Otten, Thomas J., 165–66

Park, Clara Claiborne, 210 n.8
Partisanship, 8, 18–24, 30–39, 46, 55
Passing, racial, 8–9, 109–13, 124–25, 130–37, 163–64
Pease, Donald, 201 n.6
Plessy v. Ferguson, 96, 99, 108–9, 121
Posnock, Ross, 217 n.27, 228 n.27
Possession, narratives of supernatural: American, 147–48, 154–68; British, 146–56
Prince, Morton, 177–81
Privacy, 1–7, 11–14, 23, 29, 31–32, 44–50
Punishment, 8, 13, 29, 53–68, 74–77

Quirk, Tom, 104

Racial identity, 8–10, 97, 107–37, 147–48, 155–58, 162–68
Racism, 8–9, 82–87, 96–106, 107–37, 164–68
Ragussis, Michael, 115, 117–19
Regulation, state, 4–6
Reising, Russell, 83
Renza, Louis, 198 n.5
Responsibility: individual, 6, 9, 14, 84–85, 90–107, 175–76, 181–82, 193–94; national, 5, 9, 85, 99–105
Richardson, Benjamin Ward, 144
Rollin, Horace J., 219 n.45
Rosenberg, David, 211 n.16

Sacred Fount, The: analogy in, 9–10, 172, 181, 184–88, 191–94; and desire, 171, 183–92; and divided self, 169–71, 173–83; and form, 172–73, 181–95; and homosexuality, 9–10, 170–73, 186–95; and multiple personality disorder, 177–82; and sexuality, 172–74; and the unconscious, 176–77, 182–84; and unified self, 169–71, 175–83; and vampirism, 168, 172–74, 182–85
Schrager, Cynthia, 165
Scott, Walter, 113, 115–17, 135–36
Sedgwick, Catherine, 62
Sedgwick, Eve, 151, 171
Segregation, 8–9, 99, 101, 108–10, 113–15, 119–25, 130–37, 167–68
Seltzer, Mark, 143
Sigourney, L. H., 62, 64–65
Silverstein, Alan, 125
Simmons, Judy, 53
Smiley, Jane, 82–85, 105–6, 210 n.9
Sol, Adam, 126, 128
Sorin, Gerald, 125
Southworth, E. D. E. N., 66
Stern, Julia, 200 n.18
Stevens, Hugh, 171
Stoker, Bram, 152–55
Stone, Albert, E., 216 n.12
Sundquist, Eric, 133

Thomas, Brook, 212 n.29
Thoreau, Henry David, 44–45
Tintner, Adeline, 187
Tocqueville, Alexis de, 18
Tompkins, Jane, 51, 53–55
Tort law, 6, 9, 91–95, 99–101
Tourgée, Albion, 99; *Pactolus Prime*, 99–102
Tragic mulatta, 108, 110, 124
Trilling, Lionel, 4, 81, 86
Twain, Mark: *The Gilded Age*, 93–94; *Pudd'nhead Wilson*, 96–97; "Tom Sawyer's Conspiracy," 212 n.23. See also *Adventures of Huckleberry Finn*

Vampirism, 10, 147–56, 161, 166, 168, 172–74, 182–85
Van Buren, Martin, 35

Warner, Charles Dudley, 93–94
Warner, Michael, 13, 188
Warner, Susan: *The Letter of Credit*, 68, 70–71, 77; *Melbourne House*, 57, 68; *My Desire*, 68; *The Old Helmet*, 69–73; *Queechy*, 208 n.33. See also *The Wide Wide World*
Washington, George, 34–35, 64–67
Weems, Mason, 64–65
Welke, Barbara Young, 5–6
White, G. Edward, 95
White, Isabelle, 53
Wicke, Jennifer, 148, 154
Wide Wide World, The: and child-rearing literature, 8, 62–66; compared to nineteenth-century domestic fiction, 11, 54–65, 76; and corporal punishment, 53, 57, 63, 74; and discipline, 7–8, 52–67, 76; and education, 52–67, 76–77; feminist critique of, 51–55, 59–60; and judgment, 55–56, 59, 61–62, 65–77; and limits of introspection, 53–54, 68–69; and *The Old Helmet*, 69–73; role of mentor in, 59–62, 65–69, 73–74; and self-regulation, 8, 53–67, 76–77; and George Washington, 64–67
Wieck, Carl F., 214 n.33
Wilde, Oscar, 173–74
Williams, Bernard, 90–91
Williamson, Joel, 215 n.3
Wills, Garry, 65
Wilson, Edmund, 226 n.3
Wolf, Emma, 127–28
Woodward, C. Vann, 214 n.3

Stacy Margolis is an assistant professor of English at the University of Utah.

Library of Congress Cataloging-in-Publication Data
Margolis, Stacey, 1966–
The public life of privacy in nineteenth-century American
literature / Stacey Margolis.
p. cm.—(New Americanists)
Includes bibliographical references and index.
ISBN 0-8223-3536-0 (cloth : alk. paper)
ISBN 0-8223-3549-2 (pbk. : alk. paper)
1. American fiction—19th century—History and criticism.
2. Privacy in literature. 3. Literature and society—United
States—History—19th century. 4. Intimacy (Psychology) in
literature. 5. Public opinion in literature. 6. Personal space in
literature. 7. Social values in literature. 8. Individualism in
literature. I. Title. II. Series.
PS374.P647M37 2005
813'.309353—dc22   2004023364

www.ingramcontent.com/pod-product-compliance
Lightning Source LLC
Chambersburg PA
CBHW071817230426
43670CB00013B/2479